RIBA Book of
20th Century British Housing

LIVERPOOL JOHN MOORES UNIVERSITY
Aldham Robarts L.R.C.
TEL 0151 231 3701/3634

LIVERPOOL JMU LIBRARY

3 1111 00959 5685

RIBA Book of 20th Century British Housing

Ian Colquhoun

LIVERPOOL JOHN MOORES UNIVERSITY
Aldham Roberts L.R.C.
TEL 0151 231 3701/3634

OXFORD   AUCKLAND   BOSTON   JOHANNESBURG   MELBOURNE   NEW DELHI

Butterworth-Heinemann
Linacre House, Jordan Hill, Oxford OX2 8DP
225 Wildwood Avenue, Woburn, MA 01801-2041
A division of Reed Educational and Professional Publishing Ltd

 A member of the Reed Elsevier plc group

First published 1999

© Ian Colquhoun 1999

All rights reserved. No part of this publication may be reproduced in
any material form (including photocopying or storing in any medium by
electronic means and whether or not transiently or incidentally to some
other use of this publication) without the written permission of the
copyright holder except in accordance with the provisions of the Copyright,
Designs and Patents Act 1988 or under the terms of a licence issued by the
Copyright Licensing Agency Ltd, 90 Tottenham Court Rd, London,
England W1P 9HE. Applications for the copyright holder's written
permission to reproduce any part of this publication should be addressed
to the publishers

British Library Cataloguing in Publication Data
A catalogue record for this book is available from the British Library

ISBN 07506 33074 4

Library of Congress Cataloguing in Publication Data
A catalogue record for this book is available from the Library of Congress

Composition by Scribe Design, Gillingham, Kent
Printed and bound in Great Britain, by The Bath Press, Bath

FOR EVERY VOLUME THAT WE PUBLISH, BUTTERWORTH-HEINEMANN
WILL PAY FOR BTCV TO PLANT AND CARE FOR A TREE.

Contents

Note
Reference is made in several places to the English Heritage publications all entitled *Something Worth Keeping? Post-War Architecture in Britain*, 1996. The publications were concerned with different building types and, unless otherwise stated, the references EH (followed by page number) relate to *Housing and Houses*.

Foreword

David Rock
President of the Royal Institute of British Architects

British architects throughout the century have been at the forefront of social housing – from the garden cities and the first London County Council development at Boundary Street to the recent Millennium Village at Greenwich – and visitors have come from many parts of the world to learn from our latest developments. It was a great pleasure, therefore, during the first week of my RIBA Presidency, to host the presentation of the RIBA/DETR 1997 Housing Design Awards. This, interestingly, coincided with the 50 year anniversary and celebration of Aneurin Bevin's announcement to the RIBA Council of the first housing award scheme. Society and social housing have changed considerably over 50 years, but those latest awards were a convincing demonstration of the continuing talent and commitment that exists among architects, and that can be realized by clients and housebuilders.

Quality in housing is something for which the RIBA, through successive, dedicated RIBA Housing Groups, has campaigned vigorously over the years, and this, the *RIBA Book of 20th Century British Housing*, is the latest in a long line of initiatives to focus our attention. Ian Colquhoun's book is special in that it looks at housing by reference to design (the word is used in its fullest sense, not simply that of external appearance) and the great variety of design solutions, and there can be no doubt that the meaningful involvement of architects by the volume housebuilders can raise the quality of housing. It is no coincidence that housebuilders do recognize the need to commission architects to find solutions for difficult urban 'brownfield' sites. If they would also work with architects on the 'easier' greenfield sites, we could perhaps look forward to much better quality in private housing

estates as well as in social housing. Certainly this book, while it is not afraid to illustrate failure as well as success, highlights the depth of experience in housing development that exists within my profession.

Significant change in social housing is being and will continue to be driven by changes in responsibility for housing provision. Local authorities used to be the main providers, and many had a long and proud tradition of talented in-house architect teams and of enlightened patronage in commissioning first class private practices. Now there is a range of providers from Housing Action Trusts and Housing Associations to Enterprise Agencies working with commercial firms. Community involvement in some form or another is now the norm, and communities expect more and better. With enlightened clients British architects have shown that they can lead the world in housing refurbishment and estate regeneration. We should therefore be able to expect a greater variety of answers. Regrettably many Housing Associations and many private house builders don't seem to rate quality. Their aspirations must be raised; and they must be encouraged to find out for themselves the added value they can achieve through proper involvement of chartered architects in their housing aspirations. If we and they can work together, quality could become the norm.

Ian Colquhoun's book charts progress from the housing legacy of the Industrial Revolution, through the exodus of people fron the cities to the new suburbs and the countryside beyond, to present forecasts of a need to build large amounts of new housing. Where this is to be provided, and how, are key issues at both national and local levels. The lessons to be drawn from the experience of the past century are vital to this debate. I therefore congratulate the author, and the RIBA Housing Group, on this book and I commend it to all those who will have a responsibility for, and an interest in, creating our future homes and housing environments.

Acknowledgements

Housing has been at the centre of most of my architectural life. To have been a member of the RIBA's Housing Group has not only been a privilege but an education. The group has given me continual support in writing this book, for which I am most grateful. During the last two years the group has comprised, for some or all of the time, the following: Andrew Beard, Jack Cassidy, Robert Felix, Trishia Gupta, Bernard Hunt (Chairman), Chris Johnson, Richard Lavington, David Levitt, Stuart Mackie, Mary McKeown, David Moore, David Parkes, Chris Purslow, Martin Richardson and Chris Rudolf. The RIBA Officer is Bernadette Hammerson-Wood.

David Parkes and Chris Johnson read numerous drafts of my manuscript and their comments were always most constructive. Chris Purslow and Mary McKeown helped with the research and various drafts on Scotland and Northern Ireland, respectively. The Royal Incorporation of Architects in Scotland, Jim Johnston, Roan Rutherford, Derek Lyddon, Ian and Marjorie Appleton and Dr Tom Begg's excellent books on Scottish housing helped with the section on Scotland. Professor Tom Woolley of Queen's University, Belfast and Jim McClusky of the Royal Ulster Society of Architects, the Northern Ireland Housing Executive and the Belfast office of the NHBC, helped me to understand the housing scene in Northern Ireland. The RIBA Awards Office and Nancy Mills supplied details of award-winning schemes and various RIBA Regions gave helpful advice on schemes to visit. John Bartlett provided information on MoHLG experiments into extendible housing and Bill Brown researched projects in Essex. English Heritage's listing of proposals for post-1945 buildings was most opportune and I appreciate the help which I received from Gaynor Roberts.

The book entailed endless travel throughout Britain. I was warmly welcomed by everyone I specifically arranged to meet but there are simply too many people to list. My sincere apologies go to those who very kindly provided information on schemes that was not used but space simply would not allow me to include everything.

I am extremely grateful to Chris Jones, Dean, and the staff of the Hull School of Architecture at the University of Lincolnshire and Humberside for giving me time for the research and the writing. Dr Jingmin Zhou helped with research, the preparation of plans and enabled me to understand my computer. Rita Johnson kindly assisted with typing, Lyang Sun with drawings and my son, Christopher, took the photographs for which he is credited. The developing and printing of photographs was skilfully undertaken by Richmond and Rigg (Hull) Ltd.

Authors need good support from their publishers and I must thank Neil Warnock-Smith, Marie Milmore and their colleagues at Butterworth-Heinemann for all their patience and continual encouragement.

I am particularly grateful to David Rock, President of the Royal Institute of British Architects, for writing his thoughtful Foreword which helps set the scene for the book.

Finally, the book could not have been written without the endless help of my wife, Christine, who, throughout the research and writing, helped with so many aspects of the writing, travel arrangements, photography, filing etc. and all the normal things of life which I had little time to do.

Whilst the RIBA Housing Group has contributed to the book's production, it is an independent piece of work and the RIBA has no responsibility for the views, choice of scheme illustrated and opinions expressed in the text.

Ian Colquhoun
Professor of Architecture, University of
Lincolnshire and Humberside
July 1998

Introduction

This book is about 20th century British housing and its design. The 100 years end as they began with a forecasted need for large amounts of new housing. In 1900 it was to replace the slums left by the Industrial Revolution. Today it is to accommodate a rapidly growing number of new households, the majority of which will be single people and couples with no children, often young or elderly. There is general agreement that additional housing should be centred on the re-use of existing buildings and the development of brownfield sites to offer new life to urban areas. Yet many people have little affinity for urban life and also have an inherent distrust of new concepts due to the failures of 1960s housing. The problem for architects is that the generalizations hide the achievements and in reality the century has seen an outflow of great creativity in housing design which has attracted world-wide attention and admiration.

For most of the century the interest focused on new development, mainly in the cities and new towns, but in the last two decades British architects have successfully turned their attentions to the regeneration of inner-city areas and the refurbishment of 1960s estates. They have also established a trend for more environmentally friendly and community-based development.

It was the interest from overseas that prompted the idea for this book. The RIBA frequently receives requests for information on British housing, many from people wishing to visit schemes for themselves. There is also a need for a simple up-to-date primer which can introduce the subject to visitors, students and practitioners.

The approach of the next millennium is an ideal time to celebrate the century's achievements in housing through collecting together some significant examples. Many of the projects included have received national acclaim and awards for their design quality. A number are included or have recently been recommended for inclusion by English Heritage on the government's statutory list of buildings of 'special architectural or historic interest' which now includes post Second World War housing.

The first chapter provides an historical overview. This enables the projects in the main body of the book to be seen against the political, social, economic and cultural background of the time when they were designed. Projects which are described in the later chapters are written in bold type. The overview and the description of the schemes are both brief but they are referenced to assist further research.

Anyone engaged in housing design can benefit considerably from looking at other people's work and by talking to the managers of the projects and the residents. Visits will give first-hand experience. Where schemes are within reasonable walking distance of railway, underground or Metro stations the nearest stop has been given. In some instances private transport is essential; no details have been given on travel in Northern Ireland. Most projects can be viewed from the public highway but respect for people's privacy is essential. Permission should be sought before entering private grounds and it is not possible to visit sheltered housing for elderly people and other schemes providing specialist care without first seeking the agreement of the owners of the building.

LIVERPOOL JOHN MOORES UNIVERSITY
Aldham Roberts L.R.C.
TEL 0151 231 3701/3634

FIGURE 1.1
Span housing in Cambridge has a timeless quality.

CHAPTER ONE

A century
of housing

The early years: 1900–1918

It was not until the turn of the 20th century that a real effort was made to deal with the huge legacy of poor housing handed down by the Industrial Revolution. In the nineteenth century a number of philanthropic individuals and organizations attempted to provide better housing for the working classes. Titus Salt's village at Saltaire, near Bradford, Peabody Trust housing in London and William Lever and George Cadbury's garden cities of Bourneville and Port Sunlight still remain as monuments of individual people who saw the benefits of decent housing for their workers.

Garden cities

The publication of Ebenezer Howard's *Tomorrow: A Peaceful Path to Real Reform* (retitled in 1902 *Garden Cities of Tomorrow*) [1] and the formation of the Garden City Association in 1898 led to the founding of **Letchworth Garden City** in 1902 and **Hampstead Garden Suburb** in 1906. At the same time, Joseph Rowntree started to build **New Earswick** on the outskirts of York.

Ebenezer Howard saw his garden cities in economic, social and political terms as well as physical. His vision was to create new self-sufficient 'social cities' of 250 000 people, set with their own commerce and industry in the countryside. Each social city would consist of a central core of 58 000 people connected within a circle of six independent and widely spaced garden cities, each with populations of 32 000. Letchworth reflected Howard's concept of a self-sufficient community. His plans included an agricultural belt to be farmed on behalf of the community and to serve as a barrier to limit urban development. It remains the only 'new town' where the land originally acquired for the development is still held in trust for the community [2]. Excess money from rent would be used to set up pension funds and community services. Any profit arising from development in the town must be used for the benefit of the community as a whole. In these ways he was unknowingly the first advocate of sustainable development.

Howard's ideas were ably translated in architectural terms by the architects Raymond Unwin and Barry Parker (Fig. 1.2). Their design set out to avoid the monotony of the uniform grid plans of nineteenth century housing. They restricted density to twelve houses per acre (30 dw/ha) and planned the layout carefully to use the existing landform, trees, hedgerows and other natural features of a site. Their cottage designs reflected the popular English romantic ideals of the time [3], producing an architectural quality which 'materialised the Englishman's ideal conception of home as a unit of house and garden combined' [4]. This fundamentally remains the view of most British people today.

Government intervention

Despite Howard's energy, the garden city movement merely touched the fringe of the problems and clearly a more concerted effort was required. Under the Housing of the Working Classes Acts of 1890 and 1900 local authorities were empowered for the first time to buy and develop sites to build houses for rent. The legislation was not mandatory but a few authorities were quick to respond. The London County Council (LCC), founded only a few years previously in 1888, built both tenement blocks (**Boundary Street**) and cottage estates, using two storey housing with gardens at both front and rear (Totterdown Fields, **Old Oak Estate** and **White Hart Lane**).

Homes fit for heroes: 1918–1939

It took a world war and the fear of revolution to bring about real change. Reconstruction after the war meant a totally new outlook and spirit of concern to deal with the problems. In his speech to the electors of Wolverhampton in 1918, the Prime Minister, David Lloyd George, vowed 'to make Britain a fit country for heroes to live in' [5]. His words were embodied into legislation in the 1919 Housing and Town Planning Act, introduced into parliament by the Minister of Health, Christopher Addison. The Act instructed local

FIGURE 1.2
Parker and Unwin's cottage housing at Westholm, Letchworth.

authorities to survey the housing needs of their area and prepare programmes for meeting them. For the first time local authorities could seek government subsidy to support their programmes. Subsidy in some form or other has remained a feature of British housing ever since.

Garden city ideals

There was no doubting the preference for garden city housing. The Tudor Walters Report of 1919 [6] embraced this fully. A prominent member of the committee was Raymond Unwin. His influ-ence ensured design criteria which remained in place for a quarter of a century. The key features were semi-detached houses and short terraces made up of wide frontage houses, with densities of twelve dwellings per acre in towns and eight per acre in the countryside, and a minimum planning distance of 70 ft (21 m) between adjacent rows of dwellings. In many cities and towns, the 'cottage' estates began to be laid out with great care and pride by local authorities [7].

Addison Act, 1919

This Act became the basis for all local authority housing built during the inter-war years. The Ministry of Health 'Housing Manual' of 1920 illustrated typical cottage plans. The Tudor Walters Report recommended separate parlours, but the Health Ministry preferred non-parlour types because these were considerably cheaper to build. Kitchens were merely 'sculleries' and the bathroom was on the ground floor with the coal store nearby. These houses lacked many of the facilities that are now taken for granted but, at the time, they were major improvements on previous housing.

A lowering of quality

The lowering of subsidies by the Wheatley Housing Act of 1924 and subsequent funding cuts during the recession reduced standards and general design quality. The early images of Parker and Unwin which had formed the basis of the Tudor Walter's Report were rationalized and simplified. The difference in quality became evident. The Garden City Association felt betrayed. Ebenezer Howard had campaigned for the construction of fifty new towns. In reality, Welwyn Garden City, founded in 1919, was to be the only other new town built until after the Second World War.

Slum clearance

The 1930 Greenwood Housing Act introduced subsidy to assist local authorities with slum clearance. It encouraged higher density housing and the building of flats in city centres. These were mainly in walk-up form in blocks of not more than five storeys in height. At this time the influence of contemporary housing in Amsterdam, Berlin and Vienna was strong and this can be seen in many of the design solutions.

The density issue

The building of flats in the 1930s fuelled the density debate which was to continue throughout the century. The garden city movement rejected the city as it then existed and searched for better solutions based on the countryside and the village. Layouts were to take their form more naturally from the site and the dwelling design was to reflect a rural image [8]. At this time the

debate started on how to accommodate the motor car, which began to have a severe impact on the urban scene, in terms of dealing with through traffic and congestion. It also gave access for more people to live in the new suburbs and the countryside beyond.

There was disagreement amongst architects on layout, arising from the contrast between Parker and Unwin's theories and the *beaux arts* style of straight roads and formal, symmetrical layouts advocated by Patrick Abercrombie and Professor C.H. Reilly of Liverpool University [9]. Also emerging were the new radical ideas of Le Corbusier as expressed in his proposals for La Ville Radieuse (1922) and through his creative use of reinforced concrete to produce simple artisans' housing with free-form plans.

Influence of the Bauhaus

In parallel to Le Corbusier, a number of new developments in London in the 1930s were influenced by the related architecture of the Bauhaus. Architects escaping the Nazi regime in Germany joined with young British architects to design a number of unornamented 'white' blocks of flats (**Isokon flats, Kent House, Highpoint 1** and **2, Kensal House,** and **Pullman Court** in Streatham). Highpoint 1 quickly became an icon for architects. Together these schemes, and the simultaneous publication of F.R.S Yorke's *The Modern Flat* (1935) [10], were to have a phenomenal influence on housing design in the early post-1945 years. On a much larger scale in Leeds, the eight-storey Quarry Hill flats, built in 1934, were modelled on the Karl-Marx-Hof housing in Vienna. This involved a highly experimental form of prefabricated concrete construction which, by the 1980s, had so seriously deteriorated that demolition was considered to be the only solution by Leeds City Council.

Private housing development

The most significant development between the wars was not council housing but the construction of large numbers of houses for sale. Over a quarter of a million new houses per year were sold to the new middle classes – civil servants, professional people, office workers and others whose earnings were sufficient for them to afford the regular mortgage repayments to the building societies. Some 75 per cent of the four million dwellings completed between 1919 and 1939 were built by the private sector. Private developers seldom employed architects; their housing took on an all too familiar appearance. Most layouts conformed to planning criteria set down by the Tudor Walter's Report and much of the housing was built along the new main roads leading out of the towns and cities. 'Ribbon development' and the increasing use of good agricultural land fuelled constant criticism from planners and writers, and paved the way for higher density housing after the Second World War.

Years of ambition: 1945–1951

With a few notable exceptions, such as at **Coventry** (under City Architect Donald Gibson), very little new housing was built during the Second World War. However, the war produced a revolution of socio-political ideas that previously would have been considered unthinkable. During the war, people had come to accept organization from above, and they wanted a post-war reconstruction programme which would 'win the peace'. Throughout the country the housing shortage was severe. Positive planning was called for to tackle both slum housing and the effects of the bombing which had destroyed or made permanently uninhabitable some half a million homes. All political parties accepted that the state had a major role to play in tackling the nation's housing problems.

Prefabricated housing

The Dudley Report and the Housing Manual of 1944 recommended the use of prefabricated houses as a means of building more quickly and during this period local authorities used a whole range of concrete, steel and timber systems – BISF, Spooner, Weir etc. – which were designed to look traditional. These lasted well into the 1970s and beyond without serious problems and

were generally well liked. Most interesting were the 'prefabs' built for people who had become homeless as a result of the bombing. The prefabs offered their occupants a standard of living that they could never have dreamt of. Most had built-in cookers and refrigerators as part of factory-made kitchen/bathroom units (Fig. 1.3). Under the powers in the 1944 Temporary Housing Programme, over 150 000 prefabs were built by local authorities. They were generally intended to have a life-span of around 20 years, but most far exceeded this expectation. As late as the early 1990s the 'little palaces' were still popular with their occupants. A few, which have in recent years been modernized inside and given an outer skin of brickwork and a new roof, will undoubtedly have an even longer life.

The neighbourhood unit

Both the Dudley Report and the 1944 Housing Manual [11] recommended planning new housing in neighbourhood units. These varied in size from 5 000 to 10 000 people and contained smaller homogeneous housing groups of between 100 and 300 dwellings. Neighbourhoods of this size could support a primary school, a range of local shops and other community facilities.

Scandinavian influence

The influence of post-1930 housing by Scandinavian architects was considerable in the early years after 1945. Their projects featured in many journals and government publications and they were admired for their modest domestic scale and use of natural materials. Scandinavian layouts followed principles first used in 1930 by Walter Gropius for his Seimensstadt housing in Berlin, where blocks of flats were arranged in rows on an east–west orientation in open landscape to allow maximum sunshine penetration into living rooms. Sunshine was perceived to be important to good health in Britain so the layout principle was widely accepted and no one had any doubts about separating the housing from the road system. Amongst the first schemes laid out this way were **Churchill Gardens** and **Roehampton**.

FACTORY-MADE EQUIPMENT

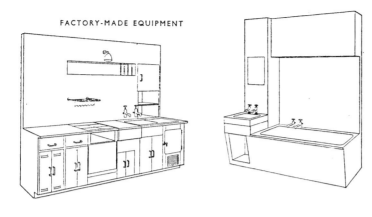

FIGURE 1.3
Post-war prefabricated housing: most contained the kitchen/bathroom combined unit made of pressed metal, shown here in a three-bedroom house and a three-bedroom flat. [From Ministry of Health/Ministry of Works, Housing Manual 1944, *HMSO, 1944, pp. 86 and 89.]*

1949 Housing Act

The Health Minister, Aneurin Bevin, was concerned to ensure that council housing would be available for a wide cross-section of society. His ideas were incorporated into the 1949 Housing Act which removed the obligation on local authorities to provide housing only for the working classes. They were now free to create balanced communities and to meet all housing need irrespective of social class [12]. Regrettably, this opportunity was never developed as local authorities concentrated on tackling their most critical problems.

The 1949 Housing Manual [13] contained minimum space standards for dwellings that have not been improved upon even by those of the 1961 Parker Morris Report. The Manual criticized the monotony of the pre-war estate: 'Unity and character are best achieved in low density areas by the use of terraces and semi-detached houses in contrast with blocks of flats, and public buildings, and in other areas by a mixture of three-storey terraces and multi-storey flats and maisonettes' [14]. Housing of all forms and densities was shown in plans and photographs. Much attention was given to the need for careful design in rural areas, which was exemplified in the new village housing in **Ditchingham, Norfolk** (Fig. 1.4). High density housing was seen as necessary in urban areas and examples illustrated in the Manual included the **Spa Green** and **Woodbury Down Estates** in London.

The Manual contained a chapter on the use of non-traditional systems of house building. It advised of the economies in time, labour and cost that could be effected by the prefabrication of internal parts and fittings for a shell of standard size built in brick or in other forms of construction.

FIGURE 1.4
Tayler and Green at Ditchingham, 1948.

Mixed development

The concept of 'mixed development' was based on the social perception that people would, in accordance with their needs, freely move from one kind of dwelling to another within an estate. The first home of the typical young family would be a flat in a tower or a four-storey block. Here the first child would be born. After the arrival of the second child a house with a garden would be more suitable. With the approach of old age, the occupants could find a house too large for their reduced needs and a more manageable flat or a bungalow would now be preferable. Mixed development appeared in every town and city (**Roehampton** and **Gleadless Valley, Sheffield**), but the concept was flawed because mobility between the various forms of dwellings never became a practical reality.

Mark 1 new towns

A major concern of the immediate post-war years was planning the overspill of population from the large cities. Patrick Abercrombie's Greater London Plan of 1944 recommended the establishment of new towns as planned settlements of balanced communities with a target population of between 50 000 and 100 000 people. In 1946

proposals were announced for the first new town at Stevenage, which was quickly followed by others at Harlow, Crawley, Hemel Hempstead, Welwyn (previously a garden city), Hatfield, Basildon, Bracknell, Newton Aycliffe and Peterlee. The planning of these new towns embraced the concepts of the neighbourhood unit and mixed development.

The Development Corporations employed architects and consultants of the highest calibre including Berthold Lubetkin at Peterlee and Sir Frederick Gibberd at Harlow. Their role was significant in the development of the master-plans and in determining the urban and housing design strategy. At Harlow Gibberd became a legend for his 'design' [15] of the new town and his name is still commonly known to many people in the town today.

The Festival of Britain

The period culminated in 1951 with the Festival of Britain in London. Whilst enjoying the pleasures on the South Bank site, people were encouraged to visit the 'live' architecture and planning show of the festival. The new Lansbury Estate, built in the East End of London, modelled all the new planning and design concepts, complete with schools, ·a pedestrian shopping centre, churches and other community buildings. The intention was to demonstrate the future to come. However, the reality in 1951 was more concerned with the general election and the return of a Conservative government, with promises of new approaches to housing development. The scene had been set for what was to be an explosion in housebuilding in the next 30 years.

In pursuit of an ideal: 1951–1979

The incoming government of 1951 introduced economies and lowered standards in order to build homes in greater numbers. Through the medium of Harold Macmillan's 'people's house' (Fig. 1.5) [16], the increased use of terraces, narrower frontages to raise density and fewer

FIGURE 1.5
'The people's house', 1951. [MoHLG, Houses 1952, 1952, frontispiece.]

internal facilities were advocated. For the first time, plans for family flats above ground-floor level were recommended. Mixed development continued until the emergence at the end of the 1950s of higher density housing.

High rise development

The 1960s and early 1970s are synonymous with high rise housing. Politicians, planners and architects alike all welcomed the move away from the suburban housing sprawl of previous years. The influence upon architects of Le Corbusier's Unité d'Habitation in Marseilles, completed in 1952, proved highly significant in promoting the modernist image. It symbolized 'the futurist view of ....modernity as the saviour of the housing crisis' [17].

Le Corbusier's vision was of clean, healthy housing in a green parkland setting with houses built in a mass-produced manner like ships and aeroplanes. His views were widely supported by contemporary architectural writers. In 1953, J.M. Richards and Gordon Cullen made bitter attacks in *The Architectural Review* on what they called the 'prairie planning' of post-war new towns [18]. Both demanded more urban and higher density development: 'Towns should be planned as towns which is denied by the present suburban sprawl' [19]. At Marseilles was the concrete embodiment of Le

Corbusier's long-standing theories and programmes concerning housing. Such an event had not occurred since Ebenezer Howard's day and it started a process of questioning and reappraisal of the housing problem in Britain: 'Where do we want to live?' and 'What sort of houses do we want?' [20]. This fuelled the imagination of an architectural profession eager to make its contribution to the reconstruction of Britain [21].

The first point block of flats constructed in Britain was Frederick Gibberd's eleven-storey block at the Lawns in Harlow New Town (1950), but the most important of the early schemes using high rise blocks were Alton East and Alton West at Roehampton. Built by the LCC between 1952 and 1958, the influence of Le Corbusier's Unité d'Habitation is clear to see. The latter of the two projects, Alton West, set the trend in Britain for the use of precast concrete components (Fig. 1.6). G.E. Kidder Smith, the leading American critic, claimed it to be 'probably the finest low-cost housing development in the world' [22]. Nicholas Pevsner 'canonized' it as 'one of the masterpieces of post-war residential design....which stood four-square in the greatest tradition of British picturesque landscaping' [23].

There were reasons other than architectural for attempting to convert Le Corbusier's image into reality. The race to build larger numbers of new dwellings took on an overwhelming political significance. Harold MacMillan's initial objective of building 300 000 homes per year was soon overtaken by targets of half a million. The Slum Clearance Act of 1955 fuelled the issue, as local authorities drew up their 10-year programmes for huge amounts of clearance and redevelopment.

There was a shortage of land within the industrial towns and cities. Local authorities favoured high density housing as it reduced their population loss. It was also firmly believed by both the government and the local authorities that the building industry could not cope with the volume of houses required using traditional craft-based methods of construction. Industrialized methods had to be employed. These could only be financially viable if development was organized on a large scale which meant building high density flats and maisonettes.

FIGURE 1.6
Alton West, Roehampton.

The peak years of 'high rise' housing construction were from 1958 to 1968. The tallest blocks, which were thirty-one storeys in height, were built at Red Road in Glasgow. In reality little more than 2 per cent of the housing built at this time was in tower block form, as the vast majority was six storeys or less. Most schemes were mundane and few reached the early expectations of the immediate post-war years [24]. They made little physical link with their surroundings and had few urban amenities within themselves (as was the case with Le Corbusier's 'Unité') nor anything around which would have made them viable communities. On urban sites these flats frequently occupied tight plots where any surrounding space was appropriated by road access and car parking. They were also built on the periphery of towns and cities from which there were inadequate public transport links to urban centres.

Streets in the sky

The influence of Le Corbusier's ideas was expressed further in the development of deck access housing. The concepts of 'streets in the sky' and 'cluster housing' were first identified in the unsuccessful entry by Alison and Peter Smithson in the 1952 Golden Lane housing competition. The Smithsons, who were members of an international modernist group known as CIAM X (Team 10), argued that 'streets would be places and not corridors or balconies, thoroughfares where there are shops, postboxes, telephone kiosks' [25]. Unlike the central corridors in Le Corbusier's Marseilles Unité, the Smithsons' streets would be 'open to the air although covered over, giving views to parkland and open space' [26]. Their *Criteria for Mass Housing* was published in the Team 10 Primer, 1957, and had a considerable impact in defining 'the new brutalism' [27].

FIGURE 1.7
Park Hill, Sheffield.

The Smithsons were ultimately to design only one scheme that reflected these principles, at Robin Hood Lane in Tower Hamlets (DLR All Saints) which proved most unpopular with its occupants.

Sheffield

The Smithsons' concepts became a reality at **Park Hill in Sheffield**, where, in the years between 1955 and 1965, the City Architect's Department, led by Lewis Wormersley, established an international reputation for its innovative housing design. Park Hill, with its 'streets in the sky', was built on a steep hillside overlooking the railway station (Fig. 1.7). Harold Macmillan said it would 'draw the admiration of the world' [28]. It had its own schools, shopping precinct, nursery, churches, pubs and community centres. Part of its initial success was due to an enlightened policy for the time of moving whole streets of families into the new 'rows' so that neighbours were kept together. Community development officers helped the people settle in and set up social activities. As it was experimental, Park Hill received extra government funding which enabled the general standard to be higher than in later schemes built by other local authorities. Most noticeable elsewhere was the reduced width of the decks which became little more than access galleries. This major development enabled Sheffield to achieve 3651 completions in 1965.

Cluster housing

The concept of cluster housing related to the Smithsons' vision of 'community' and 'feeling of identity' that had its origins in the 'unadulterated vitality of life in the East End street' [29]. The cluster block, as developed by Denys Lasdun at **Usk Street** (1952) and **Claredale Street** (1960), both in Bethnal Green, reflected these principles, but neither was to prove successful with their occupants.

Space standards

Internally, the dwellings of the 1960s were designed to good space standards. The Parker Morris report *Homes for Today and Tomorrow*, published in 1961 [30], set out a new range of overall dwelling sizes based on thorough investigations into how people lived (Fig. 1.8). It concluded that space standards should not be concerned with room sizes but with the number of occupants. *Design Bulletin 6: Space in the Home* [31], first published by the Ministry of Housing and Local Government (MoHLG) in 1963, developed the principle through defining spaces between the furniture in each room. From 1969 to 1981, the Parker Morris standards were mandatory for all public sector housing, but the Report's recommendations were never accepted by the private sector to which it was also directed.

FIGURE 1.8
How people live: an illustration by Gordon Cullen from the Parker Morris Report, 1961, pp. 1 and 49.

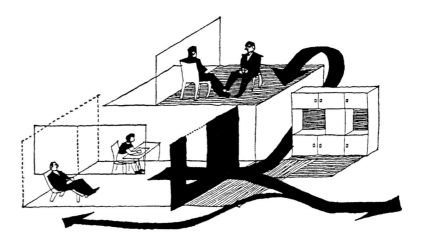

Housing Cost Yardstick System

Funding levels and subsidy for new local authority development had to be determined in relationship to Parker Morris standards. This was achieved through the Housing Cost Yardstick System introduced by the Housing Subsidies Act 1967 and set out in the accompanying manual [32]. All too quickly the yardstick became geared to density and high rise development and minimum standards became maximum.

Contractor designed housing

There was a shortage of architects both in private and public sector practice which meant that local authorities relied heavily upon the contractors who offered a combined planning, design and construction service. In the mid-1960s authorities were inundated with representatives selling their company's systems of construction. Far too many systems were untried and tested before use. Supervision on site was often poor. Prefabricated panels were damaged at the edges and in the corners during construction, which produced leaky joints. Designs failed to consider cold bridging which caused dampness and mould growth that was to become worse where tenants could not afford to run the central heating systems. Poor construction was followed by bewildered management and maintenance in local authorities whose staff lacked the skills and experience to cope with the legacy handed to them.

Radburn layout

One of the key references in the Parker Morris Report was to the use of layouts which segregated pedestrians and vehicles along the lines developed during the 1930s in Radburn, New Jersey, USA. The Radburn concept responded to a genuine fear of increasing danger from the growth in car ownership, but there were inherent problems related to building houses in terraces whereas at Radburn the houses were detached or semi-detached with access to the front door from both sides of the house. There

were also serious problems due to a lack of security in the rear parking courts and the separation of housing from the street was not liked.

Research and development (R&D)

The MoHLG's Research and Development Group, originally set up by Cleeve Barr, was supervised in the early 1960s by Oliver Cox. It experimented with new housing forms in an attempt to set standards and it collaborated with local authorities to build and test the ideas. The R&D Group developed its own 5m system which was used in a pilot project in 1961 at Gloucester Road in Sheffield. From the outset Oliver Cox expressed his concern over the way in which the development of industrialized housing was proceeding. He preferred to see a more humanistic participatory approach to housing development which later in the 1970s he was able to foster in Shankland Cox's schemes for the London Borough of Hillingdon (p. 92).

The Research Group and later the Housing Development Directorate (HDD) of the Department of the Environment, under Pat Tindale, researched key design issues and produced a whole series of Bulletins, Occasional Papers and other publications that offered guidance and feedback on design and development, much of which is still relevant today. Of particular merit were the Occasional Papers on housing for people with physical disabilities and the research on residential roads and footpaths directed by John Noble [33].

Standardization of plans

Inherent in the research into the industrialization of housebuilding was the recognition that certain elements such as staircases and bathroom fittings could be standard even though dwellings might differ in size. This theme was developed in a series of generic plans produced in 1965 by the National Building Agency (NBA). The NBA's standard range of house shells was intended to prevent abortive time being spent on house planning and to streamline production.

Flexibility and adaptability

Concepts of flexibility and adaptability were considered through the development of pilot houses by the MoHLG at the Ideal Home Exhibition in 1962 (Fig. 1.9). The arguments were further implemented after 1967 through the development of PSSHAK (Primary System Support Housing and Assembly Kits). This concept had visions of using industrialization to offer choice. The system provided movable partitions which enabled the tenants to decide on the relative sizes of rooms for themselves and, when one family moved or the children grew up, the sizes of the rooms or the size of the flat could change. A pilot scheme was built in 1977 at **Adelaide Road/Eton Road**, Camden.

The decline of high rise

Initially the new housing was accepted as people enjoyed modern facilities within the home for the first time. However, few people warmed to the modernist images. The rejection was heightened by the sheer size and scale of many of the schemes. There were also serious problems with noise transmission between dwellings, people felt isolated and they were clearly unsuitable for families with children. The problems were aggravated by a spiral of social and economic decline as communities were hit badly by unemployment following the collapse of traditional heavy industry from the 1970s onwards. The gas explosion at Ronan Point in May 1968 hastened an end to high rise and by the mid-1970s industrialized house-building had virtually ceased. No other country has since rejected it to the same extent as Britain.

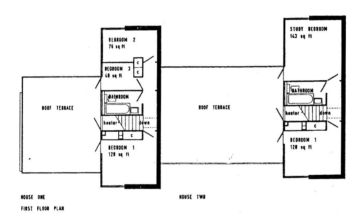

FIGURE 1.9
Expandable/adaptable houses designed by the MoHLGs Research and Development Group and erected at the Ideal Home Exhibition in 1962.

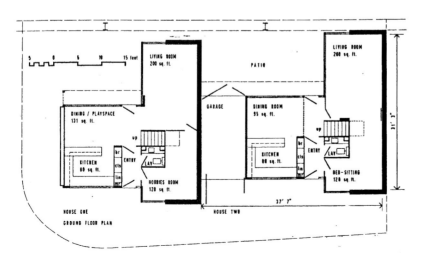

High density/low rise

The unpopularity of high rise and mixed housing development at the end of the 1960s led to a new direction to overcome its disadvantages whilst retaining high densities. Forms of housing were sought that matched the scale of surrounding buildings whilst accommodating families at ground level in dwellings with gardens. Some solutions were ingenious, but the over-complex forms required more sophisticated maintenance techniques which local authorities had difficulty in providing. A conviction for modernist housing remained an important vision in some public and private architectural practices during the 1970s.

Prominent amongst these was the **Camden Borough Architects Department**, headed by Sydney Cook. Under his direction, Neave Brown, Gordon Benson, Alan Forsyth and others designed a number of highly ambitious schemes between 1968 and 1971 at **Highgate New Town**, **Maiden Lane** (Fig. 1.10), **Alexandra Road** and

FIGURE 1.10
High density/low rise housing, Maiden Lane, Camden.

Branch Hill. Most of the Camden schemes were built on the consistent pursuit of a single idea – the linear stepped-section block, based on Le Corbusier's designs as personified in Atelier 5's 1962 Seidlung Halen in Berne.

A very different approach was adopted by Darbourne and Darke for their scheme at **Lillington Street**, Pimlico, built between 1961 and 1971. Here the buildings are clad externally in brick and tile and the modelling of the blocks is designed to express individual dwelling units [34]. The approach produced a landmark project that was much admired and copied during the 1970s.

Theoretical design models

Most influential at this time were the mathematical models of built form derived from studies at Cambridge University in the 1960s conducted by Leslie Martin and Lionel March. These proved that low rise housing could be created at the same density as high rise development. Two of their studies, published in *Urban Spaces and Structures* (1972) [35], related to 'courtyard' housing and 'perimeter' housing (Fig. 1.11).

Courtyard housing

Using hypothetical models, courtyard housing was shown to provide five times more accommodation than tower block development on equivalent site areas. It could also achieve over half as much accommodation again as a terraced layout. The concept took physical form in Neylan and Unglass' schemes at **Bishopfield** in Harlow New Town and at **Setchell Road** in Southwark. A patio form was also used by Peter Phippen and Associates in the co-ownership scheme at **The Ryde**, Hatfield. This scheme also embodied house design principles developed by Serge

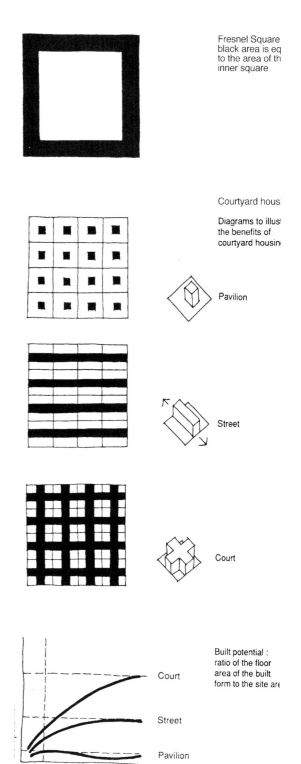

Fresnel Square black area is eq to the area of th inner square

Courtyard hous

Diagrams to illus the benefits of courtyard housin

Pavilion

Street

Court

Built potential : ratio of the floor area of the built form to the site ar

Court

Street

Pavilion

Number of storeys

FIGURE 1.11
The Fresnel Square and Court housing: diagrams to illustrate alternatives to high rise housing. [Redrawn from Martin, L. and March, L., Urban Space and Structures, *pp. 36–37, and AR, 4/80, p. 207.]*

Chermayeff and Christopher Alexander in their book *Community and Privacy*, published in 1963. The dwelling plans separated the house into 'domains', each having different requirements – family, parents and children, noisy and quiet, tidy and untidy etc. [36]. This separation of the space has proved highly successful at **The Ryde, Hatfield**, offering flexibility in the use of the internal space as the household needs change. Other courtyard schemes proved less popular due to the narrow pedestrian alley-ways between the houses which fostered crime and vandalism, and the separation of the house from the street.

Perimeter housing

The principles of perimeter housing lie in the geometry of the 'Fresnel Square' (Fig. 1.11). When translated into architectural terms the concept is that the traditional tower block isolated within a square of green could be developed as low rise housing in a ring around the edge of the green without the loss of dwellings. The principle was developed into built projects by Richard MacCormac whilst at the London Borough of Merton (p. 110). He designed a further scheme at **Duffryn, Gwent** whilst Merton constructed **Watermeads**. Both demonstrated that the principles could produce very satisfactory design solutions [37].

Byker

Almost the last and one of the most striking of all local authority high density housing projects was the **Byker** redevelopment in Newcastle, designed between 1968 and 1992 by the Stockholm-based architect, Ralph Erskine. The scheme is most noted for the unusual form of the 'wall' and tenant participation. Through his resident architect, Vernon Gracie, he maintained an open door for anyone wishing to talk with him and his architectural team. The extent to which the design genuinely reflects the views of the tenants is an issue of debate, but it cannot be denied that he influenced the subsequent development of community architecture in Britain.

New towns and planned overspill

Even with high rise housing, it was impossible for local authorities to rehouse in new developments within their boundaries all the people and facilities displaced from the slum clearance areas. New towns and planned overspill developments were therefore seen by the government as an important part of the country's overall new house-building programme. This policy of population dispersal was supported by town planners who considered that the social, economic and planning problems of the inner cities could not be tackled without some people being moved out. The GLC was particularly active through its 'Expanded Towns Policy'. Planned overspill, under the 1952 Town Development Act, took place at Basingstoke, Bletchley (later Milton Keynes), Swindon and in a number of East Anglian towns including Haverhill, Kings Lynn and Thetford.

After 1960 a further group of new towns were designated (Fig. 1.12) amongst which were Skelmersdale, Runcorn and later Warrington and Central Lancashire in the North-West, Washington in Tyneside, Redditch and Telford in the West Midlands, and Peterborough, Northampton and Milton Keynes in the South-East. Others were designated in Scotland and Northern Ireland. In total, since 1946, thirty-two 'new towns' were designated throughout Britain with a total population of 2.5 million.

The master plans for these provided an opportunity for their planners to explore a number of different models. The road grid plan at Washington and later at Milton Keynes (both designed by Walter Bor of Llewellyn Davies and Partners) were based on achieving a high level of personal mobility. Runcorn's figure-of-eight bus-only route gave an alternative emphasis on public transport. Most of the new towns experimented with new ideas in housing design. Runcorn (later Runcorn and Warrington), Washington and Telford successfully pioneered new ways of integrating the car into housing layouts. Runcorn developed the access-way (**Halton Brow**) whilst shared pedestrian/vehicular courts first appeared in Washington in the late 1960s. Milton Keynes developed complete cycle networks. High

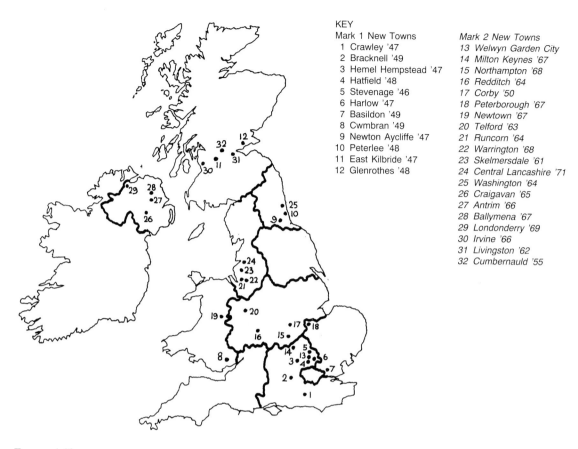

KEY

Mark 1 New Towns	Mark 2 New Towns
1 Crawley '47	13 Welwyn Garden City
2 Bracknell '49	14 Milton Keynes '67
3 Hemel Hempstead '47	15 Northampton '68
4 Hatfield '48	16 Redditch '64
5 Stevenage '46	17 Corby '50
6 Harlow '47	18 Peterborough '67
7 Basildon '49	19 Newtown '67
8 Cwmbran '49	20 Telford '63
9 Newton Aycliffe '47	21 Runcorn '64
10 Peterlee '48	22 Warrington '68
11 East Kilbride '47	23 Skelmersdale '61
12 Glenrothes '48	24 Central Lancashire '71
	25 Washington '64
	26 Craigavan '65
	27 Antrim '66
	28 Ballymena '67
	29 Londonderry '69
	30 Irvine '66
	31 Livingston '62
	32 Cumbernauld '55

FIGURE 1.12
'New towns' in Britain.

standards were set for the design of external spaces and planting. These innovations contributed significantly to the DOE's range of planning and design bulletins and occasional research papers. Their influence upon local authorities, the planning system and the general level of quality of development in Britain was considerable. Since the new towns were disbanded this gap has never been adequately filled.

Housing Associations

The Housing Association movement began in the 1830s with the Society for Improving the Conditions of the Labouring Classes. They were of little significance until in the 1950s when they became involved in building special needs housing, particularly sheltered housing for elderly people. Housing Associations received their major boost in the 1964 Housing Act when the government established the Housing Corporation as a promotional body and the channel of finance. Most new schemes were small with an emphasis on meeting special need and developing urban infill sites. Architects became experienced at designing schemes to fit the sites and the localities.

Encouraged by the 1967 Civic Amenities Act, Housing Associations became skilled in conservation and reusing old buildings for housing. This experience introduced associations to the larger and more difficult task of rehabilitating pre-1919 housing in inner urban areas. Working closely with local authorities, they established local offices and proved themselves particularly adept at working with communities, many of which included large ethnic minorities. Frequently the residents were elderly owner-occupiers whose homes were in serious disrepair. The work often went far beyond the improvement of the housing itself into areas of coordinated environmental improvement, the modernization of old commercial premises, and into helping local groups promote community activities and pursue employment-generating opportunities [38].

Improvement of pre-1919 housing

The 1969 Housing Act created a new emphasis. At this time the worst of the Victorian slums had been cleared and most of the pre-1919 housing that remained, if adequately repaired and modernized, was capable of having a much longer life. Prominent amongst the early schemes in the 1970s was **Black Road** at Macclesfield where architect Rod Hackney worked with local residents to preserve and improve two small groups of housing which, at the time, were included in the local authority's slum clearance programme.

The 1969 Act effectively brought an end to slum clearance and gave powers to local authorities to look at older housing areas as a whole. Funding was available to designate General Improvement Areas (GIAs) and later Housing Action Areas (HAAs) in which the local authority established a working relationship with house owners, landlords and their tenants to encourage them to secure improvement grants for internal works, whilst the local authority itself organized the environmental improvements through a process of participation. Many local authorities had large programmes through which they gained valuable experience of community participation.

Private housing

Home ownership grew rapidly from 1950 but most speculative housing followed the pattern established before the war with layouts of detached and semi-detached houses built to average densities of around ten dwellings per acre (25 dw/ha). A number of specialist developers produced good schemes, for example A. Cragie in Jesmond, Newcastle (pp. 184–186). Neil

FIGURE 1.13
Span housing at Blackheath.

Wates, after visiting Seidlung Halen in Berne, commissioned the architects Atelier to design a small group of hillside houses in Croydon (Park Hill Road, 1968, R. East Croydon).

However, the most exceptional private housing developments of the period were the **Span housing** schemes in **Blackheath** (Fig. 1.13), **Ham Common, Highsett** in Cambridge and at other locations in the south of England. Span Developments Ltd was established in the mid-1950s by G.P. Townsend, an architect who was formerly a partner of Eric Lyons, but who resigned from the partnership (and the RIBA) to become a 'developer' [39]. Span's architect, Eric Lyons, thereafter produced designs with unmistakable flat and monopitched roofs which set styles that became fashionable all over Britain. Lyons and Townsend shared a vision of how people might live – if shown the possibilities. It was a vision which captured the imagination of Richard Crossman who, as Minister of Housing, gave planning consent, despite official advice, for **New Ash Green**.

Eric Lyons's greatest design achievement was to demonstrate that it was possible to move away from the standard housebuilder's pattern of site layout and the highway engineer's rigid requirements for the design of roads. At **Blackheath** the roads around the sites were private (and still are). This enabled him to soften their

LIVERPOOL JOHN MOORES UNIVERSITY
Aldham Robarts L.R.C.
TEL 0151 231 3701/3634

FIGURE 1.14
Essex Design Guide at its best at South Woodham Ferrers.

visual impact and use materials such as stone
setts for curbs and a variety of materials for
paving [40].

Lyons believed that the key to successful
design was the firm control by a single architect
of every detail from briefing to site supervision.
Supported by Ivor Cunningham's landscape
design, he was able to realize these high
standards. His achievements brought public
acclaim and he was RIBA President between 1975
and 1977.

A distinct benefit to the design was the
management company set up by Span to maintain
the buildings with their roads and planting. The
residents bought long leases costing between
£2500 and £3000 (a substantial amount for the

late 1950s) – knowing that thereafter their house
and its environment, including the roads and
footpaths, would be maintained. This arrangement has been a resounding success. It has not
only preserved and enhanced the landscaping but
also ensured that the timber and tile hanging, the
flat roofs, the open entrances to flat blocks and
other features that have caused problems when
copied elsewhere, have not been an issue in Span
housing.

Design guides

Some planning authorities attempted to improve
standards through design guides, particularly for
roads and footpaths. The best of these were based

on the new concepts for the design of residential roads and footpaths that had been developed in the new towns. The *Essex Design Guide* (1973) demonstrated how, by careful design, it was possible to create townscape quality that existed in the traditional town and village (Fig. 1.14). *The Architects Journal* compared its significance to Le Corbusier's *Vers une Architecture* commenting that it 'will inevitably influence the environment of the future' [41].

New directions: 1979–1997

New policies

The new Conservative government began making a decisive change of direction for all housing sectors. An early move was to abolish mandatory Parker Morris standards in 1981 which caused sufficient concern for the RIBA and the Institute of Housing (now the CIOH) to collaborate on the publication of their own set of standards in *Homes for the Future* in 1983, followed by a series of specialist design bulletins (listed in the bibliography). New housing development by local authorities dwindled and in the 1988 Housing Act their role was redefined as 'enabler'. After much hesitation, the government passed responsibility for providing new rented housing from local authorities to Housing Associations. 'Public sector housing' became 'social housing', defined as 'housing provided by an organization which allocates accommodation on the basis of need' [42].

Right-to-buy

A cornerstone of government policy was the right-to-buy (RTB) legislation. Home ownership was essential to the government's philosophy which centred on the property-owning individual and family. Despite counter-efforts by some Labour-controlled Councils, the early years of the RTB were successful for the government. By 1982, over 200 000 council houses had been sold to their occupants, frequently with the benefit of very generous discounts off the market value of the property. By 1986, over a million houses had been sold. It was 'the sale of the century' [43].

However, by the mid-1980s sales were dwindling and the government looked for new ways of reducing the control which local authorities had over the large quantity of housing still in their possession. This it determined to achieve through estate regeneration.

Estate regeneration

The housing crisis

The 1981 riots in Brixton, Toxteth and Moss Side and those of 1985 in Handsworth and Broadwater Farm in Haringey drew government attention to the need for action to tackle the worst council estates. Lord Scarman's official enquiry [44] into the causes of the 1981 riots concluded that they were the product of unemployment and poverty which produced an alienated society. A principal recommendation was that local communities should be more involved in the making of decisions that affect their home and environment. This view was supported by *Faith in the City*, published by the Church of England in 1985 which added an important issue: 'where a community is small enough for human relations to be conducted, and for the environment to be cared for by the people who live in it, the destructiveness diminishes' [45].

Estate action

The solution determined by the government was a marriage of Conservative ideals of privatization, home-ownership and self-sufficiency, linked with the hitherto left-wing model of community participation. The Priority Estates Project (PEP), which began in 1981, was the first initiative. This was followed by the launching of the Urban Housing Renewal Unit (UHRU) in 1985, renamed Estate Action in 1986.

Estate regeneration funding was made available for a wide range of physical improvements to tackle the structural, layout and environmental problems, as well as the modernization of the dwellings themselves. High on the agenda were measures to improve safety and security, to conserve energy and to provide more community facilities. Community workshops and other buildings were intended to stimulate employment opportunities. In some instances, it has proved to be more economically and/or socially viable to demolish the estate progressively and decant the tenants into new low rise development.

In addition to improving the physical fabric of estates, the process of estate regeneration was in itself important as a means of stimulating the economic and social objectives for stabilizing the community and raising its self-esteem. This multi-faceted approach to regeneration was seen as essential to the long-term sustainability of the estates.

The 1990s saw the development of partnerships between local authorities, Housing Associations and the private sector as a means of rescuing the worst estates. Financial incentives for refurbishment were offered by the government to encourage a whole host of initiatives aimed at stock transfer to new landlords and greater tenant control. In 1990/1, through City Challenge, the government began to target expenditure on the more efficient, competitive inner-city pioneer authorities. Architects played a significant role in ensuring that good schemes were delivered in accordance with programmes.

Local authorities linked Estate Action with other areas of funding. The **London Borough of Lewisham**, for example, in their refurbishment of Pepys and Milton Court Estates, combined Estate Action with City Challenge and European Regional Development Fund (ERDF) opportunities to develop schemes which brought people back into employment. A skills audit was carried out on the estates with the intention that this would produce a pool of labour that could be employed on the improvement works. Training, supported by the Enterprise Council and the DOE, enabled people to work on a subcontracting basis to the main contractors. Measures to help people to take part included the conversion of disused garages into workshops and the building of child-care centres so that single parents could leave their children whilst working.

In building up to this inclusive approach to regeneration, Lewisham was also innovative in the use of private finance to supplement its capital programme, for instance, loans from a French bank were used to remodel the Flowerhouse Estate, now renamed The Meadows (R. Beckenham Hill).

Refurbishment of high rise

Many tower blocks have been given a new lease of life when modernized and overclad with a new outer skin. With the installation of modern door entry systems, a block can offer a high degree of safety, security and privacy. Some blocks have been successfully converted into sheltered housing for elderly people, complete with resident warden, community rooms and a laundrette. Most offer superb views. However, despite this late reprise, the consequence of the unpopularity of high rise housing still remains with the architectural profession.

Funding

In 1996 Estate Action was merged with the Single Regeneration Budget (SRB) to form a single funding body for estate and urban regeneration. The latest move is the establishment of Local Housing Companies and Joint Venture Companies between local authorities and private developers. All the options are related to the principle that some government investment would be available for rehabilitation provided the local authority agreed to lessen its direct control of the housing through stock transfers. Provided debt charges can be overcome, it is hoped that this will encourage the private sector to more actively participate, bringing with it a substantial financial contribution.

Community architecture

The architectural profession responded to housing regeneration through its experience of community architecture which had developed in the 1970s and the success in the early 1980s of schemes such as Hunt Thompson's **Lea View, Hackney**. The work of those involved arguably produced some of the most outstanding achievements by

British architects in the late 20th century. The movement received royal assent in 1984 from Prince Charles who, in his speech to the RIBA at Hampton Court, said:

'To be concerned about the way people live, about the environment they inhabit and the kind of community that is created by that environment, should surely be one of the prime requirements of a really good architect .... what I believe about community architecture is that it has shown 'ordinary people' that their views are worth having'.

The RIBA actively promoted community architecture. In 1988 it jointly, with the Chartered Institute of Housing, published *Tenant Participation* [46] which brought together examples of the best practice of the time. It highlighted how demanding the work was. Architects had to learn the skills of having a meaningful dialogue with users on a level basis. Design solutions had to be site specific to reflect the needs and aspirations of groups and individual people. Participation did not lead, however, to a reduction in design quality as was feared. There were arguments on architectural matters. Some committees detested 'the new' and related back to the past. Others wanted to be in the vanguard of innovation and were eager to try out new ideas. They were quick to recognize quality and to reject ideas which they regarded as substandard. The key to success for architects was the concept of options appraisals which highlighted opportunities and constraints. The options had to be displayed on an equal basis and presented in an easily understandable way, "without which participation ceases to be effective" [47].

Utopia on trial

Alice Coleman's book *Utopia on Trial: Vision and Reality in Planned Housing*, published in 1985 [48], came at a time of great public concern about the inner cities. Her views were vigorously supported by the then Prime Minister, Margaret Thatcher. The book made sweeping condemnations of local authority housing, both in its design and management. Assisted by a team of five researchers, Alice Coleman studied more than 100 000 houses mainly

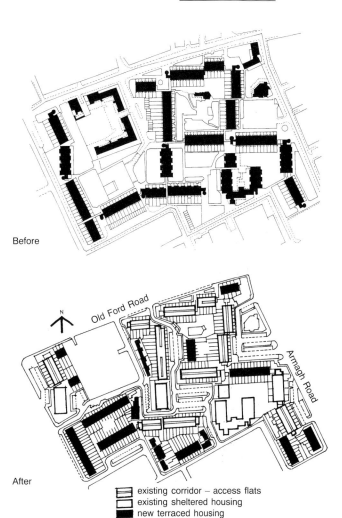

Before

After

existing corridor – access flats
existing sheltered housing
new terraced housing

FIGURE 1.15
Ranwell Road Estate, Tower Hamlets, before and after the DICE intervention (B. 7/11/97, p. 48).

in Southwark and Tower Hamlets. She concluded that people were clearly happier in housing which related to streets and where the space around had a measure of defensibility and surveillance. The use of through roads rather than culs-de-sac would reduce crime [49]. The Department of the Environment commissioned her to put these views into practice in a number of estates in Southwark, Tower Hamlets (Fig. 1.15) and Westminster. Many of her findings from this reflected those of Oscar Newman who had previously studied similar

FIGURE 1.16
Mozart Estate: new roads to increase the level of permeability. Note also the new pitched roofs and in the distance Erno Goldfinger's Balfron Tower.

FIGURE 1.17
Tower Hamlets HAT: new housing to replace the 1960s Monteith Estate. [Photo by architects.]

estates in the USA [50]. The final outcome was ultimately considered to be inconclusive but the concept of 'permeable' housing layouts (Fig. 1.16) is now widely accepted (e.g. **Hulme, Crown Street**).

Housing Action Trusts (HATs)

These were seen by the government as another way of encouraging the transfer of council estates to alternative landlords. After experience on the Tenants' Choice Programme in 1987, government officials made direct approaches to a number of estates to form HATs. However, the tenants were suspicious of the intentions and refused to cooperate. The first HAT was eventually established, after much negotiation, at Hull in 1991 which was followed by others at Castle Vale, Liverpool, Tower Hamlets (Fig. 1.17), Waltham Forest and Stonebridge. The process enables the HATs to acquire the housing stock from the local authorities by direct transfer after a favourable ballot of the tenants. During refurbishment or replacement works, the tenants can vote to return the ownership of their housing to the local authority or their estate can be taken over by an alternative landlord such as a local Housing Association. Ownership can also be taken over by the residents themselves through forming a Community Based Housing Association. An important task for the HATs is the preparation of an 'exit strategy' to protect the long-term sustainability of the physical and socio-economic regeneration measures (p. 258).

Improvement of pre-1919 housing

Whilst funding was directed between 1979 and 1997 to refurbishing local authority housing, much less was made available for the improvement of the pre-1919 housing which still makes up one in four of the country's housing stock. Rehabilitation took on its most effective form through the enveloping schemes devised most progressively by Birmingham City Council in the 1970s and continued into the 1980s. Enveloping was envisaged as a form of neighbourhood improvement which financed renovations to the external fabric of unimproved housing without a cost burden being placed on the owners. The works included new roofs, windows, chimney stacks, damp proof courses, cleaning of brick-work, etc., and a measure of environmental works. The internal improvements were subsequently organized through the system of housing improvement grants. The Housing Acts of 1984 and 1985 directed financial resources to areas of greatest need and introduced means testing for improvement grants, but local authorities could no longer support enveloping from their housing investment allocations [51].

New housing development 1979–1997

The government placed its emphasis on building new housing for home ownership and even housing association programmes were diverted from much greater needs elsewhere to achieve this objective. By 1995, home ownership had reached 67 per cent of the total housing stock but many people, particularly those who had purchased their council house through the right-to-buy legislation, encountered difficulties in maintaining their mortgage repayments, only to find their house repossessed. The plight of the

homeless grew as the social housing programme slumped. In 1996 little more than 35 000 social dwellings were built throughout the whole of Great Britain (excluding Northern Ireland). In the same year some 110 000 dwellings for sale were built by the private sector.

Local authority development

The small amount of new housing built in the 1980s by local authorities was generally of a high standard, demonstrating a maturity of approach that benefited from continuity of practice in local authorities and experience. Public sector architects departments concentrated their attention on housing regeneration and played a major part in developing community-based approaches.

New towns

A number of new towns continued to build housing for rent well into the 1990s and produced some outstanding schemes (e.g. **Warrington, Irvine**). Milton Keynes succeeded in producing some well designed private sector housing through its positive development control approach.

The major problem now experienced by new towns at the end of the century arises from the absence of any financial arrangements to fund major repairs to the infrastructure. In some instances this problem is now acute since the infrastructure and major facilities were built over a short space of time and are ageing together [52].

Urban Development Corporations

Unlike the former new towns, the Urban Development Corporations, established after 1979 [53], were not set up to be direct providers of new housing. They possessed full planning powers within their designated areas and could exert influence on quality through the briefing and land release processes. Some Corporations used these powers effectively.

The **London Docklands Development Corporation (LDDC)** was severely criticised in

FIGURE 1.18
London Docklands: Limehouse Basin.

the early 1980s for its *laissez-faire* planning when the emphasis was to secure development regardless of its quality. It will by the end of the century have produced some 25 000 new houses. Much is rubbished as 'dockney' [54], but nowhere in Britain is there the density of schemes worthy of attention (Fig. 1.18). The largest percentage of the housing is privately owned but since 1990 the LDDC has worked in partnership with Housing Associations to secure social housing for rent. In total some 5000 dwellings have been built with a further 936 for local authorities (e.g. Masthouse Terrace off Westferry Road, E14 – East Thames Housing Association, DLR Island Gardens). The LDDC has also funded the improvement of some 8000 council dwellings (e.g. Barley Mow Estate, Three Colt Street, Limehouse, E14, DLR Westferry) [55].

FIGURE 1.19
Liberty of Early sheltered housing for frail elderly people, Lower Early, Reading: view of the garden court.

Housing association development

In recent years housing associations have taken on new areas of responsibility. Many are actively involved in regenerating large 1960s council estates, working in partnership with local authorities and the private sector. Others are concerned with the ageing population, building schemes for elderly people often with nursing care facilities (e.g. **Liberty of Early, Reading**, Fig. 1.19). A number of associations have successfully promoted low energy housing (**Gwalia, Swansea**) and developed new forms of housing for young people (**Swansea foyer**) and for students (**Lincoln, Winchester**). Design quality is seriously affected by financial constraints but recent projects in London, Manchester and Glasgow demonstrate that there is still confidence in modern design. It is a pity that this quality has not percolated through to the main body of housing association development and to the private sector.

Design-build

The 1988 Housing Act imposed the current harsh financial regime upon housing associations. Most housing association development is now procured through design-build contracting methods which place more of the detailed design with the contractor. In the report 'Constructing the Team', published in 1994, the Chairman, Sir Michael Latham, gave added strength to those who advocated this method of procurement. He believed that closer working between client and builder could cheapen costs, and he considered that a target of a 30 per cent reduction by the year 2000 could be confidently set. His intentions of team work were sound but when applied to housing association development in an austere financial environment, they merely resulted in a general lowering of quality.

Housing co-operatives

The early 1980s witnessed the emergence of the housing co-operative movement. Most significant in the last quarter of the century was the growth of the par-value co-op. In normal co-operative housing, members have personal equity for their own property but in par-value co-ops they are nominal shareholders and own the development collectively [56]. From 1957 local authorities could provide them with mortgages, but more importantly from 1974 they could receive the same grants as housing associations through the Housing Corporation. The greatest concentration of co-ops was in Liverpool, arising out of unique political circumstances (p. 201), and in Glasgow (pp. 281, 300–304).

Self-build

A number of housing co-operatives have in recent years ventured into the area of self-build, notably the **Diggers** in Brighton (using the Segal method), Zenzele in Bristol, **Paxton Court**, Sheffield and the Lightmoor project in Telford. Self-build is the ultimate form of participation in the housing design and procurement process and, its supporters would argue, the most sustainable.

In addition, individual people have built their own homes on plots of land, but in total the amount of self-build in Britain is small in comparison with other countries. A study carried out by Sussex University in 1992 [57] showed that the self-help sector comprised just 6 per cent of the housing market in comparison to Germany where it was 60 per cent and the United States where it was 20 per cent. In Sweden, Stockholm City Council has had a self-build department since the 1920s which has helped build 30 per cent of all single family dwellings in the city.

The benefits of self-build for both rent and home-ownership can be considerable, provided participants accept the commitment and the time it takes, particularly that involved in acquiring the land and the finance. It can reduce construction costs by as much as 40 per cent which can produce cheaper homes or the saving can be put into improving the quality of the housing. In some self-build schemes the saving has been used to increase the level of energy efficiency. The unseen benefits are greater satisfaction, a sense of ownership leading to better standards of maintenance and a new vitality in housing [58].

Lifetime homes

One of the most imaginative concepts to emerge in recent years is that of 'lifetime homes' developed by the Joseph Rowntree Foundation. The concept builds on experience since the publication in the mid-1970s of the DOE's standards for mobility housing and wheelchair housing (p. 15). Its emphasis is on thinking ahead to ensure ease of adaptation when required and attention to detail at the construction stage to cut costs and work needed later. Dwelling plans are suitable for able-bodied and adaptable for frail or physically disabled people. Design features for lifetime homes are shown in Fig. 1.20. The additional cost at the initial construction stage of these features is small in comparison with the later cost and some housing associations have adopted the standards for all their new developments.

Private development

Private ownership increased steadily to 67 per cent of the total stock by 1997. For many people this means buying a new home in a speculative suburban development on the edge of a built-up area. The alternative use of greenfield sites or brown land in the inner cities has now focused

the attention of politicians and developers. Some house building companies have established urban renewal units to build on derelict inner-city sites. This has led to partnerships with local authorities and housing associations and in the 1990s many of these sought grant aid from the government through City Grant, City Challenge and Single Regeneration programmes. Such partnerships are generally producing the most interesting private sector housing design.

A popular trend has been the conversion into housing of former warehouses (Fig. 1.21), office blocks and factories. This includes a number of well known buildings in London such as Erno Goldfinger's 1960s office block – Alexander Fleming House – at Elephant and Castle and the 1962 Piper Building, at Carnwath Road, SW6 (u. Putney Bridge) [59].

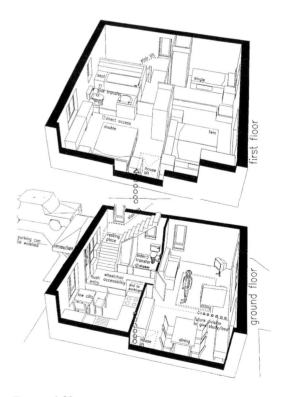

FIGURE 1.20
Lifetime homes: design features of a three-bedroom house. [By courtesy of the Joseph Rowntree Foundation.]

FIGURE 1.21
Plymouth Docks: warehouses converted into housing.

Living over the shop

Some success came out of this initiative developed in the the early 1990s by Ann Petherick and Ross Fraser [60] with the support of the Joseph Rowntree Foundation. Unfortunately, whilst there have been some excellent schemes, for example those run by Coventry Churches Housing Association in Granby Street, Leicester, and the Soho Housing Association at 9 Berwick Street in London, the goverment programme was not fully taken up.

Concern for quality

By the mid-1990s concerns about quality in the built environment and the future impact of urban growth were being expressed in high places. Prince Charles' books *A Vision of Britain* (1989) [61] and *Urban Villages* (1992) [62] brought the issues to the public's attention. In 1994, John Gummer, the then Secretary of State for the Environment, outlined his views in a remarkable publication for the government of the time, *Quality in Town and Country* [63]. The publication emphasized the importance of architecture in creating quality of place which can reinforce a sense of community and create local pride. There was need to pay more attention to urban details such as street signs and furniture. Above all it commented that 'quality is sustainable'. These were admirable recommendations but they were received with scepticism by those who had been voicing the same concerns to a disinterested government for the previous 15 years.

Rural housing

John Gummer's publication concerned itself considerably with the need for good design of new housing in rural areas. This has to be seen in the context that the availability of affordable housing in the countryside is no less severe than in towns and cities. In the past 20 years, the countryside's population has increased by more than one million people due to the greater mobility of the affluent commuter. The impact of this and the demand for second homes in the countryside has squeezed the existing rural population out of the housing market. The supply of cheap housing is now extremely limited and the need for affordable housing for people who already live and work in rural areas, the elderly and young people, is immense.

Furthermore, low-income households are caught between rich commuters who push prices up and conservation lobbyists who object to any new development taking place. The pressure that this places on the countryside is intense. Within villages it calls for sensitively designed housing on infill sites and an attitude towards design that ensures it suits the setting and reflects local architectural tradition. A number of good examples exists (e.g. **Broadwindsor**, Dorset, Fig. 1.22) but generally it is extremely difficult to achieve this quality due to the current funding regime for housing association development [64].

Sustainable housing development

John Gummer also commented on the need for sustainable development which he defined as 'taking the longer term perspective and not cheating future generations out of the quality of life we enjoy' [65]. A whole host of guidance has since emerged, amongst the best of which has

FIGURE 1.22
Broadwindsor: new rural housing adding to the structure and character of the existing village.

come from research sponsored by the Joseph Rowntree Foundation [66]. There is hope in initiatives such as the urban villages movement and the '2000 Homes' Project.

Sustainability has now become a central issue and there is particularly a growing desire by government to reverse the exodus from the cities which has been so much a part of this century's housing scene. The solution calls for a new determination to make towns and cities better places in which to live and work, where it is possible to enjoy the cultural and intellectual benefits of being part of a lively and supportive community. Well designed housing built to a

good standard is essential to this aim.

Urban villages as a concept originated in the plans for the unsuccessful attempts in the early 1980s by consortia of housebuilders to develop 'country towns' within the greenbelt around London [67]. It is now being developed through the Urban Villages Forum originally established by Prince Charles. The Forum sees urban villages as mixed-use developments covering 100 acres (30 ha) for 5000 residents. Housing is to be built at an average density of 20–25 dwellings per acre (50–60 dw/ha). There will be a focus on public transport and reducing car travel by building

FIG. 1.23
Millennium Village, Greenwich: impression by Ralph Erskine.

work-space as part of the development. The difficulty of genuinely achieving mixed-use development is not underestimated and English Partnerships (the National Urban Regeneration Agency) has allocated funds to ensure that the first schemes will include community facilities. These funds will be used for site assembly and land reclamation as well as for rent guarantees and loan mortgages to support the mixed-use set-up.

A new kind of developer is envisaged, the 'promoter' who will have to guarantee a commitment to the urban village principles. Central to the arrangements will be the unified control of the whole site by the landowner and/or promoter. Their responsibilities will be set out in the constitution of an 'urban village trust'. Local people will be represented on the urban village trust through the establishment of a 'community trust'. Two new economic appraisal techniques – social financial appraisal and community impact appraisal – will assess the costs beyond those of normal housing development [68].

Poundbury in Dorset has been identified by the Forum as its first demonstration project as well as **Crown Street**, Glasgow and **Silvertown**, in London Docklands. Others are being developed including the Lightmoor Urban Village in Telford, Little Germany in Bradford and

Gallions Reach in Thamesmead. The most ambitious project is the **Millennium Village** proposed for the Greenwich peninsular (Fig. 1.23).

The '2000 Homes' project

A concern for quality is the focus of '2000 Homes'. This RIBA-backed project was the subject of a millennium bid in 1996 which failed to gain support because the Millennium Commission considered that housing projects benefit individuals or families rather than the public at large. The project is now supported by a number of major housing associations, the National Housebuilding Council (NHBC) and the Joseph Rowntree Foundation. Its aims are to increase public awareness in housing, and particularly to demonstrate that contemporary housing offers more than what is currently available. It proposes to achieve this through a year-long, nation-wide exhibition in the year 2000 which will draw to the public's attention many innovative housing schemes at the design or completion stages.

Housing for young people

The 1980s witnessed a huge rise in the number of homeless people in Britain, particularly amongst young people aged 16–26. This coincided with the severe cutbacks in public funding for social housing. In 1995 the CHAR Inquiry into Youth Homelessness Report [69] estimated that there were between 200 000 and 300 000 homeless young people in Britain. The numbers are now a little less but the problem is still acute. The rise in homelessness in the 1980s also came at the same time as the huge rise in unemployment. With no work, the young people are unable to find anywhere to live and with no home they cannot get a job.

A number of initiatives emerged to meet the need, although these have merely touched the problem. Amongst these are the **Young Builders' Trust** and a whole host of other small but important projects (e.g. Grimsby Doorstep) in which young people undertake the improvement of pre-1919 terraced housing whilst gaining training and experience in the building industry and undergoing vocational training.

The most significant development in housing for young people in the 1990s was the rise of the **Foyer** movement. The idea originated in France in the 1940s. The UK network was spearheaded by Shelter and Grand Metropolitan plc from 1992. Foyers provide accommodation, training and a job network for young people between the ages of 18 and 25. Most have been located in cities and large towns, close to transport and work opportunities. By mid-1997 there were fifty-one operational Foyers in Britain and many more planned. Sizes vary between eight and over 150 bedspaces, amounting to a total of 2500 bedspaces nation-wide. The average length of stay is 12 months. Rents are low and Foyers raise additional income from statutory grants and revenue from catering in their cafe/restaurants and training facilities.

Agenda for the 21st century

It is important that the housing agenda for the next century should respect the lessons from the past 100 years. The successes came from a care for quality whilst the failures resulted from a gulf between design, management and use. In its 1997 policy paper 'Building the Future', the RIBA set out its housing agenda by recommending that, to produce 'better homes', the government must take the following action:

*   Undertake an audit of the nation's housing, identifying numbers, locations, types and conditions.
*   Develop a national housing policy based on need, ability to pay and choice of tenure.
*   Require local authorities to produce local housing plans, based on an audit of local need.
*   Establish a unified housing budget to relate government expenditure on development to the housing benefit support given to those in need.
*   Adopt new procurement methods to achieve long-term quality rather than short-term gain.

- Establish a national programme of research, and in particular to encourage innovative, adaptable and affordable housing solutions to match the rapid change in the pattern of need.
- Provide incentives for the private sector to build more housing for single people in the areas of greatest need.
- Adopt housing standards, suitable for well into the 21st century and applicable to all housing sectors, with priority given to energy-conscious design.
- Encourage greater choice and greater opportunity for choice within both public and private housing.
- Develop a government agency 'UK Homes' along the lines of English Partnerships, but with the specific brief to develop land for building.

Government leadership is essential but there needs to be vision in all parts of the housing and building industries. Quality in housing means getting the right decisions on what should be built, where it is built and how it is managed and maintained. It means resolving issues such as land costs which currently represent too high a proportion of development costs and it means involving people in designing their home. The question for the future is whether the lessons of the 20th century have really been learnt or whether the past mistakes will be repeated. Hopefully this book and the continued work of the RIBA Housing Group who stimulated its production will influence the debate.

References

[1] Howard, E., *Garden Cities of Tomorrow*, Attic Books, 1997 (reprint).

[2] Reiss, R.L., The significance of Welwyn Garden City, *AR*, 1–6, 1927, pp. 175–182; Girardet, H., *The Gaia Atlas of Cities*, Gaia Books Ltd, 1992, pp. 54–55.

[3] Taylor, N., *The Village in the City*, Temple Smith, London, 1973, p. 73.

[4] Hawkes, D., The architectural partnership of Barry Parker and Raymond Unwin, *AR*, 6/78, pp. 327–332.

[5] Swenerton, M., *Homes fit for Heroes*, Heinemann Educational Books, 1981, p. 79.

[6] Tudor Walters Report, *Report of the Committee to consider questions of building construction with the provision of dwellings for the working classes*, 1918.

[7] Housing and town planning after the war: a valuable report, *AR*, 9/18, pp. 19–22.

[8] Unwin, R., Town planning: formal or irregular, *AR*, 11/11, pp. 293–294.

[9] Swenerton, M., *Homes Fit for Heroes*, Heinemann Educational Books, 1981, pp. 64-66.

[10] Yorke F.R.S., *The Modern Flat*, The Architectural Press, London, 1937.

[11] Ministry of Health/Ministry of Works, *Housing Manual*, HMSO, London, 1944.

[12] Smith M., *Guide to Housing*, The Housing Centre Trust, London, 1971 (Third Edition 1989), p. 13

[13] Ministry of Health, *Housing Manual*, HMSO, London, 1949.

[14] Ibid., p. 14.

[15] Lock, D., Harlow: the city better, *Built Environment*, 3/4, 1983 pp. 210–217.

[16] MoHLG, *Houses 1952: Second Supplement to the Housing Manual 1949*, HMSO, London, 1952.

[17] Nuttgens, P., *Homefront*, BBC, 1989, p. 68.

[18] Richards J.M., Failure of the new towns, *AR*, 7/53 pp. 29–32; Cullen, G., Prairie planning in the new towns, *AR*, 7/53, pp. 33–35.

[19] Ibid., p. 33.

[20] *RIBA J*, 12/62, pp. 447–469.

[21] Failure of the new densities (editorial and letters to the editor), *AR*, 12/53, pp. 355–361.

[22] English Heritage, *Something Worth Keeping? Post-War Architecture in Britain: Housing and Houses*, 1996, p. 3.

[23] *AR*, 7/59, pp. 21–35; Taylor, N. *The Village in the City*, p. 16.

[24] Ravetz, A., *The Place of Home*, p. 51.

[25] Glendinning, M. and Muthesius, S., *Tower Block*, pp. 121–131.

[26] Scoffham, E.R., *The Shape of British Housing*, p. 85.

[27] *AD*, 9/67, pp. 393–394.

[28] English Heritage, *Something Worth Keeping? Post-War Architecture in Britain: Housing and Houses*, 1996, p. 3.

[29] Glendinning, M. and Muthesius, S., *Tower Block*, p. 121.

[30] MoHLG, *Homes for Today and Tomorrow*, London, HMSO, 1961.

[31] MoHLG, *Design Bulletin 6, Space in the Home*, HMSO, London, 1963 and 1968.

[32] MoHLG, *Housing Subsidies Manual*, HMSO, London, 1967.

[33] DOE/DOT, *Design Bulletin 32, Residential Roads and Footpaths* (2nd Edition 1992), HMSO, London, 1977; DOE/HDD, Occasional Paper, 2/74, *Mobility Housing*; DOE/HDD, Occasional Paper, 2/75, *Wheelchair Housing*.

[34] Scoffham E., *The Shape of British Housing*, p. 91.

[35] Martin L. and Marsh, L., *Urban Space and Structures*, Cambridge University Press, 1972.

[36] Chermayeff, S. and Alexander, C., *Community and Privacy*, Doubleday, New York, 1963.

[37] Colquhoun, I. and Fauset, P.G., *Housing Design in Practice*, pp. 53–56; *AR*, 4/80, pp. 205–219.

[38] Smith, M., *A Guide to Housing*, p. 241.

[39] *AR*, 2/59, pp. 108–120.

[40] *The Architect*, July 1971, p. 42.

[41] *AJ*, 14/8/74, p. 366; *AJ*, 22/9/76, pp. 533–552.

[42] *Planning*, 10/10/97, p. 3.

[43] Nuttgens, P., *The Homefront*, p. 112.

[44] Scarman (Lord), T. (Inquiry Report Chairman), *Brixton Disorders, April 10–12*, HMSO, London, 1981.

[45] Church of England, *Faith in the City: A Call for Action by the Church and the Nation*, Church House Publishing, 1985, p. 333.

[46] RIBA/CIOH, *Tenant Participation*, 1988.

[47] McCafferty, P., Working in association, *Prospect*, Summer 1994, p. 25; *AJ*, 8/8/84, pp. 18–19.

[48] Coleman, A., *Utopia on Trial, Vision and Reality in Planned Housing*, Hilary Shipman, 1985.

[49] This view is still not shared by all police crime prevention officers.

[50] Newman, O., *Defensible Space – People and the Design of the Violent City*, Architectural Press, 1973.

[51] Smith, M., *A Guide to Housing*, pp. 95, 301–302, 296–297, 301–306.

[52] Parry, N. The new town experience, *Town and Country Planning*, 11/96, p. 302.

[53] Urban Development Corporations: Bristol, Central Manchester, Cardiff (Cardiff Bay), Leeds, Liverpool (Merseyside), London (London Docklands, LDDC), Manchester (Trafford Park), Sheffield, Stoke on Trent (Black Country), Teesside, Tyne and Wear.

[54] *London Docklands*, A Builder Group Supplement, March 1998, p. 30.

[55] Ibid., pp. 38–39.

[56] Ravetz, A., *The Place of Home*, pp. 112–113.

[57] Duncan, S., and Rowe, A., *Self-help housing: the world's hidden housing arm*, Centre for Urban and Regional Research, The University of Sussex, 1992.

[58] *AJ*, 7/11/96, pp. 48–50.

[59] *AJ*, 21/9/95, pp. 8–9; *AJ*, 26/9/96, pp 39–44; *Independent on Sunday*, 18/7/8, pp. 71–73; *Independent on Sunday*, 15/6/97, pp. 62–65. *AJ*, 24/9/98, pp. 37–44.

[60] Petherick A. and Fraser, F., *Introduction to Living over the Shop*, The University of York, 1992.

[61] Charles, Prince of Wales, *A Vision of Britain – A Personal View of Architecture*, Doubleday, 1989.

[62] Aldous, A., *Urban Villages* (Foreword by HRH The Prince of Wales), Urban Villages Group, 1992.

[63] DOE, *Quality in Town and Country*, HMSO, London, 1994.

[64] *Building Homes* (Supplement to *Building*) 14/6/91, pp. 20–22.

[65] DOE, *Construction Monitor*, Issue 9, 2/95, p. 1.

[66] URBED (David Rudlin and Dr Nicholas Falk), *21st Century Homes, Building to Last*, Joseph Rowntree Foundation, May 1995; Girardet, H., *The Gaia Atlas of Cities. New Directions for Sustainable Urban Living*, Gaia Books Limited, 1992.

[67] Colquhoun, I. and Fauset, P.G., *Housing Design in Practice*, pp. 68–69.

[68] *Urban Villages Forum Newsletter*, Autumn 1997, p. 9.

[69] Evans, A., *We do not choose to be homeless*, CHAR – Campaign for Homeless and Rootless (recently renamed Natural Homeless Alliance), 1996.

FIGURE 2.1
Crescent House, Golden Lane Estate (p. 66).

CHAPTER TWO

London

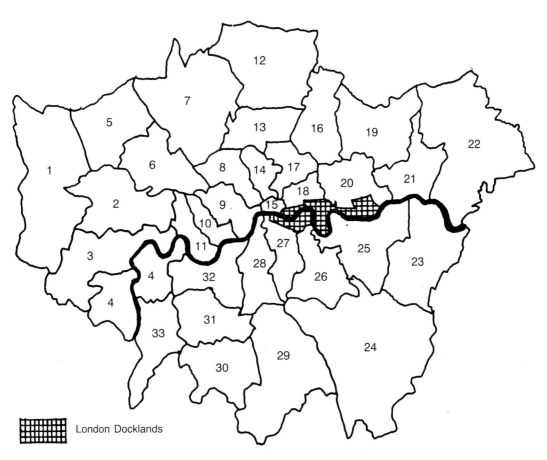

| London Docklands

1 Hillingdon	10 Kensington and Cheksea	19 Redbridge	28 Lambeth
2 Ealing	11 Hammersmith and Fulham	20 Newham	29 Croydon
3 Hounslow	12 Enfield	21 Barking and Dagenham	30 Sutton
4 Richmond upon Thames	13 Haringey	22 Havering	31 Merton
5 Harrow	14 Islington	23 Bexley	32 Wandsworth
6 Brent	15 City of London	24 Bromley	33 Kingston upon Thames
7 Barnet	16 Waltham Forest	25 Greenwich	
8 Camden	17 Hackney	26 Lewisham	
9 City of Westminster	18 Tower Hamlets	27 Southwark	

FIGURE 2.2
London Boroughs and location of London Docklands Development

BROMLEY

107 Westmorland Road, terrace of houses and flats.

1979. Edward Cullinan Architects. R. Bromley South

Edward Cullinan's housing of the 1970s and early 1980s offered fresh, new solutions to traditional design problems. His design of rented housing at Westmorland Road for the Solon Housing Association of thirty-six, one- to four-bedroom dwellings is an ingeniously designed six-storey broad-fronted terrace.

The bottom two floors have access from the pavement. Taking advantage of the sloping site, short ramps from the street lead to a second floor walkway from which the middle two levels of dwellings are reached, thus eliminating the need for lifts. From the elevated walkway the top storeys are reached by a flight of stairs (open-air but contained within the building) which feed to a high level walkway. In this way the architects endeavoured to bring the street to every door. The solidity of the street facade is contrasted with the glazed garden elevation (Fig. 2.3). On the garden side, ground floor dwellings lead out on to small terraces. The dwellings above have indented balconies or roof terraces according to

their location within the terrace. The timber detailing and colouring are excellent.

AJ, *19/9/79, p. 583; BD, 5/10/79, pp. 20–21; Toshi-Jutaku (Tokyo), 10/80; L'Industria Delle Costruzioni (Rome), 11/81; Edward Cullinan Architects (Academy Editions), 1995.*

CAMDEN

Hampstead Garden Suburb, NW11.

Started 1906. Parker and Unwin, Lutyens, Baillie Scott and others. U. Golders Green.

Founded in 1906 by Dame Henrietta Barnet, this development had a most significant influence on British housing design for half a century. Here Barrie Parker and Raymond Unwin produced some of their finest planning (Fig. 2.4). Culs-de-sac were used for the first time. In his book *Town Planning in Practice* (1909), Unwin described these as being 'specially desirable for those who like quiet for their dwellings....particularly since the development of the motor car' [1]. A special Act of Parliament was required to enable culs-

FIGURE 2.3
Westmorland Road: the front elevation.

FIGURE 2.4
Plan of Hampstead Garden Suburb by Parker and Unwin with Sir Edwin Lutyens. [Plan reproduced by courtesy of the New Hampstead Garden Suburb Trust Ltd.]

FIGURE 2.5
Hampstead Garden Suburb: Corringham Road neo-Georgian housing by Parker and Unwin.

de-sac to be built and a maximum density of eight dwellings to the acre was stipulated by Parliament due to concern regarding possible traffic problems. The central area was planned by Sir Edwin Lutyens whose designs were more formally structured than Parker and Unwin's work elsewhere in the Suburb.

The housing was designed by several architects. Amongst the finest groups are Sir Edwin Lutyens's 'Wren' inspired housing (1908–10) at Erskine Hill (on the west side of the street below the Free Church), and M.H. Baillie Scott's Waterlow Court, Heath Close (1908–9) and 6–10 Meadway with 22 Hampstead Way (c.1910). Most of the housing designed by Parker and Unwin takes the form of simple terraced cottages but at Corringham Road (1911) Unwin successfully combined a neo-Georgian style with the intimate character of a small-scale quadrangle (Fig. 2.5). Their Temple Fortune shops and flats (1900) at the junction of Finchley Road and Hampstead Way form a powerful composition at the gateway to the Suburb. A visit should include a walk up Erskine Hill to Lutyens' Central Square with its two massive churches and Institute (1909–10);

crossing the Square to Heathgate reveals the open heathland beyond.

After the First World War desirable but less interesting dwellings, mostly neo-Georgian, were built. Hampstead Garden Suburb is now a middle and upper class dormitory of some 16 000 people and as such has lost much of its former social objectives [2].

[1] Unwin, R., *Town Planning in Practice*, 1909; [2] *AR*, 10/57, pp. 259–262.

Ossulston Estate (Levita House, Chamberlain House and Walker House), St Pancras.
1929. G. Topham Forrest. U. Euston.

These high density flats built by Camden Borough Council illustrate the influence of the continental modern movement in architecture in the 1920s as exemplified by the Karl-Marx-Hof housing in Vienna. Here the new architecture is tempered by the English neo-Georgian tradition which is reflected in the windows, bays, the roof and eaves

FIGURE 2.6
*Ossulston Estate. [Photo by
Christopher Colquhoun.]*

and other design features. The flats are grouped around small greens and courtyards which are accessed through archways on Ossulston Street and Chalton Street where there is also the remains of a row of single-storey shops built with the scheme. Parts of the original avenues of trees in the court-yards still remain but the external spaces generally are in urgent need of refurbishment (Fig. 2.6). *AJ*, 12/9/73, pp. 588–590.

Isokon flats, Lawn Road, Hampstead, NW3.
1933. Wells Coates. U. Belsize Park.

This block of thirty-two mainly single-person flats, with its powerful white balconies and stair-cases, was the first British housing development to be built in the modernist manner. Designed for Jack Pritchard who lived for many years in the penthouse, the flats were aimed at young professionals. They were let furnished, with services offered to the tenants such as shoe and window cleaning, bed making, dusting and refuse collection, for rents of £96 per year [1]. The project included the Isobar restaurant which was envisaged as the social hub of the community. Commenting in 1970 on the design, Jack Pritchard said 'we had just been hit by the Bauhaus, which in fact we went to see with Wells and Chermayeff. We were very much bowled over by that episode. We were not consciously pioneers: it just seemed the right thing to do' [2]. [1] *AR*, 11/79, p. 290; [2] *AJ*, 11/3/70, p. 595.

FIGURE 2.7
Kent House: white 1930s housing which has survived well.

FIGURE 2.8
The houses at 1–3 Willow Road: large windows enable occupants to enjoy the view of the Heath.

Kent House, Ferdinand Street, NW1.
1935. Connell Ward and Lucas. U. Chalk Farm.

Built for the St Pancras Housing Association, this was Connell Ward and Lucas' only social housing commission. It is one of the few inter-war examples of modern movement architecture applied to housing for low income people. The development is in two-, five- and six-storey blocks with a small amount of open space, containing children's play equipment. The white walls and metal horizontal windows which are the hallmark of this architectural style have survived extremely well. The large balconies are very usable spaces and add considerably to the appearance of the scheme which was listed in 1993 (Fig. 2.7).

1–3 Willow Road, NW3.
1939. Erno Goldfinger. U. Hampstead.

These three houses which overlook Hampstead Heath are very significant to the history of British housing, as their style has been so frequently copied. Three storeys in height, the main living rooms are at first floor level, emphasized externally by the projection of the framing around the large windows set in predominantly brick elevations (Fig. 2.8).

Writing about the design in 1970, Goldfinger said, 'they are not eccentric, what I call Casbah architecture – that very early international style, white walls and horizontal slit windows, which always look avant-garde because it never caught on, except with spec builders in the Côte d'Azur. I really tried to build a late Georgian or Regency terrace in a modern way' [1]. Despite this, it is a genuine building of the modern movement. The reinforced concrete frame offers open plans internally which can be readily subdivided and modified. The only fixed point is the staircase with a plumbing duct in the middle. The National Trust has acquired Goldfinger's

FIGURE 2.9
*St Anne's Close: elegant, functional
simplicity.*

house, which Avanti Architects restored in 1996
to enable it to be open to the public [2].
[1] *AJ*, 11/3/70, p. 597; [2] *AJ*, 28/3/96, pp. 41–44;
AJ, 28/3/96, pp. 24–26.

St Anne's Close, Highgate West Hill, N6.
1947–48. Walter Segal. U. Kentish Town.

This group of eight semi-detached houses
designed by Walter Segal for himself and his
friends resembles the work of Tayler and Green
(p. 163) about which he had written at this time.
The simple brick and tiled houses are practi-
cally detailed with large living room windows
overlooking a communal wooded area and deep
overhanging eaves to shade the bedrooms from
the sun (Fig. 2.9). In its proposals to list the
scheme, English Heritage, describes it as
'elegant' with open staircases and high quality
finishes despite a £2000 cost ceiling.
EH, p. 8.

FIGURE 2.10
Brunswick Centre: 1960s concrete and glass.

Brunswick Centre, Brunswick Square and Guilford Street, Camden, WC1.

1965–73. Patrick Hodgkinson (design) and Bickerdike Allen (construction). U. Russell Square.

Of all the housing projects built in London during the 1960s, this is possibly the one that most profoundly symbolizes the spirit of its age. It is large, prominent and entirely unlike any other London development before or since (Fig. 2.10). A whole city block in the heart of Bloomsbury was cleared to make way for a scheme which possesses all the mixed development ingredients common of such an area – housing for 1600 people comprising one-, two- and four-person dwellings at a density of some 200 persons per acre, shops, offices, a cinema, pubs, restaurants and garaging for nearly 1000 cars. Yet its raised central plaza is lifeless; this was originally intended to be a glazed arcade but the developer cut it out to save money. Patrick Hodgkinson could not concede this change and subsequently resigned the commission. *AR*, 10/72, pp. 195–214; *RIBAJ*, 12/89, pp. 28–33; *AJ*, 29/7/92, p. 15; *AJ*, 15/9/93, pp. 19–20; (Refurbishment proposals) *AJ*, 4/7/96, p. 16.

PSSHAK flexible and adaptable housing, Adelaide Road/Eton Road.

1977. GLC Architects. U. Chalk Farm.

The ideas of flexibility and adaptability in the 1960s and 1970s were embodied in this housing for rent scheme built by the GLC. The development, which contained a mixture of forty-four family and elderly persons flats and maisonettes, was the result of a long struggle on the part of the GLC and the job architect, Nabeel Hamdi, to adapt the theories of Nicholas Harbraken to the realities of the British housing system. The idea of the design was known by its initials as PSSHAK which stood for Primary Support Structure and Housing Assembly Kit.

The exterior of the scheme was a basic structural shell of brick and timber with a tiled pitch roof. Inside, the flats were formed from kits, complete with bathroom, kitchen, ductwork, timber

FIGURE 2.11
PSSHAK, Adelaide Road. Sample plans: solid lines show the support structure; hatched areas show demountable party walls; open blocks show the 'kit'. [AJ, 21/5/75, p. 1073.]

stud walls and doors. These were prefabricated in The Netherlands, their design allowing considerable flexibility in the internal planning, and the partitions could be rearranged after erection (Fig. 2.11). The system had the advantage that the architect was able, within defined limits, to design the interiors to suit the requirements of the individual household at quite a late stage of the building contract, when the prospective tenants would have been identified. This gave a level of flexibility that was not possible with traditional methods of construction and enabled the tenants to participate in the design of their future home. *AJ*, 21/5/75, pp. 1070–1073; *AJ*, 12/10/77, pp. 692–693.

Highgate New Town, Dartmouth Park Hill and Chester Road.

1975–81. London Borough of Camden Architects Department. U. Archway.

The redevelopment of a slum clearance site at Dartmouth Park Hill excellently illustrates the

FIGURE 2.12
Highgate New Town, phase 1.

change of political and architectural climate in Camden Borough Council during the mid 1970s.

Stage 1 at Chester Road, completed in 1975, is typical of the earlier schemes of the Camden Borough Architects, with split-level house plans reflecting the principle of the stepped section. In this instance the white modernist image comes from the predominant use of light coloured concrete blocks (Fig. 2.12). The mixture of houses, flats and maisonettes is arranged in terraces along the contours to take full advantage of the slope of the site and the superb views across Highgate Cemetery to Parliament Hill (Fig. 2.13). Every dwelling has a south-facing private open space screened from its neighbours. The scale of the buildings was kept low, to not more than two and a half storeys, but a density of some 200 bedspaces per acre (approximately 70 dw/acre or 173/ha) was still achieved. A network of pedestrian streets and play-squares runs between the terraces. These are overlooked from the kitchens, allowing for the supervision of children and natural policing of streets. A high

FIGURE 2.13
Highgate New Town, phase 1: site layout.

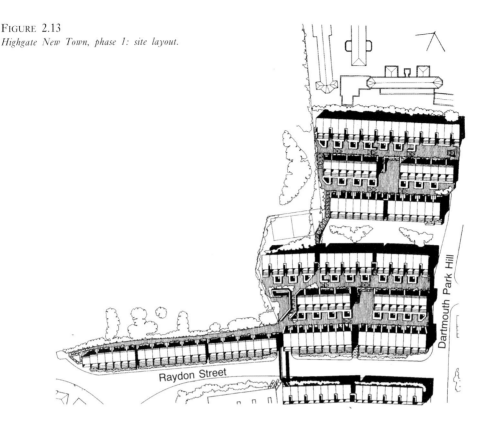

level of car parking was provided underground in lock-up garages [1].

Stage 2 (site C) is very different. By 1976, the Borough Council had written a new design brief. This insisted that all families be housed at ground floor level in brick, low rise housing with pitched roofs. The layout, containing 107 flats and houses, now relates the buildings to the former streets which were retained or made into pedestrian routes that pass under decorative archways of the main barrier block along Dartmouth Park Hill (Fig. 2.14).

The houses and flats are in two- and three-storey terraces. Colourful brickwork reflects the conventions of traditional housing in the area and balconies are light and decorative. Communal areas, kept to a minimum to reduce maintenance, were well planted and have now matured.

AD, 3/72, pp. 145–164; *AR*, 9/73, pp. 159–162; *AJ*, 10/8/77, pp. 236–238; *RIBAJ*, 11/79, pp. 483–489; *AJ*, 12/8/81, pp. 294–306.

FIGURE 2.14
Highgate New Town, phase 2C: site layout.

Branch Hill, Hampstead, NW3.
1978. London Borough of Camden Architects Department. U. Hampstead.

Branch Hill is much smaller than the other Camden schemes of this period. It comprises forty-two houses clustered tightly on a steeply sloping site in a woodland setting in one of the most select areas of London close to Hampstead Heath. Restricted covenants required that the buildings were to be in semi-detached form and not higher than two storeys, but the design interprets these requirements in most liberal manner.

The houses are clustered close together about a series of pedestrian alleys and steps; they follow the slope of the ground with stepped levels internally (Fig. 2.15). Only the lowest row of dwellings have gardens at ground level; the roof of the dwelling below is used as a garden for the dwelling above. From within the dwellings the large areas of glass make it possible to fully appreciate the changing landscape of the site and its surroundings (Fig. 2.16). The house plans ingeniously separate the activities of parents and children by creating a communal zone in the middle of the house with private bedroom areas at each end of the dwelling.
AJ, 20/6/79, pp. 1261–1276.

Alexandra Road, Abbey Road, Boundary Road and Loudon Road, NW8.
1979. U. Swiss Cottage.

The most complete and extensive exposition of Camden's modernist approach to housing design in the 1970s was Alexandra Road where a very high density was achieved with predominantly low rise housing whilst ensuring for many dwellings an outlook over the four acre central park. The scheme comprises 520 dwellings in two banks of eight- and four-storey blocks which are separated by the park (Fig. 2.17). The proximity of the site to the railway determined the need for the eight-storey barrier block to overcome the noise problems. This contains a mixture of flats and maisonettes which face south, each dwelling having a garden or open

FIGURE 2.15
Branch Hill: cross-section of the site.

FIGURE 2.16
Branch Hill: refinement in concrete and glass.

terrace off its living room. Two brick pedestrian streets run the entire length of each bank of dwellings and provide the principal means of access. Car parking and garages were located in the basements. At the north-eastern end of the site, the scheme included a school for mentally handicapped children, a community centre, a youth club and a building department depot. A district heating plant was accommodated below the community centre.

It is a brilliant architectural set-piece which has recently been recognized in its grade II* listing by English Heritage. The white concrete and matching white rendered blockwork are well contrasted by the dark stained timber windows (Fig. 2.18). Regrettably over the years it has been poorly maintained and particularly the environment and car parking areas are neglected.

[1] *AR*, 9/70, p. 180; *AJ*, 14/9/70, pp. 62–64; *AJ*, 1/9/93, pp. 14–15; *AR*, 8/79, pp. 76–88; *AD*, 11/69, p. 593–601.

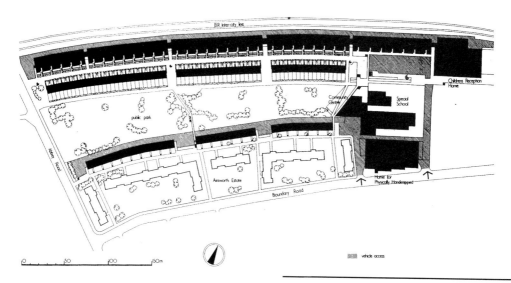

FIGURE 2.17
Alexandra Road: site layout.

Maiden Lane Stage 1, Agar Grove/St Paul's Crescent, NW1.
1982. U. Camden Town.

Maiden Lane was the last of Camden Borough Council's large modernist housing schemes of the 1970s and the most controversial. The basic layout contains 225 dwellings in two, four-storey, L-shaped blocks of flats and maisonettes with two rows of two-storey houses within each 'L'. All dwellings are planned on a 4.1m grid (Fig. 2.19).

FIGURE 2.18
Alexandra Road: large balcony to every dwelling.

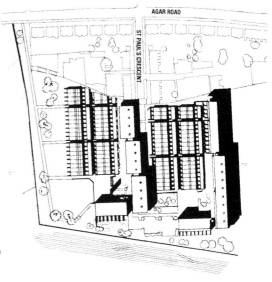

FIGURE 2.19
Maiden Lane: site layout.

FIGURE 2.20
Maiden Lane: typical terrace.

Living rooms in the houses are at first floor level to enjoy the view, with bedrooms on the ground floor, and each dwelling has a private, walled garden at the front and the rear. Car access is restricted to two culs-de-sac from St Paul's Crescent and York Way, which connect to garages located below the podiums between the houses and flats (Figs 2.20 and 1.10).

The scheme received rave reviews in the architectural press but its design meant little to the tenants who described it as 'looking like Alcatraz, a modern prison'.[1] Its concrete finish and the complex arrangement of levels which separate many of the dwellings from the roads were disliked. Six years after the completion of the scheme, serious problems of crime and vandalism had developed. There was high unemployment and poverty in the estate combined with high child density, technical

LIVERPOOL JOHN MOORES UNIVERSITY
Aldham Roberts L.R.C.
TEL. 0151 231 3701/3634

failures, unsatisfactory arrangements for refuse collection and poor management [1]. As arguments raged architects Hunt Thompson were called in to prepare a rescue plan. John Thompson condemned the modern movement architecture, claiming it to be 'out of touch with ordinary people'. The scheme was fiercely defended by the architectural press which claimed that the problems had mainly arisen from the social stress that the scheme was under [1]. This is true but what cannot be denied is that the tenants at Maiden Lane have a very different culture to people living at Seidlung Halen in Switzerland from where the architects gained their inspiration.

[1] *AR*, 11/88, pp. 74–78; *AR*, 1/80, p. 34; *AR*, 4/83, pp. 22–29; *AJ*, 19/10/88, pp. 83–84.

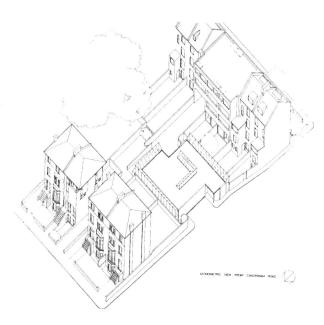

FIGURE 2.21
Caversham Road/Gaisford Street: axonometric drawing showing the inclusion of the once proposed meeting hall.

---

5 Caversham Road, 6–10 Gaisford Street, Camden, NW5.
1979. Colquhoun and Miller. U. Kentish Town.

Colquhoun and Miller produced a number of housing schemes in London in the late 1970s/early 1980s which were much admired for the way in which their design made a conscious play between traditional and modern architectural forms. This small scheme of rented housing, built by the London Borough of Camden, is an imaginative solution to the problem of filling gaps in two adjacent nineteenth-century streets (Fig. 2.21).

At Gaisford Street the gap was filled with a four-storey block comprising five maisonettes. Direct access to front doors at upper levels is by two flights of external stairs. The first flight, reflecting the stairs of the adjoining Victorian houses, leads to a landing at first floor level. From here a separate stairway leads to entrance doors at second floor level. In Caversham Street one half of the semi-detached house was rebuilt to form two maisonettes, both having access directly off street level. This block was topped with a hipped roof to match the adjoining house. The buildings respect the heights of their neighbours, and roof-line, parapets and windows line match similar features on the adjoining buildings.

Unfortunately the meeting rooms at the rear of the new buildings were never built.

BD, 10/8/79, pp. 2–13; *AR* 1/78, p. 9; *AD*, 3/04, 81, pp. 10–11; *Baumeister*, 11/82, pp. 1078–1080; *A+U*, 4/82, pp. 92–4.

Field Court, Fitzjohn's Avenue/ Arkwright Road, Hampstead, NW3.
1979. Pollard Thomas and Edwards. U. Hampstead.

This scheme of nine houses and twelve flats in Hampstead, designed for Camden Borough Council, is located on a prominent corner site of approximately half an acre (1.25 ha). One of the main aims of the design was to respect the character of the surrounding large-scale Victorian villas with their dominant sloping roofs.

This was achieved by placing the flats and two of the houses in a four-storey block fronting Fitzjohn's Avenue and by using dark stock and red trim bricks. A block of two-storey houses was located at right-angles forming a courtyard. A third block contains a single house and the heating plant. The roof of the large block cleverly slopes down to two-storeys to link the scale of the different building heights. The natural slope across the site enabled the maximum number of dwellings to be entered half a floor above or below ground level, this way reducing the walk-up distance. *AR*, 2/80, pp. 94–97.

Leighton Crescent, Camden, NW5.
1980. Edward Cullinan Architects,
U. Kentish Town.

This small scheme reflects the quality of Camden's new housing built in the late 1970s/early 1980s. The four-storey block of twelve, one bedroom, two-person flats replaced a derelict house in the centre of a mid-nineteenth century London crescent (Fig. 2.22). Its yellow brick architecture with well proportioned openings fits well into the space. Each floor is divided into four flats or maisonettes occupying each corner with the main

stair in the centre of the block. The dwellings are wide frontage: bedroom, living room and kitchen are placed in a row with large double doors connecting them, which means that they can be occupied as one, two or three rooms. The dwellings have French windows opening out onto balconies which are connected to the coloured steel grid of poles that support the slim overhanging roof. This introduces a scale to the elevations that helps match the building to its surrounds, making it a suitable centre-piece for the Victorian crescent. Toshi-Jutaku (Tokyo), 10/80. Abitare (Milan), 7–8/81, pp. 38–39; Edward Cullinan Architects (Academy Editions), 1995.

Coutts Crescent, 13–23 St Alban's Road, NW5
1986–9. Chassay Wright Architects.
U. Kentish Town/Archway.

This superb terrace of eleven, three-storey houses is a stylish solution to the design of private housing in an urban location. The terrace forms a shallow crescent with each end emphasized by the curved roofs of taller towers, the extra height forming double-height bedrooms (Fig. 2.23). The architectural language is more 20th century

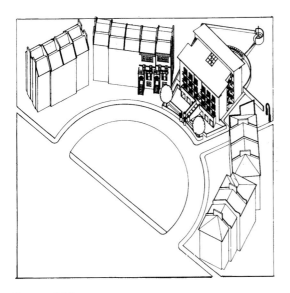
FIGURE 2.22
Leighton Crescent, showing its relationship with the other buildings in the crescent.

FIGURE 2.23
Coutts Crescent: a classical curve to the front elevation.

European than traditional English. The front elevation, characterized by its brick banding and two-storey high windows at ground and first floor levels, reads as one composition rather than a series of linked houses. Setting the crescent back from the road has provided ample space at the front for a planted brick-paved parking forecourt that is a well conceived space.

AJ. 8/3/89, pp. 34–41.

Supermarket and Housing, 17 Camden Road, NW1.

1988–90. Nicholas Grimshaw and Partners. U. Camden.

The futuristic design of this small row of houses caused a sensation when it was first built. Camden Borough Council had long wished to see

the site redeveloped with mixed uses. After protracted negotiations, the outcome was a Sainsbury's supermarket, workshops and a terrace of houses of most unusual design fronting the Regent's Canal (Fig. 2.24). The single aspect houses face north over the canal and back on to Sainsbury's car park. A private path runs along the edge of the canal, giving access to the front doors. These open into the entrance hall and a ground floor bedroom/study. On the first floor are the living, kitchen and dining areas. The dining area is a double-height space with a completely glazed wall looking out over the canal; glazed strips in the roof above the double-height space allows sunlight to penetrate. Part of the interest these houses created was the possibility that the lower part of the glazed wall could be raised electronically so that the space could flow out to a balcony perched over the canal. Added to this was the curved aluminium walls to the

FIGURE 2.24
Futuristic housing at 17 Camden Road.

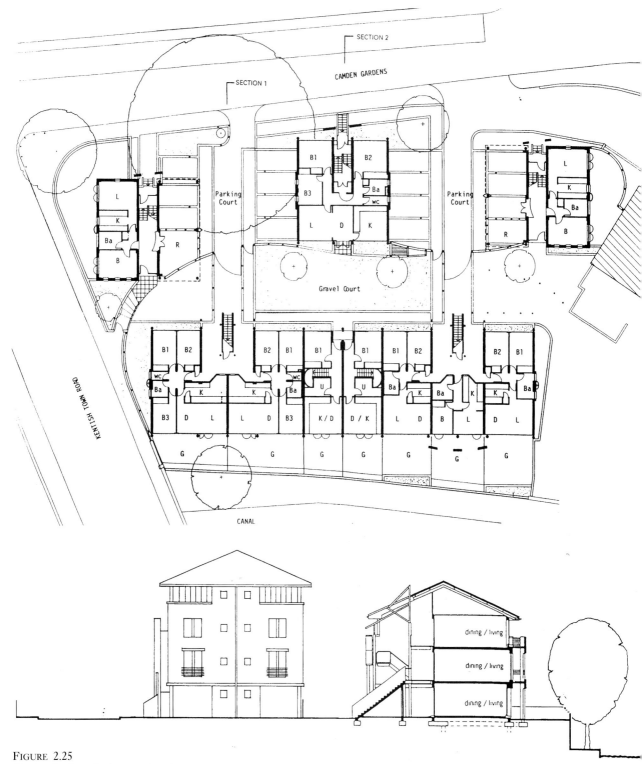

FIGURE 2.25
Camden Gardens: site layout and section.

FIGURE 2.26
Camden Gardens: looking into the internal courtyard.

living room and master bedroom with its thin window slots.

AR, 10/89, pp. 36–49; *AJ*, 4/10/89, pp. 56–59; *RIBAJ*, 4/90. pp. 52–63.

Camden Gardens, Kentish Town Road, NW1.
1993. Jestico + Whiles. U. Camden Town.

Jestico + Whiles was commissioned by the Community Housing Association to design this rented housing scheme on a restricted site in Camden overlooking the Grand Union canal. Its twenty-seven dwellings are distributed between a three-storey terrace of houses and flats along the side of the Grand Union Canal and three square 'villas' facing Camden Gardens which accommodate flats and maisonettes (Fig. 2.25). Parking courts situated between villas at the entrance give the 50 per cent required provision which frees the centre of the scheme for pedestrian use (Fig. 2.26).

The appearance of the terrace is characterized by the treatment of the external communal stairs. A large double-height curved trellis for planting supports two frameless glass canopies which give the whole area a light and transparent quality. A wide stairway passes through the trellis to a deck of timber slats at first floor level, where a second staircase leads to the upper level. The villas are entered through free-standing portals of terracotta painted masonry. Light buff bricks are used throughout in a simple stretcher bond with raked pointing. The result is a most elegant scheme.

AJ, 9/3/94, pp. 45–55; *AJ*, 13/10/94, p. 30.

Russell Nurseries, Aspern Grove/ Haverstock Hill, NW3.
1993. London Borough of Camden. U. Belsize Park.

The aim of this development was to design housing in which people would feel comfortable without compromising urban design principles.

The layout of two- and three-storey terraces of flats and houses is based on a pattern of linked shared-surface roads and footpaths. The houses front on to tightly spaced streets and have private, enclosed gardens at the back (Fig. 2.27). The flats have ingenious open stairways with glazed canopies to the upper floors, but the purpose of the substantial overhang at the gable of the roofs of some blocks is not clear. The external works and landscaping are particularly well executed.

AT, 4/93, p. 39.

Camden Goods Yard urban redevelopment, Chalk Farm Road, NW1.
1996. Pollard Thomas and Edwards and (novated architects) JCMT. U. Camden Town.

This social rental housing scheme, developed by the Community Housing Association with others – Ujima, ARHAG, Centrepoint, Soho and John Grooms – was a large development for the mid-

FIGURE 2.27
Russell Nurseries: entrance to the scheme.

FIGURE 2.28
Camden Goods Yard: children's playground.

1990s. The site was a narrow triangle of land isolated by railway lines on both its long sides and the Regent's Canal on its southern short boundary. Development was only viable because Safeway was allowed to build a supermarket on a proportion of the land through a joint planning agreement, enabling a new access road to be built under the railway from Chalk Farm Road.

The housing is in two groups on either side of the supermarket. Whilst maintaining a similarity in the design and materials used, the two sites required different design solutions. The southern area by the canal had a strong industrial history including two former railway buildings which now accommodate the headquarters of Worldwide Television News and the Henson Corporation. The design contains a mixture of three-storey terraced mews houses with private back gardens and four-storey blocks of flats which form a courtyard with the refurbished railway buildings.

The northern site was more affected by the railway, so consequently the scheme turns its back on it with the housing arranged in a semi-circle around a large landscaped court. There are two small openings into the court, one for pedestrians and the other for cars. Gardens and principal rooms inside the dwellings all face the court and small back windows help reduce noise from the railway. The grouping of the housing provides a variety of building heights and fenestrations, which breaks down the scale of the space, and this is complemented with excellent planting and a profusion of play equipment (Fig. 2.28).
AJ, 7/11/96, pp. 32–33.

Bruges Place, mixed-use development, Baynes Road/Randolph Street, NW1.
1987. Jestico + Whiles. U. Camden Town.

Bruges Place sets high standards for mixed-use development in inner-city areas. Its design successfully demonstrates that light industrial uses and housing can be combined provided access is carefully organized. The former bomb site was zoned by the planners for industrial use even though it was surrounded by housing. They preferred two-storey industrial development but the architects successfully argued that the urban grain of the area dictated that the development should be four-storeys in height and of mixed use (Fig. 2.29).

FIGURE 2.29
Bruges Place.

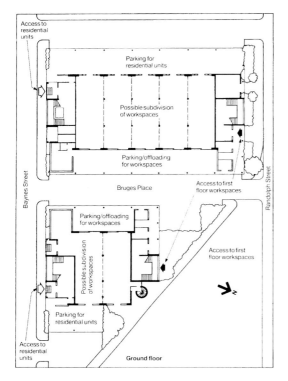

FIGURE 2.30
FIGURE 2.30
Bruges Place: ground floor plan indicating entrances into the various parts of the building.

AJ, 15/7/87, pp. 32–37, 41–54; Housing Design Awards 1989, A *Building* Publication, p. 26; *RIBAJ*, 11/90. pp. 6–7.

112–124 Haverstock Hill, Hampstead, NW3.
1995. Pollard Thomas and Edwards (PTE).
U. Belsize Park.

This scheme demonstrates what can be achieved in a Conservation Area through a combination of sensitive refurbishment and new infill development. During the 1970s, a number of 1880s Victorian villas on Haverstock Hill were taken over by squatters. The houses were in an extremely poor condition but by 1980 the group determined to renovate them to accommodate local homeless people.

They formed a co-operative, Belpark 2, named after Belpark 1, a similar co-operative which had campaigned successfully to save other nearby houses. Unfortunately, no. 118 and no. 120 Haverstock Hill became structurally unsound and had to be shored up. In 1989, the Borough Council threatened to sell the site which caused Belpark 2 to take urgent action. Consequently, Circle 33 was invited to produce development proposals and to negotiate the purchase of the

The scheme ultimately included 20 000 sq. ft (2000 sq. m) of industrial space in multiple units on the ground and first floors. Entrance to the ground floor is from the central mews with access to the first floor at the northern end (Fig. 2.30). The residents of the twenty-one dwellings on the two floors above the workspace park their cars in two side streets and gain access via staircases and lifts in the south of the complex, which overlooks the Regent's Canal. The stairs lead to landscaped courtyards at second floor level from where the housing is entered. The dwellings all have good views out from private balconies on the outer faces of the building. The yellow brick and orange banding is striking and contrasts well with the dark green joinery and metalwork. Much credit is due to the architects' determination to see the site correctly developed.

FIGURE 2.31
Haverstock Hill: sensitive design in a Conservation Area.

property from Camden Borough Council. The ASRA Greater London Housing Association also became involved and PTE was appointed to produce design proposals.

Nos 114, 116, 122 and 124 were converted into flats whilst no. 118 and no. 120 were rebuilt with front elevations matching the former Victorian facade, as requested by Belpark 2 who wished the new development to be in keeping with the conservation area (Fig. 2.31). New link buildings were constructed between no. 112 and 114, and 120 and 122. The conservatory adjacent to no. 116 was rebuilt in the original form and an additional one built beside it, forming a winter garden to new houses behind.

Restoration of the gardens included preserving an area of rare trees and plants developed by a previous tenant who was a Kew Gardens botanist.

AJ, 11/7/96, pp. 40–41.

Endsleigh Gardens, Bloomsbury, WC1.
1994. Avanti Architects. U. Euston.

This small development close to Euston Station demonstrates a modern approach to the design of infill housing. The site, which formerly housed the LCC Weights and Measures Building, came into the ownership of Camden Borough Council in the mid-1980s as part of the abolition of the Greater London Council. Its redevelopment involved a developer who wished to construct offices on Euston Road and the Community Housing Association who proposed to build a mixture of one- and two-bedroom flats and maisonettes.

The architecture reflects the historical Bloomsbury area. The six-storey height matches the Georgian housing and forms a strong visual stop at the end of Endsleigh Street. This street elevation is divided into brickwork and rendered panels of proportions that echo the narrow frontages of the neighbouring housing. Rendering at ground floor level and the setting back of the top floor creates a continuous open terrace at the front. A curved glass block wall is a strong

FIGURE 2.32
Endsleigh Gardens: modern Bloomsbury infill housing.

feature marking the entrance to the flats above (Fig. 2.32)

AJ, 3 & 10/1/90, pp. 32–63; AT, 2/95, no. 55, pp. 13–14.

Coptic Street, WC1.
1991. Avanti Architects.
U. Tottenham Court Road.

Housing for rent of this quality is vital to the future of inner cities, both in architectural and social terms. This vacant bomb site, once the site of Mudie's lending library, remained undeveloped as it was designated a possible site for the British Library. The community housing association became interested in it in 1977 and, four years later, Avanti Architects started to produce housing designs.

FIGURE 2.33
*Coptic Street: corner tower and balconies. [Photo by
Christopher Colquhoun.]*

The twenty-three flats offer accommodation
to a range of households, several being suitable
for people with physical disabilities. The block
is L-shaped and four storeys in height with an
additional two storeys to form a tower on the
Coptic Street corner (Fig. 2.33). The simple
brickwork is enhanced by well proportioned
windows which are deeply inset and finished
with light steel balconies on the corner tower.
Within the internal court the walls are finished
in white render reflecting the architects' belief
that a new building in this historic part of
London should respect the past but be of
modern appearance.

AJ, 2/10/91, pp. 31–43; *RIBAJ*, 6/91, pp. 54–55.

King's Cross Estate Action, Cromer Street, WC1.

*1996–2001. AFH Shaw Sprunt, Camden Building
Design Services, The Floyd Slaski Partnership,
Hunt Thompson Associates, Tibbalds Monroe.
U. Kings Cross, Euston.*

Kings Cross has had an image of deprivation
which is now changing. The community of over
1000 council and housing association properties
based on Cromer Street south of Euston Road
has, since 1996, been involved in the £46 million
Kings Cross Estate Action project phased over 5
years. This is one of the largest local authority
building projects in London and tenant involvement is high.

The housing includes a mixture of pre-1919
brick tenement housing of fine architectural
quality and substantial 1950s high rise slab
blocks. A number of architectural practices were
employed to ensure variety of design approach.
The post-1950s housing has been colourfully
overclad which, with the new entrance structures,

FIGURE 2.34
Kings Cross Estate Action: a new image for 1960s housing.

FIGURE 2.35
Kings Cross Estate Action: environmental improvement plan.

boundary walls, fencing and planting, has completely transformed the area (Fig. 2.34). Considerable attention has been given to increasing security by provision of concierge-controlled access or new door entry systems and improved lighting. A range of energy-efficiency measures includes new central heating which will be connected to a combined heat and power scheme.

The brick tenement housing has been carefully and sensitively restored. Its newly painted metal balconies and freshly cleaned brickwork emphasize the architectural qualities.

FIGURE 2.36
*Golden Lane tower clad in yellow
curtain walling.*

The environmental improvement proposals build on the quality of the existing urban structure of streets and squares (Fig. 2.35). They include a self-enforcing 20 mph speed zone with speed tables and pinch points, the introduction of pedestrian/cycle routes and renewal of pavements. Designs for open spaces between the blocks are low maintenance and simple, with children's play areas situated away from densely populated areas. The three urban squares, Regent, Argyle and Bamber Green, have been upgraded to relate to their local environment. Generally all have been given higher railings, improved entrances, new seating and extensive planting.

In line with current regeneration practice, the project includes a number of training initiatives for local people.

AT, 9/97, pp. 57–58; *AJ*, 14/5/98, pp. 33–36.

CITY OF LONDON

Golden Lane and Crescent House, Goswell Road/Baltic Street, EC1.

1962. Chamberlin Powell and Bon. U. Barbican.

Against a wealth of talented architects including the Smithsons, Geoffrey Powell won a most prestigious architectural competition in 1952 for the development of a site on the northern boundary of the City of London which had been heavily bombed during the war.

Golden Lane, with its seventeen-storey tower clad externally in yellow curtain walling, was much admired for its bold approach to the design of urban housing (Fig. 2.36). It epitomized everything that was good about mixed development. The tower stands as the centre-piece of a series of linked landscaped pedestrian courtyards formed by four- and six-storey blocks of flats and maisonettes (Fig. 2.37). In the tradition of Le Corbusier's Unité, the roof of the tower was laid out as a terrace for the tenants of the upper floors. Its most distinctive feature, the oversailing canopy on the roof, covers the water tanks, lift motor rooms etc. The dwelling units were very varied in size and type to cater for a wide range of people. The scheme has a wealth of community facilities including shops, sports facilities, a swimming pool, a community hall, tennis courts and a creche. It is proposed for Grade II listing.

Crescent House is rated Grade II* (Fig. 2.1). In its description of the scheme, English Heritage likens the design of the curved terrace to 'the brick and concrete idiom of Le Corbusier's Maisons Jaoul but adapted for its urban setting' [1]. The stepping of the block to follow Goswell Road was particularly well handled by the architects.

[1] EH, pp. 3 and 6; *AR*, 6/57, pp. 414–425; *AJ*, 7/11/96, p. 25; *AJ*, 29/12/60, pp. 931–942.

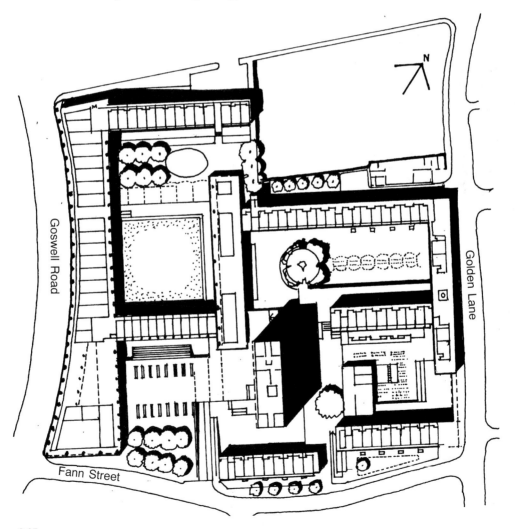

FIGURE 2.37
Golden Lane Estate: site layout.

LIVERPOOL JOHN MOORES UNIVERSITY
LEARNING & INFORMATION SERVICES

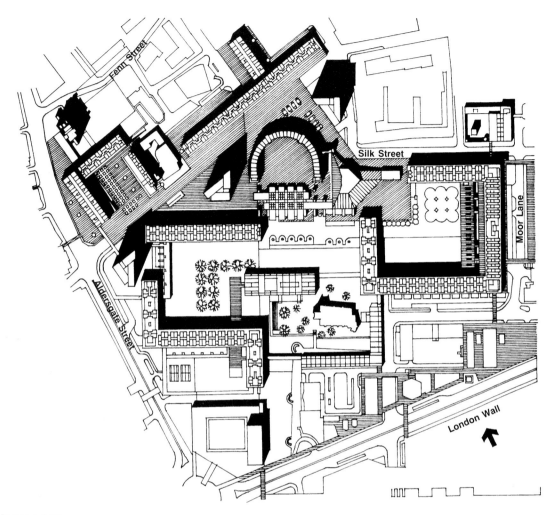

FIGURE 2.38
The Barbican: site layout.

The Barbican, bounded by London Wall, Beech Street and Moorgate, EC2.

1973. Chamberlin Powell & Bon (Barbican).
U. Barbican, St Paul's, Moorgate.

At the end of the Second World War the resident population of the City of London had declined to as few as 5000 compared to some 125 000 a hundred years previously. This meant that, during the day, the City bustled with half a million commuting workers but by evening it was reduced to a ghost town, a 'city of cats and caretakers'.

The vision of the City of London Corporation was to change this by building on a bomb-site at the Barbican, 'a genuine residential neighbourhood incorporating schools, shops, open spaces and other amenities.... even if this meant forgoing a more remunerative return for the land' [1].

The solution was perhaps the closest that British housing design has ever got to applying Le Corbusier's planning theories. Its 125 m (415 ft) high triangular towers – the tallest in Europe when first built – tower above interlinking court-yards of medium rise flats. Some 6500 people are housed in 2113 flats with parking for 2500 private cars underground below a pedestrian podium level (Fig. 2.38). Built for the middle to high income group, the design avoids the balcony and deck

FIGURE 2.39
The Barbican, with the theatre on the left.

access so favoured at the time for council flats. Entrance to the flats is by closely spaced lifts and staircases which are rigidly controlled by concierge and door entry systems.

The buildings themselves are imaginatively sculptured and the spaces are well proportioned and landscaped. Yet, the overriding feeling is one of bleakness. The large areas of empty paving are hard and windswept and there are few people about. Even the presence of the Barbican theatre complex in the centre of the development makes little difference (Fig. 2.39). It may be 'a haven of quiet' [2] but it is hardly a city. Regrettably the vision was not fulfilled.

AR, 8/73, pp. 71–90; [1] Ibid., p. 71; [2] Ibid., p. 74; *AR*, 8/81, pp. 239–251.

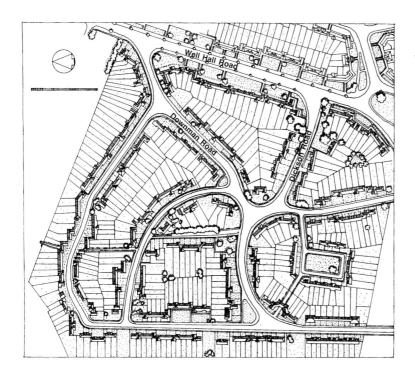

FIGURE 2.40
*Well Hall Estate, Eltham. [Redrawn
from MoHLG,* Design in Town
and Village, *HMSO, 1953, p. 69.]*

GREENWICH

Well Hall Estate, Ross Way/
Phineas Pett Road, SE9.
1915. LCC Department of Architecture.
R. Eltham.

The Housing and Town Planning Act of 1919
was considerably influenced by the programme of
housing development implemented during the
First World War to provide housing for
munitions workers in London and elsewhere [1].
Raymond Unwin headed a team of architects in
the Ministry of Munitions which included Frank
Baines, whose Well Hall Estate in Woolwich was
the finest achievement of the programme.

The scheme of 1298 houses was conceived
and built at great speed. Its design was firmly
rooted in the tradition of Unwin's pre-war garden
city ideology using a wide variety of materials
and external finishes including timber framing,
tile hanging, stone, brick and render. This was
matched by a generous use of gables, dormers,
overhangs, tunnels and various other projections
and recessions, 'to produce an architectural

ensemble that seemed centuries apart from an age
of total war' [2] (Figs 2.40 and 2.41).

After the war, the Well Hall Estate attracted
considerable attention from overseas and from civil
servants preparing the 'Homes fit for Heroes' legislation. However, the average cost per dwelling was
£622 [3], which was reduced by at least half in
most local authority development that followed.
Consequently Well Hall stands as a symbol of what
might have been had standards been maintained.

[1] *AR*, 6/78, pp. 366–375; [2] Ibid., p. 367; [3]
Swenerton, M., *Homes fit for Heroes*, pp. 54–55.

85–91 Genesta Road, SE18.
1935. B. Lubetkin and A.V. Pilichowski.
R. Woolwich Arsenal.

These four, three-storey houses successfully
applied the new modernist ideal to the traditional
terraced house. With their rendered walls and
projected first floor windows and integral garages,
they set a theme for the design of town houses
that was frequently copied.

FIGURE 2.41
Well Hall Estate: high quality streetscape.

Span Housing, Blackheath, SE3.
1956–79. Eric Lyons. R. Blackheath.

In a small area of London, at Blackheath, it is possible to see almost the whole range of Span housing designed by its architect Eric Lyons between 1956 and 1979 (p. 21) much of which is subject to listing by English Heritage.

Foxes Dale (1956–57) comprised only three houses including the showhouse and it was Lyons' earliest work at Blackheath.

Hallgate (1958) is a stepped line of twenty-six, three-storey flats occupying a prominent position at the entrance to Span's larger development – The Hall.

The Hall (1958) is a mixed development of flats and houses. The two- and three-storey flats

FIGURE 2.42
The Hall, Blackheath: Span housing preserved in its original 1950s form.

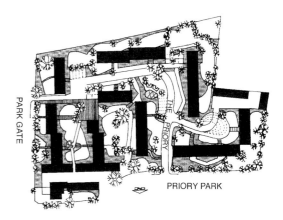

FIGURE 2.43
The Priory, Blackheath: site layout.

are grouped around courtyards with the lush planting sweeping across the site. As at Hallgate, the blocks contain large areas of colourful painted timber and tiled infill panels between party walls. The houses front onto roads and have large picture windows and tile-hung first floor facades (Fig. 2.42)

The Priory (1959) is a group of two- and three-storey blocks of flats set in the gardens of a former priory. Some have timber and glass panels between cross-walls but others have long horizontal bands of tile hanging without expressing the cross-walls (Fig. 2.43).

The Keep (1959). Eric Lyons considered the Keep, with its two-storey tile-hung terraces of houses, to be his least satisfactory scheme.

Corner Green (1959) is a development on a sloping site comprising three terraces designed with simple cross-walls and white weatherboarding with yellow brick infill panels which were copied all over Britain. The layout had the simple idea of a central green pedestrian area with the ground formation and the planting forming strong shapes to underline the functional use of the space.

Southrow (1963). This scheme is a long, mainly three-storey, terrace of flats facing the Heath and small pond on the corner of Southrow

and Montpelier Road/Prince of Wales Road. Its elevations, which express the concrete frame, are quite different to the other Span housing in the area.

Brooklands Park and Blackheath Park (1964) comprise nine houses with staggered pitch roofs that give clerestory lighting. Two houses at right angles skilfully complete the composition.

Holmwalk (1980) is the last of Span's housing in Blackheath. Ten, two- and three-storey brick-fronted dwellings arranged in four groups have a delightful appearance when approached from the south-west corner.

EH, pp. 9–10. [1] *The Architect*, 7/71, pp. 38–40; *AR*, 1/57, pp. 42–43; *AJ*, 27/3/58, p. 458; *AR*, 2/59, pp. 108–120; *AJ*, 21/1/70, p. 138; The Architect, 7/71, p. 36–42; *AJ*, 9/7/75, pp. 54.

Thamesmead, Abbey Wood, SE2. phases 1 and 2.
1972. GLC Department of Architecture and Civic Design. R. Abbey Wood.

Thamesmead was the product of the forecast in the early 1960s that London needed 500 000 new homes within the next 10 years. After the GLC's unsuccessful bid in the late 1950s to build a new town for 100 000 people at Hook in Hampshire, it looked to less environmentally sensitive sites

FIGURE 2.44
Thamesmead: lakeside terraces of concrete housing.

like the flat marshland of Erith. The GLC's Master Plan of 1965 envisaged a population of 60 000 people living in a mixture of council and private housing in a roughly 65/35 split. It was to be a self-reliant community with its own shops, schools, pubs, health centre and other community buildings, together with factories and workshops offering local employment. Traffic and pedestrian segregation was to be given a high priority in the planning of the development. The images of new housing built in an environment of canals and lakes were most seductive and many visitors came from home and overseas to see what a 'city for the 21st century' looked like [1] (Fig. 2.44).

The public sector housing was to be constructed using the most advanced systems of prefabrication, and a factory was established on the site. The first two phases, containing 2741 dwellings, were completed in 1972. A third of the dwellings were family houses with gardens mostly grouped around pedestrian courtyards. The thirteen-storey tower blocks of flats were designed for two and three people. To meet a local bylaw concerned with the possible flooding of the site the whole scheme was raised above ground level. Walkways forming a continuous route through the tower blocks separated pedestrians from the streets below which resulted in both levels lacking life and activity (Fig. 2.45).

By 1972, the development had proved expensive and unpopular and the spirit to continue had gone. Later developments were

FIGURE 2.45
Thamesmead: thirteen-storey towers.

traditional in both form and layout. Thamesmead's problems became compounded by
unemployment and poverty during the 1980s and
public transport connections with London
remained tortuous as the promised road link
across the River Thames was never built.

Gallions Reach Urban Village (PRP
Architects, R. 1998+ Plumstead). The construction of Thamesmead is still ongoing and an urban
village has been planned by a group of housebuilders for the land immediately to the north of
the 1972 council development. The proposals
envisage that most of the houses will be for sale
but with a proportion built by housing associations for rent. The plan also includes a new riverside walk, a canal-side park and a new local
centre at Battery Road (Fig. 2.46).

AR, 9/70, p. 158–160; *AJ*, 11/10/72, pp. 817–831; *AJ*,
18/10/72, pp. 879–896; *RIBAJ*, 1/88, pp. 60–67;
RIBAJ, 1/98, pp. 60–67; [1] Ibid, p. 61.

Nightingale Heights, Nightingale Vale, SE18.
1994. Hunt Thompson Associates.
R. Woolwich Arsenal.

The refurbishment of this twenty-four-storey
tower block of 93 flats, built by the London
Borough of Greenwich at the end of the 1960s,
resulted from a successful Estate Action Bid for
phase II of the improvements to the Woolwich
Common Estate in south-east London. The block
suffered from problems of inadequate heating and

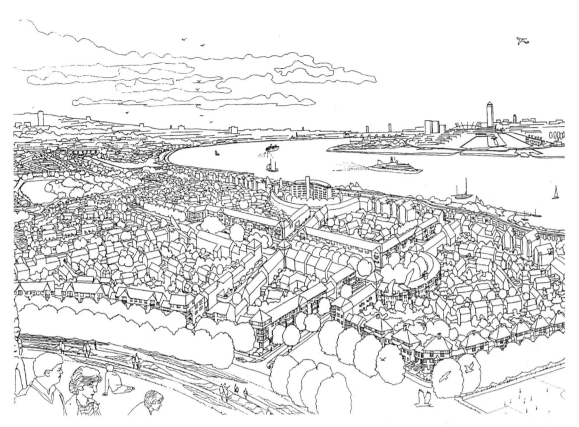

FIGURE 2.46
Gallions Reach looking over the River Thames.

insulation, high condensation, poor windows and a lack of security. There was a high level of tenant dissatisfaction, low morale, and the flats were hard to let, but there was a willingness on the part of the tenants to participate in resolving the problems.

The tower was fully encased with a high performance aluminium cladding system which incorporated aluminium clad timber windows (Fig. 2.47 and back cover). Each balcony was enclosed to create a warm, dry conservatory. A new central, gas-fired, heating system serving all the dwellings was installed in the roof space, resulting in a substantial reduction in the heating costs. Security was improved by eliminating two of the three entrances and employing a concierge and a TV monitoring system. A common room was provided for the tenants and this leads off the lobby. The ground immediately around the block was enclosed and planted and private gardens were formed for the residents.
AJ, 7/11/96, pp. 28–30.

The Millennium Village, Greenwich Peninsular.
End of 1999. Ralph Erskine with Hunt Thompson Associates.
U. North Greenwich (Jubilee line extension)

The aim of the Millennium Village proposed for the site next to the Dome is to challenge the way that houses are built in Britain. The design, by Ralph Erskine working with Hunt Thompson Associates, was the subject of a competition which sought to promote new thinking on how to achieve sustainable urban development for the 21st century.

FIGURE 2.47
Nightingale Heights: overclad tower block.

The proposals (Figs 2.48 and 2.49) envisage a Greenwich Riverside development on the 13 ha (32 acre) site that will contain 1,079 flats and 298 houses (to be developed by a consortium comprising Taylor Woodrow, Countryside Properties, Moat Housing Group and Ujima Housing Association). There will be 4500 sq. m mixed commercial development, as well as a primary school, health centre, shops, community buildings and workshops amongst the housing. Different housing tenures will be integrated so that personal status is not evident through location, form or appearance of the housing. Most controversially, the use of cars will be discouraged in favour of a pool of hire vehicles on the site and public transport. The housing will be arranged around courtyards to encourage a sense of community and provide shelter from the east winds that blow across the site. The units will be will be designed to be flexible, adaptable and extendible to accommodate changes in family size.

The design aims to achieve targets of an 80 per cent reduction in primary energy consumption, 30 per cent in water demand, 80 per cent

FIGURE 2.48
The Millennium Village.

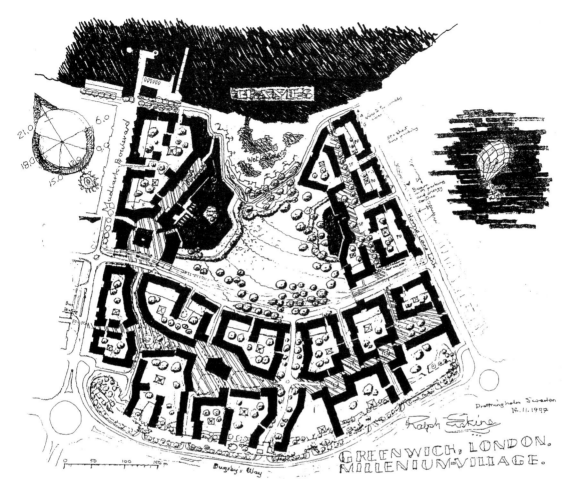

FIGURE 2.49
The Millennium Village: site layout.

recyclable building and zero CO_2 emission. Housing will face south to maximize the benefits of orientation, and the scheme will have its own combined heat and power plant and recycling processes. Construction methods will be highly industrialized, with large sections of the dwellings made in factories with the plumbing pre-installed. This, claim the consortium, will reduce costs by 30 per cent, enable a 25 per cent shorter construction period and quality control will be higher than is possible during site operations.

Many projects have previously had these ideals with limited success. The consortium feel that, in this instance, the commercial companies and housebuilders are all committed to their objectives and are confident that the outcome will now be achievable.

AJ, 26/2/98, pp. 10–15.

HACKNEY

Woodbury Down Estate, Stoke Newington.
1946–48. LCC Architects Department. U. Manor House.

Woodbury Down was the first LCC post-1945 experiment in building new communities complete with a health centre and comprehensive

LIVERPOOL JOHN MOORES UNIVERSITY
Aldham Robarts L.R.C.
TEL. 0151 231 3701/3634

FIGURE 2.50
Woodbury Down Estate: 1951 demonstration of housing of the future.

school in England. Its four tall blocks were the first high rise flats to be built of concrete by the LCC which was made possible by using lifts to increase the height from the previous limit of five to eight or nine storeys. High horizontal rendered balconies were designed as fire escapes. These, with the flat roofs and distinctive wide eaves, suggest a Viennese influence [1]. The scheme has been recommended for Grade II listing by English Heritage (Fig. 2.50).

EH, Something Worth Keeping? p. 4; [1] Ibid. p. 4.

Lea View House, Springfield Road and Jessam Avenue, E5.
1987. Hunt Thompson Associates. R. Clapton.

Lea View has become a model for the regeneration of council housing estates. Built in 1939, it contained 250 flats and maisonettes which had

become difficult to let, plagued with crime, vandalism and racial tension, and the vast majority of the tenants wanted to move elsewhere.

Following a successful campaign by the tenants, architects were appointed to work directly with them from an office on the site. The key features of the improvements include accommodating large families at ground floor level in two- and three-storey maisonettes, all of which have their own front entrance and private front and rear gardens (Fig. 2.51). Entry to the upper floor flats is via new lift towers which have become the scheme's notable architectural feature (Fig. 2.52). Access to the courtyard was restricted to improve privacy and security.

The quality of the scheme and the process of development has enhanced the environment and empowered the tenants. Crime and vandalism have been virtually eliminated and there is a new sense of community spirit.

AJ, 20/7/83, pp. 52–55; *AR*, 4/85, pp. 60–61; Housing Design Awards 1987, A *Building* Publication, p. 77; *RIBAJ*, 6/85 pp. 53–55.

Mothers' Square, Sladen Place, Clarence Road, Hackney, E5.
1990. Hunt Thompson Associates.
R. Hackney Central, Hackney Downs.

A partnership between the Hackney Health Authority, Newlon Housing Trust and Access Homes Housing Association created a model for new mixed-tenure housing (and medical facilities) on the site of the former Mothers' Maternity Hospital.

Mothers' Square is enclosed by an unbroken three-storey neo-Classical terrace, with raised four-storey elements at key points. The square has an internal perimeter road around a central green area (Fig. 2.53). The architects' initial proposal was for a more permeable through road but this was rejected by the local planners. The end result is extremely safe for children's play and is generally secure; intruders are instantly noticed. Most of the central space is taken up with car parking, but pergolas and landscaping reduce its impact.

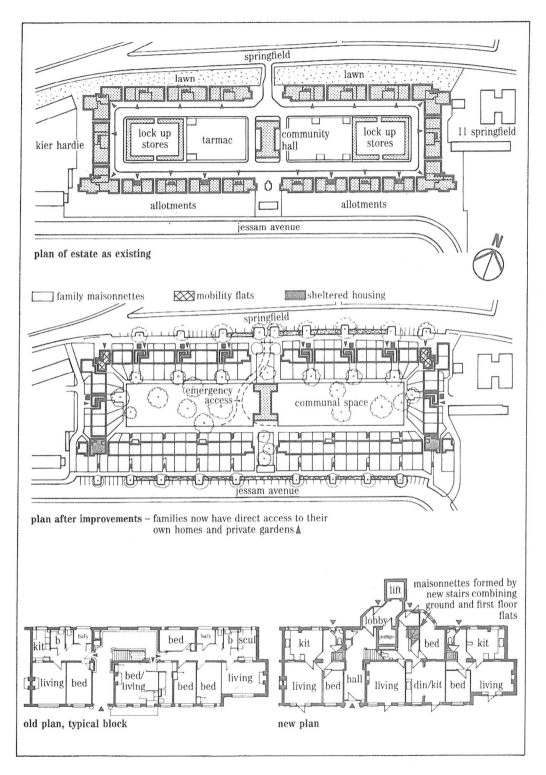

plan of estate as existing

☐ family maisonnettes ⧓ mobility flats ▨ sheltered housing

plan after improvements – families now have direct access to their own homes and private gardens ▲

old plan, typical block

new plan

FIGURE 2.51
Lea View: before and after plans.

Figure 2.52
Lea View: stairs and lift towers.

The housing association development comprises twenty-one family houses and six one- and two-bedroom flats for rent. In addition there are twenty-four shared-equity one- and two-bedroom flats, and warden-assisted sheltered flats for elderly people. All the dwellings have their living rooms looking into the square, which the architects claim is what the people like. To meet the 'Care in the Community' legislation which was coming into force in the late 1980s a nursing

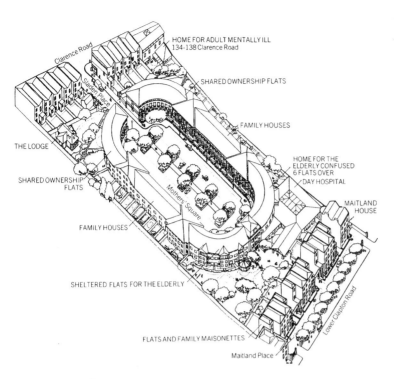

HOME FOR ADULT MENTALLY ILL
134-138 Clarence Road

Clarence Road

Slader Place

SHARED OWNERSHIP FLATS

FAMILY HOUSES

THE LODGE

HOME FOR THE
ELDERLY CONFUSED
6 FLATS OVER
DAY HOSPITAL

SHARED OWNERSHIP
FLATS

Mothers' Square

MAITLAND
HOUSE

FAMILY HOUSES

SHELTERED FLATS FOR THE ELDERLY

Lower Clapton Road

FLATS AND FAMILY MAISONETTES

Maitland Place

FIGURE 2.53
Mothers' Square.

home for elderly, mentally confused people was included. Hackney Health Authority was most anxious that this part of the project should not be segregated and consequently it too looks into the square. It is connected at the rear to a small day hospital which also serves a new home for adult mentally-ill people that has recently been built at nearby Clarence Road.

AJ, 8/8/90, pp. 34–44; Aldous, T., *Urban Villages*, p. 34–35; *Voluntary Housing*, 2/95, pp. 15–16.

Holly Street Estate Regeneration, Dalston, E8.
1997+. Levitt Bernstein Associates.
R. Dalston Kingsland.

Hackney is one of London's most deprived areas. In 1991 a Comprehensive Estates Initiative (CEI) was formed to tackle the problems on five of the council's worst 1960s estates: Holly Street, Nightingale, Clapton Park, Trowbridge and New Kingshold. The Hackney CEI offered a radical new approach to estate action by aiming to

improve the worst physical conditions and the social, economic and environmental problems. To achieve this, partnership arrangements were established between the local authority, central government, the residents, housing associations and private housing developers. Circle 33 was appointed the lead housing association in the consortium. In 1993 Holly Street Estate became the flagship project in the Dalston City Partnership, Hackney's successful City Challenge bid.

Holly Street Estate was a system complex built of sixteen five-storey blocks called snake blocks by residents. They had internal access corridors and had acquired a reputation as oppressive and 'prison-like'. Opportunity for criminal activity was high. Four, twenty–storey towers were also unpopular due to structural problems that included defective waterproofing between panels which also cracked, and spalling concrete.

Initial surveys indicated that most of the residents would like to leave. An options appraisal ranged from carrying out major repairs throughout to the total demolition of the estate and its

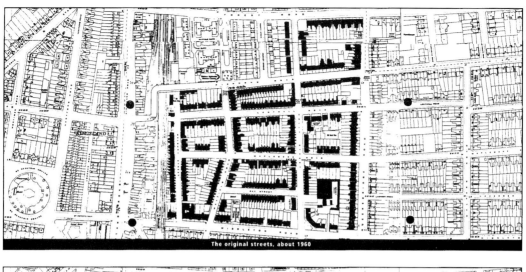

The original streets, about 1960

The old estate, 1990

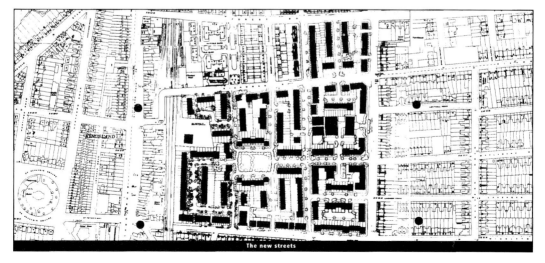

The new streets

FIGURE 2.54
Holly Street, Dalston: three stages of redevelopment since 1960.

replacement with new two- and three-storey housing. The outcome was complete renewal except for one tower block which would be refurbished. To integrate the new housing into its surroundings the pre-1970 street pattern was largely reinstated (Fig. 2.54). Mixed tenure was seen as vital to the creation of a more balanced social and economic community, and low-cost housing for sale, shared ownership and self-build housing were planned.

New ways of managing the housing encouraged the local people to participate actively in the regeneration process. This included the establishment of tenants management committees and the construction of community facilities with support to ensure that the residents had the ability to plan and manage them. Economic regeneration was initiated through a Community Access Centre where people could be offered help, employment training, educational opportunities and advice on forming their own businesses. Builders were contracted to employ a percentage of their workforce from the local community and training was made available. *AJ*, 7/11/96, pp. 28–30; *AJ*, 30/4/98, p. 44.

Navarino Manions Refurbishment, Dalston Lane, E8.

1904, refurbished in 1990. Hunt Thompson Associates. R. Hackney Downs.

Constructed in 1904 by the Four Per Cent Industrial Dwellings Society, Navarino Mansions were solidly built with robust detailing which had survived well but by the 1990s they were in need of modernization (Fig. 2.55). The architects have

FIGURE 2.55
Refurbishment of Navarino Mansions.

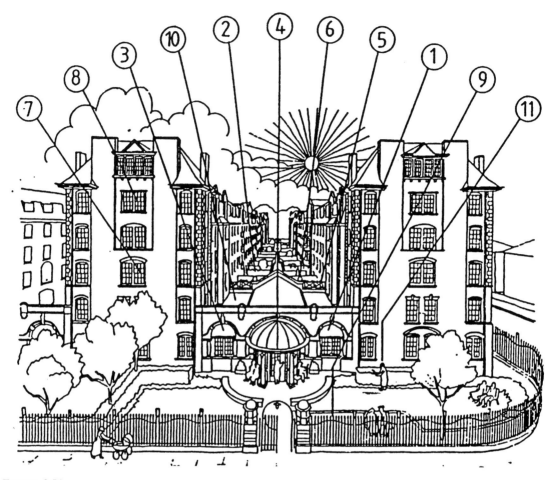

FIGURE 2.56
Navarino Mansions: tenants have had an influence on design decisions. 1, Warden control sheltered housing; 2, ground/first floor maisonettes; 3, new link block with facilities; 4, single new entrance; 5, selected landscaping out of 3 options; 6, separate garden for sheltered housing; 7, kitchens separate from living room; 8, windows chosen out of options but vetoed by planners; 9, sheltered block not screened; 10, roof terraces for keen gardeners; 11, tenants of sheltered housing want involvement in gardening.

achieved a remarkable transformation through sensitive and imaginative conservation and working closely with the tenants (Fig. 2.56).

The five- and six-storey housing is in two long courtyards restored to reflect their original image. The housing now meets a wide range of needs including warden-controlled sheltered housing. Ground and first floor accommodation was converted into maisonettes for families, with gardens in the space between the blocks. Lifts and entry phone systems were installed at communal entrances. The laundrette was enlarged and children's play areas provided. The balconies to the upper units, which had been removed in the 1960s, were reinstated.
AT, 9/93, p. 36.

The German Hospital, Dalston Lane, E8.
1997. Hunt Thompson Associates.
U. Hackney Downs.

The redevelopment of the former German Hospital by a development consortium comprising New Islington, Newlon and North London Muslim

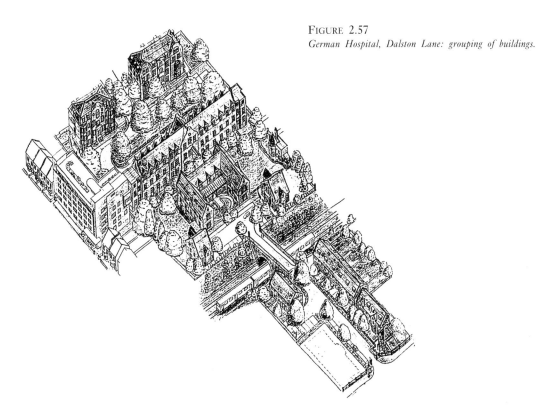

FIGURE 2.57
German Hospital, Dalston Lane: grouping of buildings.

Housing Associations and MacIntyre Care has brought new life to this group of Grade II listed buildings built in 1845 (Fig. 2.57).

The brief from the consortium was to provide housing for rent and shared ownership, new health care facilities and to find new, appropriate uses for the large hospital blocks. The outcome was the construction of fifteen new, large family houses and the conversion of some of the hospital buildings into flats and maisonettes which included the provision of small split-level studios financed from the government's Rough Sleepers Initiative.

The houses were built in the northern part of the site (Fig. 2.58) together with a new GPs practice building (Jefferson Sheard and Partners). These are approached from Dalston Lane and Ritson Road where the two lodge buildings were converted into single family houses.

The focus of the southern part of the site is a new 'London Square' which is accessed off Graham Road and Clifton Grove. This area contained a ward block, the nurses' home and the

FIGURE 2.58
German Hospital: new houses at the entrance to the site.

doctors' residences. The upper floors of the ward block were converted into the studios. High ceilings enabled a mezzanine to be built in each studio for the bathroom and sleeping space, overlooking the

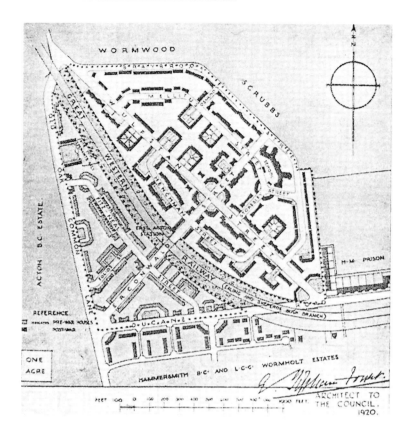

FIGURE 2.59
Old Oak Estate. [From London
Housing, *LCC, p. 136.]*

living area and separate kitchen below. The ground floor of this block was adapted for family use by constructing a tall glazed extension at the front which also formed a terrace for the first floor studio above. The nurses' home and doctors' housing were adapted into a range of one-, two- and three–bedroom flats with little change to the external appearance of the buildings.

HAMMERSMITH AND FULHAM

Old Oak Estate, Wulfstan Street, W12.
*1909–post 1945. LCC Architects Department
(A.S. Souter).U. East Acton.*

The 1890 Housing of the Working Classes Act enabled the LCC to build new housing for some 25 000 people between 1890 and 1913. One of the largest developments was the Old Oak Estate built on a 54 acre site where from 1909

to 1914, 304 houses and 5 shops were built (Fig. 2.59).

It was the first scheme to follow the new design principles embodied in the 1909 Town Planning Act which had largely been written by Raymond Unwin. At Old Oak this was interpreted in a layout of U-shaped terraces grouped around small public gardens or greens with their end gables facing on to the streets. Access to many of the dwellings was by footpath only which produced savings on the amount of road required.

There were many similarities in the design to Hampstead Garden Suburb, particularly Unwin's concept of the 'street picture'. Terraces varied in length and appearance and steep tiled roofs overhung the bedrooms with low eaves and dormers, and bedroom windows were frequently positioned in front and side facing gables. Most of the external walls were built in brick but the occasional gable was picked out in half-timbering or tile hanging.

Swenerton, M., *Homes Fit for Heroes*, pp. 16–18.

FIGURE 2.60
Thames Reach.

Thames Reach, 80 Rainville Road, Hammersmith, W6.
1987. Richard Rogers Partnership.
U. Hammersmith.

Richard Rogers has only occasionally designed grouped housing but his scheme at Thames Reach, on a site overlooking the river near the Hammersmith Bridge, is outstanding. The design is 'bold and contemporary' [1] (Fig. 2.60). It is housing at the luxury end of the market which presented a design opportunity not normally available to most architects.

The scheme comprises three linked five-storey pavilions, each with two flats per floor and two double-height penthouses with roof terraces. The southern-most block is non-standard, with an extra storey. The riverside elevation is totally glazed to take advantage of the views. A strong 'nautical' feel comes from the profusion of metal balconies located between the pavilions and at the ends.

On the entrance side, each pavilion has its own staircase and lift, approached along a 'gangplank' from a well landscaped courtyard where visitors' car parking is located. Parking for the residents is off this courtyard in an underground communal car park. The roadside elevation is a complete contrast to the lightness of the river-side front. Built in purple brick, the curved stair-case and lift towers present a feeling of great solidity.

[1] Housing Design Awards 1989, A *Building* Publication, pp. 46–47; *AJ* 4 and 11/1/89, pp. 33–49.

Vespan Road, conversion of a Victorian school into housing.
1997. Pollard Thomas and Edwards.
U. Shepherds Bush (Central Line).

This scheme illustrates how redundant school buildings and grounds can be successfully reused for housing purposes. The Victorian Northcroft school, designed by E.R. Robson, was built around two sides of a playground. A later single-storey annex enclosed the third side.

The scheme developed by the Shepherds Bush Housing Association involved the conversion of the Victorian L-shaped block into twenty-nine maisonettes with the annex accommodating a further ten maisonettes. A terrace of six new family houses was built on the corner of Vespan Road and Hadyn Park Road, together with a further three on a small playground fronting Vespan Road. The conversion of the existing buildings was very skilfully handled. The Victorian block was divided down its length to form three close-knit groups of six to eight maisonettes, each with its own stairs. The annexe was 'cored' along its length to create a small open courtyard, off which the dwellings are entered. Most of the dwellings have their own private outdoor space or roof garden.

The scheme has breathed new life into sound, but redundant buildings, and provided additional homes in an established neighbourhood, within easy reach of transport and shops. It is the kind of scheme that should be encouraged in every city.

Adjacent to the site is Becklow Mews, an earlier scheme of considerable merit by the same architects.

AJ, 9/10/97, pp. 39–42.

Figure 2.61
Richford Gate offices converted into housing: central courtyard.

Richford Gate, Off Goldhawk Road, W6. Conversion of offices into housing.
1995. *Keith Norman Associates.*
U. Goldhawk Road.

There are large empty offices in every town and city which could be used for housing. The Richford Gate project, situated off the Goldhawk Road and developed by the Kensington Housing Trust (KHT), shows how effectively this can be done. Originally built as open plan offices in the 1960s, it failed due to the recession in the 1980s leaving 88 000 sq.ft. (880 sq. m) of office space unused. The buildings had been designed to blend in with their predominantly residential surroundings which made them suitable for conversion into housing (Fig. 2.61). To achieve a mixed-use scheme KHT formed a partnership

with Yarrow Housing, Bringing Up Baby Ltd, The Grove Health Centre and the Ealing, Hammersmith and Hounslow Health Agency.

The scheme comprised fifty-seven dwellings of different sizes ranging from one-bedroom flats to four-bedroom maisonettes. Dwellings were grouped together so that not more than eight share a common access point. Conversion from offices to housing made compromises unavoidable but often flat areas exceeded Parker Morris standards. Six of the dwellings on the ground floor are designed to full wheelchair standards. Most of the ground floor of one block was converted into a day nursery which offers places for fifty children. Two of the four bedroom furnished maisonettes managed by Yarrow Housing provide 24–hour support for adults with learning disabilities to help them gain experience in independent living. Yarrow also manages 'The

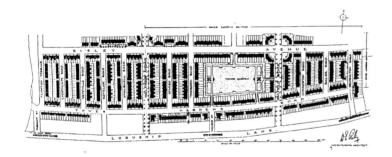

FIGURE 2.62
White Hart Lane: portion developed before 1913 and cottage plans.
[From Swenerton, M., Homes Fit for Heroes, *pp. 36–37.]*

Types of three-room changes

Four-room cottages

Five-room changes

Gate' – a training space offering therapeutic, educational, social and leisure-based opportunities to people with learning disabilities.

The development also includes a community health centre, a tenants' meeting hall and an area office for Kensington Housing Trust.

RIBA, *Building Homes as if Tomorrow Matters*, p. 7.

HARINGEY

White Hart Lane, Risley Avenue, Lordship Lane, N17.
1904–12 and 1921–28. LCC Department of Architecture (W.E. Riley). U. Wood Green.

White Hart Lane was built on 177 acres (77 ha) of land which made it the largest of the LCC's cottage estates built before 1914. Unlike the Garden City form of Old Oak Estate (p. 84) the phase of White Hart Lane built before the First World War followed a grid layout which was more familiar to the speculative builder of the day (Fig. 2.62). To achieve a density of twenty-seven dwellings per acre (67 dw/ha), plans for narrow frontage houses, as little as 12–15 ft wide, were developed. This was abhorrent to Raymond

FIGURE 2.63
White Hart Lane.

Unwin who strongly advocated using only the more expensive wide frontage types.

Nevertheless the appearance of the scheme takes its cue from the Garden City movement (Fig. 2.63). The houses have long roofs, low eaves, porches, two-storey projecting bays and elaborate chimney stacks, and a great variety of materials were used. At the junction of Risley Road and Awfield Avenue the houses were set-back around the intersection in true garden city style. Behind the houses at Risley Avenue, Tower Gardens, Shobden Road and Wilfield Avenue, a large green area was provided for recreational use including facilities for tennis and bowls.

Swenarton, M., *Homes Fit for Heroes*, pp. 35–38; Jones, E. and Woodward, C., *A Guide to the Architecture of London*, p. 358.

Highpoint 1 and 2, North Hill, N6.
1936 and 1938. Lubetkin and Tecton. U. Highgate.

Lubetkin and Tecton's masterpiece at Highgate has been described as the only international class pre-war Modern building in Britain [1] (Fig. 2.64). It was a watershed in the design of housing. When completed, the scheme was beautifully illustrated in the architectural magazines. In his article in *The Architectural Review* of January 1936, Le Corbusier commended the scheme by saying that it was 'the seed of a vertical garden city' [2]. To a profession eager to shake off the shackles of public timidity towards the new architecture, the building and these observations were a revelation.

The project was commissioned by the Gestetner family to accommodate their factory workers, but quickly they realized the commercial potential of selling the dwellings. Highpoint 1 comprises fifty-six dwellings grouped in the form of two linked crosses with one flat occupying each of the eight arms on every floor (Fig. 2.65). The lifts and staircases are at the intersections of each of the two crosses. This way, with one exception per floor, the flats are not connected, which prevents any possibility of noise transmission. It also provides each flat with cross-ventilation,

FIGURE 2.64
Highpoint flats.

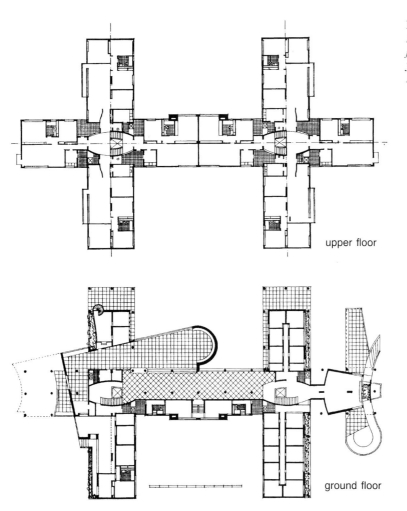

FIGURE 2.65
*Highpoint flats: ground and upper
floor plans. [Redrawn from Richards,
J.M.,* An Introduction to Modern
Architecture, *p. 141.]*

upper floor

ground floor

which at the time was seen as most important for healthy living. The construction involved poured reinforced concrete using a newly patented climbing shuttering system which gave a smooth continuous finish to the external walls.

The appearance of Highpoint 1 was disliked by the local council and when designing phase 2 in 1938, the architects had to submit a number of alternative elevational treatments to persuade the local authority to accept their design. To meet the criticisms, the elevations now contained a mixture of tiles, bricks and glazed bricks to contrast with the white concrete finish of the main structure. In addition, the entrance canopy was supported by replicas of Greek goddesses – the Caryatids of Athens.

[1] Pawley, M., Obituary: 'Berthold Lubetkin, A Modernist Maestro', *The Guardian*, 24/10/90, p. 5; [2] *AR*, 1/36, pp. 15–23.

HILLINGDON

Highgrove, Eastcote Road, Ruislip.
1977. Edward Cullinan Architects. U. Pinner.

This scheme is one of a number which developed from research on suburban forms and

FIGURE 2.66
Highgrove: typical house quad plans.

section

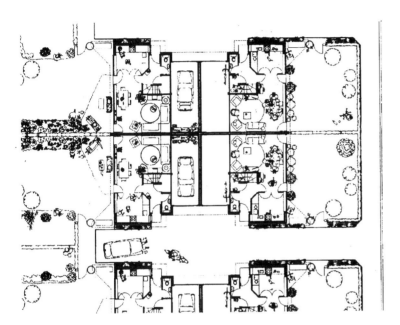

ground floor

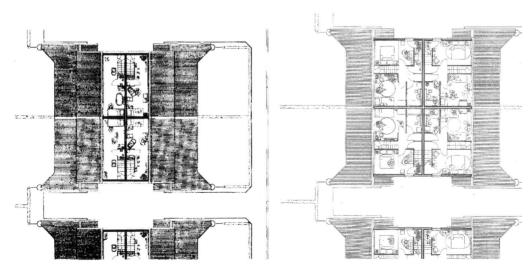

first floor   second floor

models initiated at Cambridge University in the 1960s under the leadership of Leslie Martin and Lionel Marsh (p. 18). The design was based on the principle of grouping single aspect houses in clusters of four in a back-to-back manner, arranged on either side of two culs-de-sac with parking spaces on the plot (Fig. 2.66). This arrangement had the advantage that dwelling plots and gardens were wider (9 m or 30 ft) than usual and in addition it achieved a density of 13.6 dwellings per acre (34 dw/ha). It also gave the living, dining and kitchen areas access to the garden, where the stepped section of the houses allowed maximum sunshine to penetrate. This concept required the housing to be orientated on a north-south axis. The roofs were covered with a blue lightweight coloured metal sheet (since removed) which was one of the scheme's most distinctive features.

AD, 5/74, p. 303–304; *BD*, 27/5/77, p. 15; *AJ*, 27/7/77, pp. 159–167; Toshi-Jukatu (Tokyo), 10/80; Edward Cullinan Architects (Academy Editions), 1995.

FIGURE 2.67
Hayes Court: non-estate housing.

Hayes Court, Church Green/ Freemans Lane, Hayes.
1978. Shankland Cox Partnership.
R. Hayes and Harlington.

Hayes Court is a small group of thirty-six terraced houses in an old part of Hillingdon. The design was commissioned by Thurston Williams, the Borough Architect of Hillingdon, who did much to encourage innovative design. The scheme contained twenty-six two- and three-storey houses, ten two-storey flats and seventeen garages. The design offered most of the houses views of the park but its main quality was the extent of individuality given to the dwelling externally. This was achieved through a variety of elevational treatments, stepping and staggering of varying roof heights and using a wide range of materials. The result was, in Oliver Cox's words a 'non-estate' which contrasted so greatly to the monolithic nature of most council housing built at this time (Fig. 2.67).
AR, 10/78, pp. 248–251.

ISLINGTON

Spa Green Estate, Rosebury Avenue and St John's Street, EC1.
1938–49. Skinner and Lubetkin. U. Angel.

Following their success with the design of the Finsbury Health Centre (1938), Lubetkin and Tecton were commissioned by Finsbury Council to design the Spa Green Estate but the war intervened.

In 1943 every local authority was asked to compile a one-year programme of development, set to start immediately the war ended. In London much of this was to be in the form of blocks of flats, which gave the opportunity for the Spa Green Estate to be built. The delay gave the engineer, Ove Arup, the opportunity to develop the 'box frame' concrete structure brought from Denmark where it had been designed during the war. This freed the facades for the lively pattern-work of contrasting brick-work and balconies that so characterized Lubetkin's work after 1945. The scheme comprised two eight-storey and one four-storey curvilinear block of flats (Fig. 2.68). It was built to a lavish budget having wood-block floors and waste disposal units in the kitchen sinks which still work today. In its support of Grade II* listing of the estate, English Heritage comments

FIGURE 2.68
Spa Green Estate. [Photo by Christopher Colquhoun.]

that 'Spa Green represented the ideal in clean, comfortable, modern living at high densities in the inner city' [1]. There is a lot to learn today from how well the scheme has survived.
AJ, 1/8/46, p. 77; *AJ*, 9/10/52, p. 441. [1] *EH*, p. 3.

Priory Green Estate, Collier Street, N1.
Bevin Court, Holford Street, WC1.
1953. Skinner Bailey and Lubetkin.
U. Kings Cross.

As the design of Priory Green Estate and its structural system had also begun in 1938, it was possible to make an early start on construction after the war. The layout of the blocks follows the original street pattern and is grouped around enclosed greens. Nearby at Holford Place is Bevin Court. The single Y-shaped block was designed by Lubetkin, so that as much as possible of the land left over could be incorporated into a public park. The form also ensured that no flat faced north. The central drum between the wings contained a most imaginative staircase. English Heritage, in recommending Grade II listing for the scheme, considered it must have been 'conceived as a penguin pool ramp for humans' [1].

Cuts in funding, first by Stafford Cripps in 1947 and then from 1951 by the Conservative government, meant that these two schemes and Spa Green are the best exponents of the short-lived optimism that existed at the end of the war.
AJ, 9/10/52, pp. 433–442; [1] *EH*, p. 5.

FIGURE 2.69
*Mercers' sheltered housing and health
centre.*

Mercers' House, sheltered housing, Essex Road, N1.
1992. John Melvin and Partners. U. Angel.

The Worshipful Company of Mercers commissioned John Melvin to design this monumental sheltered housing project on a main road site only a mile from the City of London (Fig. 2.69). The scheme consists of twenty-eight flats with a warden's flat and communal facilities, including sitting rooms and a laundry. They are arranged in three groups, each accessed by a staircase and lift tower. A central fourth floor corridor connects the tower and the warden's flat.

The height of the block of four floors above the basement is accentuated by eight stacks each of four flues and three lift motor rooms which, with their generous cornices, attract much comment. The apparent height of the building is further increased by the bold brickwork sizes and patterns. The 50 mm high bricks, gauged at five courses to 300 mm, were chosen to provide a heightened scale which, according to John Melvin, was a technique widely used by Sir Edwin Lutyens and Frank Lloyd Wright [1]. The chequer pattern of bricks forms giant architectural orders, framing the entrances and marking the corner, leading the eye to the lower health centre on Mitchison Road which, complete with cornice, acknowledges with good manners the fenestration of the adjoining houses.

The scheme has become known locally as 'millionaires' row' due to its grand scale.

[1] *BB*, Summer 93, pp. 14–15: *AJ*, 10/3/93, pp. 43–35.

Self-build housing, Nicholay Road, off Fairbridge Road and Sussex Way, N19.
1996. Architype. U. Archway.

Britain regrettably lags far behind other European countries in the development of self-build social housing schemes but one success in recent years is a shared ownership scheme built on two sites by the Community Housing Association. The design was significantly influenced by the Housing Corporation's tight financial limits but the scheme still manages to reflect the architect's personal agenda to seek ecological solutions and client empowerment.

The larger of the two sites at Nicholay Road contains six two-storey and seven three-storey houses compactly built on a most unlikely site adjacent to a council estate of high density housing. The scheme has a very different appearance to previous Segal housing due to cost limits. The houses are narrow-fronted using a

FIGURE 2.70
Self-build housing at Nicholay Road.

construction arrangement that is half-Segal and half-conventional. Only the front and rear walls are timber-framed. The party walls between the dwellings are Thermalite blockwork with a plaster finish which called for the self-build group to include a bricklayer and a plasterer which had not been necessary on previous Segal schemes where wet trades were eliminated.

The houses are tightly grouped, with gardens screened by high timber fencing (Fig. 2.70). Five of the residents opted for their gardens to be communal which makes good use of the small amount of private space between the dwellings. These are overlooked from spacious timber balconies at first floor level.

The second site at Sussex Way comprises a row of three, single-storey, L-shaped bungalows built within the perimeter brick wall of a former estate playground. These are much more recog-

nizable as Segal houses, but are hidden behind the wall, which makes them difficult to find. *AT*, 2/97, pp. 26–33.

Royal Free Square, Liverpool Road, N1.
1992. Pollard Thomas and Edwards and Levitt Bernstein Associates.
U. Highbury and Islington.

The Royal Free Hospital on Liverpool Road was designed by Charles Fowler in 1848. It was one of the early hospital closures and stood empty until 1986 when the Circle 33 Housing Trust and the New Islington and Hackney Housing Association (NIHHA) jointly bought the site and all its listed buildings. The two architectural practices collaborated to produce an overall scheme and

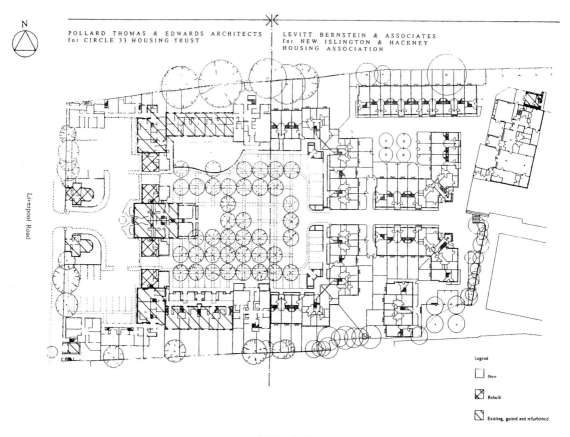

SITE PLAN   OLD ROYAL FREE
RESTORATION & REGENERATION   1:1000

FIGURE 2.71
Royal Free Square: site layout

FIGURE 2.72
Royal Free Square: urban housing of great quality.

planning permission was granted in 1987 (Fig. 2.71).

The development provides housing for families, couples and single people as well as disabled persons. A third of the dwellings were designed for elderly people and a number are suitable for wheelchair use. The design respects the scale of the listed buildings on the Liverpool Road frontage. Matching pavilions were built at each side of the entrance courtyard to help emphasize the gateway into the project. The focus is a new square similar in terms of size and scale of buildings to the eighteenth and nineteenth century squares in the neighbourhood (Fig. 2.72). Beyond the square at the Upper Road end of the site the buildings are two and three storeys where the streets and spaces become narrow. A public footpath passes through the site to prevent the development becoming an isolated housing estate.

The development at the Liverpool Road end of the site comprises a mixture of new buildings and the refurbishment and conversion into housing of the listed hospital buildings. The housing at the Upper Street end is almost entirely new houses and flats except for the original water tower which was converted to accommodate young people. This part of the scheme also includes a new psychiatric day care centre, built as part of the Care in the Community programme. All family houses have private gardens and all flats have a patio or balcony except where prohibited by the listing of the old buildings.

The urban quality of the scheme is outstanding, especially the treatment of the block-paved pedestrian/vehicular areas. The central square garden is enclosed by railings and gates which were designed by the residents and their children in collaboration with the sculptor, Jane Ackroyd.

AJ, 15/7/92 pp. 20–23; *AJ*, 11/93, p. 31; *B* (Supplement), 5/94, pp. 12–13.

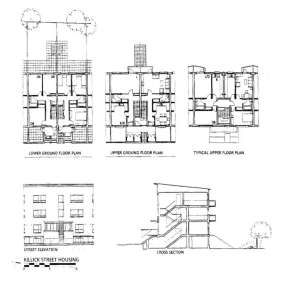

LOWER GROUND FLOOR PLAN   UPPER GROUND FLOOR PLAN   TYPICAL UPPER FLOOR PLAN

STREET ELEVATION   CROSS SECTION

KILLICK STREET HOUSING

Killick Street, Kings Cross, N1.
1995. Avanti Architects. U. Kings Cross.

Just a few streets behind Kings Cross Station Avanti Architects have given the traditional terraced house a new image. The site was almost the whole of the urban block bounded by Killick Street, Lavina Grove, All Saints Street and Wharfdale Road, the General Picton public house being one of the few buildings that remained. The architects were originally asked to design a medical centre on the site but the selected piece of land was too large. Consequently they approached the Peabody Trust to purchase the whole site for housing and make part (on Killick Street) available for the health centre. To secure funding from the Housing Corporation, the Kush Housing Association became partners in the scheme and they have twenty-four of the seventy-five dwellings.

The scheme comprises sixty-six flats and family maisonettes, including two flats adapted for wheelchair users. In addition, there are nine flats fronting Wharfdale Road which were financed for homeless people from the Rough Sleepers Initiative.

The development is arranged around the perimeter of the block and along Lavina Grove, which was converted from a cul-de-sac to a through road to reduce its potential for antisocial

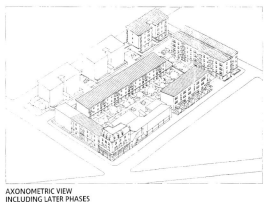

AXONOMETRIC VIEW
INCLUDING LATER PHASES

FIGURE 2.73
Killick Street: axonometric and typical dwelling plans.

use (Fig. 2.73). Three- and four-storey blocks consolidate the street pattern whilst reflecting the scale of the surrounding Georgian streets. The distinctive appearance of the housing results from the architects' reinterpretation of the traditional brick facade. The yellow stock bricks at ground floor level and smooth buff bricks on the upper floors are separated by a precast concrete string course. Painted render on the stair towers contrasts with this. Bin stores and meter cupboards are handled ingeniously in a series of front extensions to the elevations on Killick Street and Lavina Grove. These too are rendered.

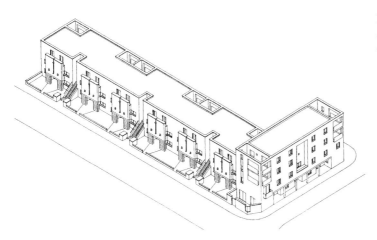

FIGURE 2.74
Lambton Road/Nugent Road: an axonometric layout.

The effect is a calm, consistent and well proportioned modern architectural expression.

AJ, 14/9/95, pp. 28–29; *AR*, 6/97, pp. 51–53; *AT*, 11/96, pp. 36–43.

Lambton Road/Nugent Road, N19.
Avanti Architects. U. Archway.

This three- and four-storey development comprises in total eighteen family dwellings and nine one-bedroom flats (Fig. 2.74). The Lambton Road frontage is a three-storey terrace containing six pairs of maisonettes with flats above. Each pair is separated by external staircases leading directly to the entrance of the flats on the top level. The four-storey apartment block on Nugent Road contains one-bedroom flats. The scheme makes a bold architectural statement. Materials and details – red brick, stone portals, a stone band course, blue concrete columns, metal balustrades, blue glazed brickwork by the entrances – were selected to provide a contemporary, visual analogy of Victorian architecture.

AJ, 13/2/97, pp. 29–37.

FIGURE 2.75
Kensal House, Ladbroke Grove.

KENSINGTON AND CHELSEA

Kensal House, Ladbroke Grove, W10.
1936. E. Maxwell Fry. U. Kensal Green,
Ladbroke Grove.

Kensall House was perhaps the most significant working class housing scheme built in the modernist manner before the Second World War (Fig. 2.75). It was built on the site of an old gas works by the Gas Light and Coke Company to house its workforce, and the circular foundations of one of the gasometers were cleverly reused as part of the construction of the nursery school built with the scheme. The two long six-storey, curving blocks were arranged on an approximately north–south axis so that the morning sun could penetrate the bedrooms and the afternoon sun the living rooms. The scheme included communal features, such as a laundry and a residents' social club, that were innovative at the time.

The external walls are finished in white render and, despite the lack of regular painting, the scheme still looks well.
CIOH, *Taking Stock*, 1996, p. 21.

FIGURE 2.76
Trellick Tower.

Trellick Tower, Golborne Road, W10.
1972. Erno Goldfinger. U. Westbourne Park.

Trellick Tower was one of two very tall towers designed by Erno Goldfinger in London during the 1960s. His earlier Balfron Tower (Grade II listed) at St Leonard's Road, Poplar, E14 (DLR All Saints; *AJ*, 22/5/68, p. 1133), built in 1965, was effectively a prototype for the far more sophisticated thirty-one-storey Trellick Tower. It was Goldfinger's last major building and the culmination of his ideas on housing (Fig. 2.76). A detached service tower was intended to reduce noise. The combination of flats, shops, a doctor's surgery, nursery and Goldfinger's own offices owes much to Le Corbusier's Unité in Marseilles, but the sophistication of the plan, the careful attention to every detail and the precision of the bush-hammered concrete are features that make it stand out.

Trellick Tower is popular with its current residents, some of whom stoutly defend it against its critics. They praise the spacious interiors, many of which are over the Parker Morris minimum areas. They enjoy the exceptionally wide bay frontage (6.75 m or 22 ft 2 in) which helps the proportions of the rooms and they like the large south-facing balconies.

This popularity was not always the case and nothing makes for greater comparison than Martin Richardson's 1973 appraisal of the scheme in *The Architects Journal* and English Heritage's support in 1996 of their recommended Grade II* listing. Richardson gave a stark reminder of the rigours of living in high rise housing – vandalism of the lifts and public areas, lack of open space, unsuitability of the development for children etc.; life was almost intolerable. By the late 1980s these problems had reduced the tower to part of a sink estate into which the poorest residents of the Royal Borough of Kensington and Chelsea were transferred. In contrast English

FIGURE 2.77
St Mark's Road housing.

Heritage wrote that, since the block had been refurbished by the council in the early 1990s and made much more secure, 'no smart Kensington-ian living in stucco comfort gets to see London as do the residents of Trellick Tower. The views are inspirational and, in the right light, almost spiritual'.

AJ, 25/11/87, pp. 28–29; *AJ*, 19/1/73, pp. 79–94; *EH*, 1996, p. 4; Glancy, J., High rise arisen, *The Guardian*, 22/11/97, p. 71.

St Mark's Road/St Quintin Avenue, W10.
1980. Jeremy Dixon. U. Ladbroke Grove.

This scheme of forty-four flats and houses superbly captures the scale and character of the surrounding Victorian terraces of North Kensington by grouping three dwellings behind each gable (Fig. 2.77). At the lowest level is a single aspect, two person semi-basement flat and above are two narrow frontage houses entered up a small flight of steps. The houses fronting St Mark's Road are angled which helped the architect resolve the prominent design of the corner with St Quintin Avenue where there are single-person flats and community rooms. Rear gardens back onto a parking street. The design of the front facades incorporates large timber-framed entrances and bay windows which, with the white coping to the gables and front walls, gives the scheme its distinctive character. The rhythm of large brick gateposts capped with large pyramid copings hides the bin stores. These combine with the railings and stairs to separate the houses from the street in the best tradition of the English street.

AR, 12/80, pp. 342–347.

Alan Morkill House, St Mark's Road, W10.
1991. PRP Architects. U. Ladbroke Grove.

Further along St Mark's Road from Jeremy Dixon's project is an equally significant scheme which meets a different brief. The concept of extra-sheltered housing for frail elderly people is a recent innovation in a fast growing area of housing development resulting from people living much longer.

FIGURE 2.78
Housing for frail elderly people, St Mark's Road.

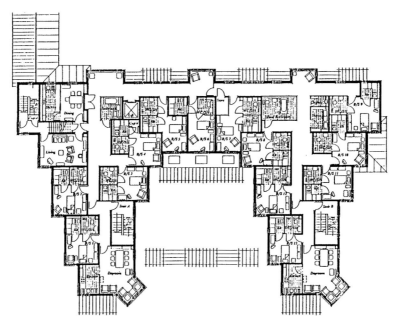

first floor

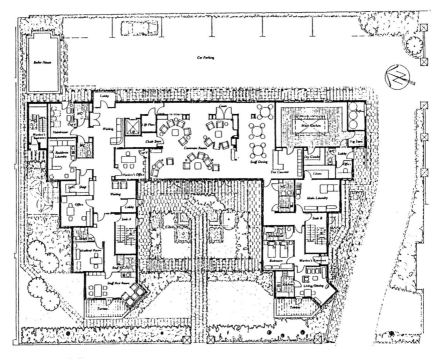

ground floor

FIGURE 2.79
Alan Morkill House, St Mark's Road: ground and first floor plans.

Alan Morkill House, developed by Servite Homes, has 24–hour support for the residents provided by a manager and care staff. Meals are available on request in a restaurant. Independent accommodation is in thirty-seven bedsitting rooms of just under 20 sq. m. (200 sq. ft), each containing its own *en suite* toilet, shower and kitchenette. These are clustered in small, self-contained 'family' groups of six to ten dwellings around a day lounge/dining room and main service kitchen. This produces a plan form which avoids long corridors and large dining/communal areas which can give developments an institutional feel. The whole complex wraps around three sides of a well planted courtyard that overlooks St Mark's Road.

The staggered form of the plan enables all the bedsits to have corner windows from which the residents can sit and look up and down St Mark's Road (Fig. 2.78). External materials are traditional yellow stock bricks and dark blue concrete bricks which helps the building nestle into its surroundings (Fig. 2.79).

B (Housing Supplement), 5/3/93, pp. 18–22; *RIBAJ*, 8/90, p. 43.

LAMBETH

Pullman Court, Streatham Hill, SW2. 1935.
Frederick Gibberd. R. Streatham

During the inter-war years flats for sale or rent became popular with middle class people in London. These were intended mainly for single, childless and retired people who wished to live in a pleasant location close to transport links and public facilities. Although the flats themselves were often small, they were marketed as luxurious and labour-saving and they had a degree of stylish living attached to them. Designs frequently leaned towards the new architecture of white rendered walls, flat roofs and horizontal windows. A number fully embraced the pioneering modernist principles, and Frederick Gibberd's Pullman Court was the most significant of these (Fig. 2.80).

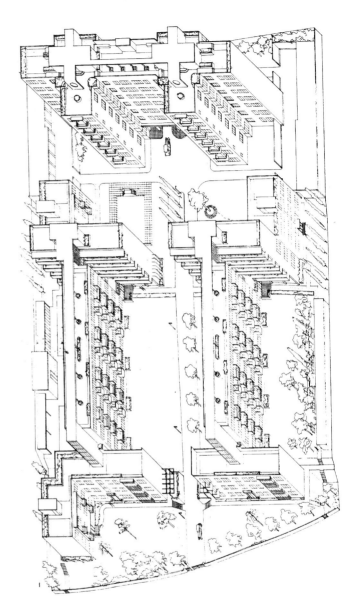

FIGURE 2.80
Pullman Court. [AR, 1/36, pp. 28.]

The scheme comprises 218 flats, built on a site of just under 3 acres (7.5 ha). The flats fronting Streatham Hill are three storeys and are set well back to preserve the existing trees. Behind these and forming two linked linear courtyards are five- and seven-storey blocks. The flats were designed to offer varying sizes from one to three-rooms. The three-roomed flats had two double bedrooms and were thought to be suitable for families. The five and seven storey blocks were served with lifts which opened on to external galleries leading to the individual dwellings.

The buildings were constructed with a reinforced concrete frame and panel walls. The external walls were to be painted every 5 years and a permanent steel cradle rail was installed at roof level for this purpose. The flats were centrally heated from a single plant beneath the seven-storey block. To attract purchasers a swimming pool was provided in the furthest courtyard.

Ravetz, A., *The Place of Home*, p. 43; *AR*, 1/36, pp. 28–30.

Central Hill, Lunham Road, SE19.
1974. London Borough of Lambeth Architects Department. R. Gypsy Hill.

During the 1970s Edward Hollamby and his architects in Lambeth Borough Council made strident efforts to humanize the design of high density housing as they maximized the use of scarce housing land. Taking its cue from Seidlung Halen (p. 18), the scheme at Central

Hill took full advantage of the sloping site to achieve this aim (Fig. 2.81).

The scheme comprises 374 dwellings which includes 212 three- to six-person houses and 162 one- and two-person flats. Fourteen garages were provided with 117 covered car spaces and a further 129 parking spaces. Most of the housing is in the form of parallel rows of three- and four-storey terraces running along the hillsides. This achieved a density of seventy-five dwellings per hectare (30 dw/acre). The dwellings are in the form of overlapping and interlocking two-storey units stepping down the site one below the other which affords almost everyone with good views and small gardens or balconies. The scheme has a network of brick-paved footpaths, and car parking and garaging is kept to the perimeter of the scheme on the high side of the site

The development was conceived as a single set-piece by its architects who strongly believed that this would create a harmonious community through the strength of its architecture. In this respect the scheme was extremely well executed. *AR*, 2/76, pp. 97–106.

FIGURE 2.81
Central Hill: site layout. [Lambeth Architects Department.]

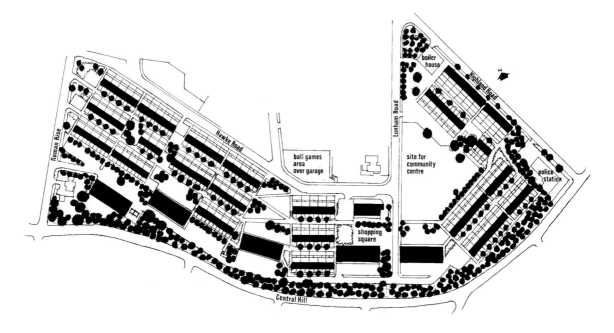

Vining Street, housing for young people, Brixton, SW9.
1989. *MacCormac Jamieson Pritchard.*
U. Brixton.

The Vining Street housing in Brixton built by the Tudor Trust and Metropolitan Trust met a real need in the mid-1990s arising from an increasing level of homelessness amongst young people in London. Its design evolved after extensive consultation with neighbourhood groups and community leaders in the area who were anxious that the development should be of familiar scale and fit into the character of the area, which meant producing a building of three/four storeys in height constructed with traditional materials.

The design avoids common staircases and corridors which would give the development an institutional feel. Instead the entrances are carefully arranged so that as many flats as possible have a direct relationship with the street. Dwellings on the first floor are entered from external staircases that resemble the front steps of traditional London terraced houses. The top landings of these are protected from the weather by glass canopies (Fig. 2.82).

FIGURE 2.82
Vining Street housing for young homeless people.

The scheme contains a range of different flat plans to meet different needs. This includes bedsitting rooms for longer stay people which are grouped in pairs with a shared kitchen and bathroom, and rooms which are shared by a number of young people who need immediate care. The scheme set a very high standard for young people's housing in the future.

RIBAJ, 12/91, p. 35; *B* (Housing Design Awards), 11/91, pp. 16–17.

Wiltshire Road/Sisulu Place, SW9.
1992. London Borough of Lambeth, Technical Services Department. U. Brixton

---

During the 1990s public sector architects were given fewer opportunities to design new housing for rent for their authorities. Edward Hollamby's department at Lambeth in the 1970s comprised seven architectural groups but by the end of the 1990s it was a merely a section of the Housing Directorate. Despite this decline, Abe Hayeem and his team's Wiltshire Road scheme, described in *Building Design* as 'a bit of decent architecture with a human face' [1], reflects the enthusiasm that once existed.

The brief was to provide two- or three-storey dwellings 'with no flat roofs, individual entrances and car ports in front of the houses'. The architects' response was to produce a layout for forty-eight dwellings that met these requirements but in a way that created the sense of a small urban village. The dwellings are mainly four-, five- and six-person family houses and a small number of flats. A large number are mobility and wheelchair dwellings and consequently the whole scheme is accessible to people with physical disabilities. The accent of the design was to create clearly defined streets, mews and courtyards in the form of continuous terraces. Three-storey houses form the spine along the east of the site, terminating in a staggered terrace of six-person houses. Corner blocks of three-person flats define the 'entrance' to the site (Fig. 2.83), and specially designed family houses serve as 'nodes' to take up the odd angles of an awkwardly shaped

FIGURE 2.83
Wiltshire Road: modernism with a human feel.

site. Two-storey terraces of four-person houses front Wiltshire Road and bound the southern part of the site. In keeping with Lambeth Borough Architects tradition, the context for the design is 'modern movement', linking a Victorian setting with a reflection of Bauhaus, Corbusian and De Stijl influences in the white walls and curved windows. The result is a striking scheme that its occupants clearly enjoy.

[1] *BD*, 15/11/91, pp. 18–19; *Access by Design*, Issue 57, 1–4/92; *AT*, 4/93, p. 24.

Broadwall Housing and Oxo Tower Wharf, Coin Street, SE1.
1994 and 1996. Lifschutz Davidson Limited. U. Waterloo.

'The battle of Coin Street' became a legend of how a local community changed the minds of politicians and developers. Faced in 1980 with the threat of a giant office and commercial development, the Coin Street Community Builders (CSCB) successfully lobbied for and secured the alternative use of the 5.3 hectare (13 acre) site

FIGURE 2.84
Coin Street: high quality co-operative housing with the Oxo Tower in the distance.

for housing, open space and community enterprise. The GLC and the Greater London Enterprise Board eventually assisted them with the purchase of the land.

This small start began a remarkable transformation of the area. CSCB formed a separate, legally registered Housing Association, the Coin Street Secondary Housing Co-operative (CSS), which was able to secure funding for housing development from the Housing Corporation. CSS in turn formed co-operatives to take on the management of the schemes. The residents joining the co-operatives were nominated by Lambeth and Southwark Councils on a 50–50

LIVERPOOL JOHN MOORES UNIVERSITY
Aldham Robarts L.R.C.
TEL. 0151 231 3701/3634

basis. To qualify these people had to be working in the area and they had to agree to participate in the management of their new housing through being members of their respective co-operative.

CSCB's first project was fifty-six low cost dwellings for the Mulberry Housing Co-op overlooking the newly laid out Bernie Spain gardens. The twenty-five dwellings for the Palm Co-operative, Broadwell, was the subject of a limited architectural competition. The scheme contains eleven three-storey houses with gardens designed as a long terrace with towers of flats at each end. The nine-storey tower at the river end contains one-bedroom flats – one flat per floor served by double lifts.

The architects' intention for the exterior was to use materials that 'grow old gracefully'. No fewer than nine were used – red brick, treated hardwood, zinc, copper, painted metalwork, bright metalwork, white soffit panelling, stone copings and timber trellises. These are beautifully composed with large windows from which there are superb views (Fig. 2.84).

This was followed by the conversion of the Oxo Building, with its famous art deco tower, into mixed development including seventy-eight one- to three-bedroom flats on the third to the seventh floors. Below the flats are commercial areas consisting of shops and workshops. Above the flats the building has been capped by a new floating roof structure which accommodates two very smart restaurants run by Harvey Nichols.

AJ, 5/81, pp. 273–276; *AT*, 10/94, pp. 40–48; *B* (Housing Design Awards), 27/10/95, p. 6; *AJ*, 13/6/96, pp. 24–45; *AR*, 2/97, pp. 56–60; *BB*, pp. 8–9; *AJ*, Brick Bulletin supplement, 12/6/97, pp. 8–9; *B*, 28/11/97, p. 50; Cunningham, J., Winners in the OXO game, *The Guardian*, 11/9/96, pp. 6–7. N.B. Part of the development falls within the L.B. Southwark.

LEWISHAM

Segal self-build housing.
1980+. Walter Segal, Jon Broome, Architype.

Walter Segal had already enjoyed a successful career when in the early 1960s he designed and constructed a temporary timber house in his garden at Highgate whilst his house was being renovated. That was the beginning of the 'Segal' method of house building which was to occupy him until his death in 1985.

Segal never liked describing his houses as 'system houses'. He was more concerned with their architectural philosophy and their radical approach to building techniques. He considered the building industry to be technologically and economically backward. The structure of its organization was archaic and inefficient and its methods of production chaotic. Unlike most industries, it had never changed with industrialization.

The aim of Segal's methods was to use materials which could be obtained easily and required minimal cutting. Ready-made components should be used wherever possible. He preferred the timber post-and-beam structure with columns 10–12 ft (3–4 m) apart which he considered gave maximum planning flexibility. His structure stood on ground slabs which enabled different site levels to be accommodated and facilitated the easy distribution of services. The plans varied according to the users' needs within the constraints of the modular construction system and the sewer positions which dictated the location of the bathrooms.

The first sites made available by Lewisham Borough Council were considered almost impossible to develop but Walter Segal rose to the challenge. They are as follows:

11/13 Elstree Hill, Bromley (R. Ravensbourne)
Longton Avenue, SE26 (R. Sydenham)
30/31 Brockley Park, SE23 (R. Catford)
Walter's Way, SE23 (R. Honor Oak Park)
Segal Close, SE23, 1981 (R. Catford/Catford Bridge) (Fig. 2.85).

Funding for the schemes was devised through an equity sharing rent/purchase leasing scheme and everyone was guaranteed a council mortgage (from Lewisham) to cover the cost of the lease. After completion the self-builder was responsible for maintenance even though they did not own all the scheme.

FIGURE 2.85
Segal Close: one of the early Segal
self-build schemes (designed by
Walter Segal and Jon Broome).

Other developments by Architype using the Segal system are at the following locations:

Prospect Vale, 1–8 Parish Wharf, Greenwich, SE18 (1995). London and Quadrant Housing Association and built by the Greenwich Self-Build Co-operative. R. Woolwich Dockyard.

Timberlands, Hope Wharf, corner of Peckham Hill Street/Commercial Way, Southwark, SE15 (1996). South London Family Housing Association and the SE London Consortium. R. Queen's Road, Peckham. This scheme of one-bedroom dwellings for young, single, homeless, unemployed people incorporated a training programme leading to NVQs in building trades.

Birchdene Drive, Thamesmead, Greenwich, SE2 (1995). Twelve houses funded by the London Quadrant Housing Trust and built by Greenwich Self-Build Housing Co-operative. R. Plumstead. This is a low-energy scheme using masonite composite timber construction and grass roofs.

The Walter Segal Trust which was set up immediately after his death now actively promotes the concept throughout the country.

AJ, 23/3/66, pp. 763–769; *AJ*, 30/9/70, pp. 769–780; *AJ*, 17/12/80, pp. 1183–1205; *AJ*, 20/6/84, pp. 35–38; *AJ*, 5/11/86, pp. 31–68; *AJ*, 7/11/96, pp. 48–50; *AJ*, 25/5/95, p. 45.

MERTON

Watermeads, London Road/Rawnsley Avenue.
1977. London Borough of Merton Architects Department, Borough Architect, Bernard V. Ward. R. Mitcham.

Watermeads was perhaps the most successful of the perimeter housing schemes built by the London Borough of Merton in the late 1960s and the 1970s. It was built on a 4 hectare (10 acre) site which contained a number of very mature trees and overlooked the River Wandle. The brief called for a dwelling mix of approximately 50–50,

FIGURE 2.86
Watermeads: perimeter housing preserving large areas of open space.

six-person houses and two-person flats plus a small number of four-person flats for disabled people.

The design of the scheme benefited from the experience of two earlier perimeter projects built by Merton Borough Council in the late 1960s on sites at Pollards Hill, South Lodge Road, Mitcham (R. Norbury) [1] and Eastfields, Acacia Road (R. Mitcham Junction) [2]. Pollards Hill was surveyed to obtain feedback and a major criticism was its monotony. The construction system used was Wimpey no-fines encased in white vitreous enamelled steel panels which was difficult to change (Fig. 2.86). Therefore, to achieve variety all the trees on the site were preserved and the development was wound around them in a continuous terrace (Fig. 2.87). This arrangement formed two culs-de-sac off which the dwellings are entered. Garages were integral with the houses which was fortunately then permitted under the cost yardstick.

[1] *AR*, 4/71, pp. 201–208; [2] *AJ*, 23/1/74, pp. 177–179; *AR*, 4/80, pp. 215–220.

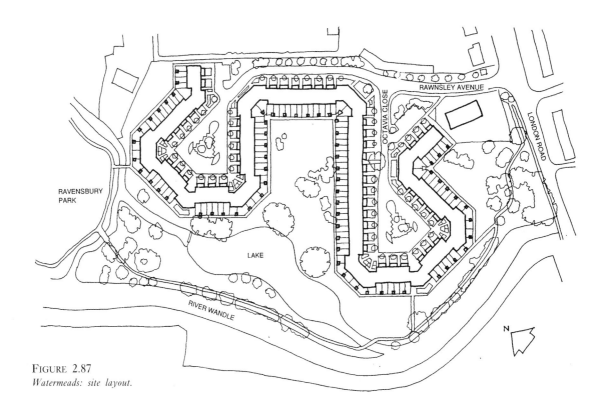

FIGURE 2.87
Watermeads: site layout.

FIGURE 2.88
West Silvertown Urban Village housing fronting the Royal Victoria Docks.

NEWHAM

West Silvertown Urban Village, Royal Docks, Silvertown Way/North Woolwich Road.

+1997. Tibbald Monro. DLR Royal Victoria.

West Silvertown Urban Village comprises 1000 dwellings on 11 hectares (27 acres). Two-thirds is private housing built by Wimpey Homes with the remainder being social housing for rent provided by the Peabody Trust and the East London Housing Association (ELHA) (Fig. 2.88). A genuine attempt has been made to mix the tenures on the site with some of the rented housing located on the better parts of the site.

A series of 'village codes' were produced to give design guidance. These propose landmark projects in key locations, one of which is the imposing CRESCENT, (Tibbald Monro), located around the central dockside piazza. This contains fifty-three flats, including twenty dwellings for elderly people on five storeys above shops on the ground floor (Fig. 2.89). The Peabody Trust is also building landmark projects in the form of flats and three-storey town housing at gateway locations and around some of the main urban nodal points. ELHA is developing most of its housing around a village green. The first housing overlooking the Royal Docks is most impressive (Fig. 2.88).

AJ, 7/11/96, pp. 36–37; *Planning Week*, 6/2/97, pp. 14–15; *RIBAJ*, 11/96, p. 11; *RIBAJ*, 3/98, pp. 31, 33 and 78–79.

FIGURE 2.89
The Crescent

FIGURE 2.90
Span housing at Parkleys, Ham Common, preserved in its original form.

RICHMOND-UPON-THAMES

Parkleys, Ham Common.
1956. Eric Lyons. R. Richmond + local bus.

This was Eric Lyons's first large private housing development for Span. The site was a former nursery garden which contained some fine trees and plants, most of which Eric Lyons was able to incorporate in his designs. The scheme is a mixture of terraced houses forming partially enclosed inter-linking courtyards (Fig. 2.90), and three-storey flats set amongst the trees. Car parking is in small groups close to the dwellings (Fig. 2.91).

The dwellings themselves are quite small and the construction of extensions and alterations

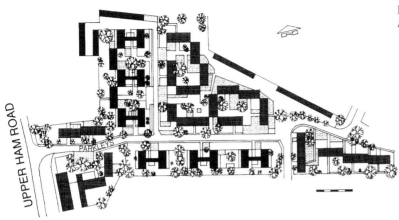

FIGURE 2.91
Parkleys: site layout

would have normally been expected, but not at Parkleys, not even a conservatory. The housing looks exactly as it did when completed, with flat roofs, tile and timber cladding, open layouts etc.; all as Eric Lyons intended.

Features of this scheme were regularly copied in both private and public sector housing but unfortunately rarely with the same success.

Langham House Gardens, Ham Common, Ham Street.
1961. James Stirling and James Gowan. R. Richmond + local bus.

Stirling and Gowan's thirty flats built in the gardens of Langham House, a large Georgian

FIGURE 2.92
Langham House Gardens, Ham Street.

house, had a great influence on British housing design in the 1960s. The appearance owes its origins to the Dutch De stijl movement of the 1920s and to Le Corbusier's Maisons Jaoul in Paris (1956). During the 1960s the brickwork panels and full height windows with wide window transoms at knee height were to be seen everywhere in both public and private sector housing (Fig. 2.92). Unlike much of the other housing designed by Stirling and Gowan, Ham Common has survived intact and unaltered.

AR, 7/11/58, pp. 218–225.

Mallard Place, Strawberry Vale, Twickenham, Middlesex.
1984. Eric Lyons Cunningham Partnership. R. Strawberry Hill.

This last scheme by Eric Lyons bears testimony to his experience over many years and his mastery of the art of housing design. The scheme followed the re-emergence of Span after years of inactivity. It comprised thirty-five houses and twenty-nine apartment flats in two- and three-storey terraces, plus a semi-basement in most cases. It included a riverside lawn, moorings and a swimming pool. The density of twenty-nine

dwellings per hectare (71 dw/acre) is high for private sector housing, yet Eric Lyons' design makes for a spacious feel. It takes full advantage of a much prized site with a strong edge of patio houses overlooking the River Thames (Fig. 2.93).

The apartments, which form much of the inner part of the development, were designed around different kinds of courts, one of which is a garden focusing on fountains playing in a heart-shaped pool. The warm brick and wall tile-hanging emphasizes the sculptural quality of the buildings, but overriding everything is the interplay of landscape with architecture, designed by Ivor Cunningham, which bears all the hallmarks of the Span developments of earlier years.

BD, 21/6/83, p. 10; *B*, 24/6/83, pp. 39–46.

SOUTHWARK

Setchell Road, SE1.
1978. Neylan and Unglass. U. Elephant and Castle.

Setchell Road was one of the finest and most successful of the 1970s high density, low rise housing developments. It is a large scheme comprising 311 dwellings built at a density of 100

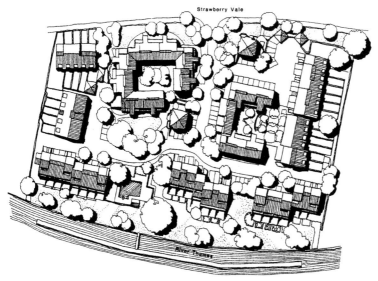

Strawberry Vale

River Thames

SITE LAYOUT PLAN

FIGURE 2.93
Site layout at Mallard Place, Eric Lyons' last Span development.

Figure 2.94
Setchell Road: successful 1970s high density/low rise housing.

dwellings per hectare (40 dw/acre). The housing is a mixture of one-, two- and three-storey terraces arranged along a series of pedestrian streets with grouped car parking courts at the rear.

The predominant use of brick and tiles and the scheme's familiar pattern of streets successfully relates it to its surroundings. The architects' handling of the different kinds of pedestrian space in the scheme is masterly. These vary according to their use, ranging from main spine routes (Alscot Way) to smaller squares and narrow lanes. The focal point is a tenants' meeting hall raised on a low plinth which is part of a two-level central square (Fig. 2.94). There is a row of corner shops fronting Dunton Road which is the only location where the buildings show signs of deterioration.

Approximately two-thirds of the dwellings were designed for one- and two-person households and the remainder were family housing of various sizes. There are three basic types of dwelling: terraced houses, courtyard flats and three-storey flats The house frontages are extremely narrow (3.9 m or 13 ft) but this is compensated by the internal plan which, in some types, includes an internal courtyard that creates a remarkable feeling of spaciousness and light.

LIVERPOOL JOHN MOORES UNIVERSITY
LEARNING & INFORMATION SERVICES

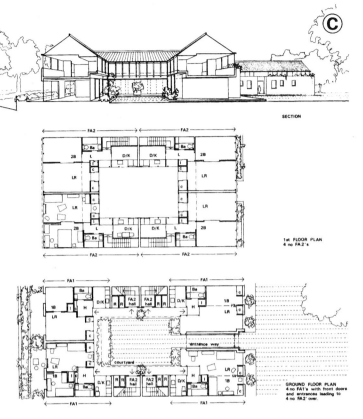

FIGURE 2.95
*Setchell Road: plans of the
courtyard housing.*

SECTION

1st FLOOR PLAN
4 no FA2's

GROUND FLOOR PLAN
4 no FA1's with front doors
and entrances leading to
4 no FA2' over.

The courtyard flats are ingeniously planned in groups of eight, entered through gated arches (Fig. 2.95). These courts are well cared for by the tenants who, in many instances, have filled them with plants.

AJ, 12/10/97, pp. 694–695; *AJ*, 9/8/78, pp. 252–265.

Greenland Dock, Redriff Road, SE16.
1987–96. LDDC. U. Surrey Quays.

The masterplan for Greenland Dock by Conran Roche in 1982 was one of the first urban design exercises commissioned by LDDC (p. 29). A number of the schemes that were subsequently built have special qualities (Fig. 2.96).

Greenland Passage (1989). Kjaer and Richter of Aarhus. This forms a gateway on either side of the passage leading into Greenland Dock. It

is distinctively European in character and reminiscent of the 1987 Berlin IBA. It is made up of two large courtyards designed in the manner of the traditional London Georgian square but the most memorable feature is the circular garden planted out with exotic herbs and low shrubs.

AR, 4/89, pp. 50–51; *RIBAJ*, 3/89, pp. 38–41.

Finland Quay (1989). Richard Reid and Associates. This development comprises sixty-seven dwellings in seven linked pavilions on the north side of Greenland Dock. The dwellings are lifted up half a storey from the quay level with car parking below. Their large bay windows and the great central windows to studio apartments give the pavilions a character quite different from anything else in London Docklands (Fig. 2.97).

AR, 4/89, pp. 52–54; *AJ*, 2/11/88, pp. 52–57; *L'Architecture d'Aujourd'hui*, 12/89, pp. 106–107; *RIBAJ*, 3/89, pp. 38–41.

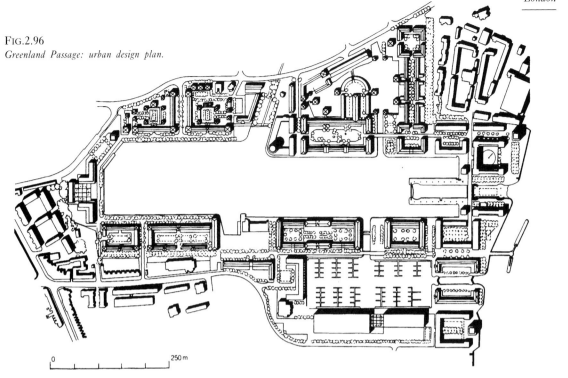

Fɪɢ.2.96
Greenland Passage: urban design plan.

0   250 m

Fɪɢᴜʀᴇ 2.97
Finland Quays.

FIGURE 2.98
The Lakes

The Lakes (1997). Shepheard Epstein and Hunter (with N. Pishavadia of Persimmon Homes). The Lakes comprises 275 town houses built on the site of the partly filled in Norway Dock and designed in the form of villas and terraces around the water's edge. In many instances the houses are accessible only across timber bridges (Fig. 2.98).

B (Homes Supplement), 14/6/91, p. 10; *B* (Brick Awards), 11/97, pp. 52–53; *RIBAJ*, 6/91, p. 56; *RIBAJ*, 3/98, p. 34.

South-east of Tower Bridge, SE1.
LDDC. U. London Bridge/Tower Hill.

The stretch of Waterfront development from Tower Bridge to London Bridge and Rotherhithe to the east has some of the finest streets in Docklands and some of the best of the LDDC housing.

Horselydown Square, Shad Thames (1989). Julyan Wickham Associates. This was the first

FIGURE 2.99
*Horseleydown Square: entrance from
Tower Bridge.*

scheme to introduce new urban spaces relating to
the existing building form and pattern of use in
the area. The scheme is mixed-use comprising
shops on the ground floor and a combination of
offices and seventy-six flats on the four floors
above. The scheme is designed around two courtyards entered at positions which reflected existing pedestrian routes across the site to the river.
The north-west approach, close to Tower Bridge,
is framed by two partially glazed drums which
signify 'entrance' (Fig. 2.99). The architecture
contrasts sharply to the warehouses around but
the distinctiveness of the spaces gain much from
the exuberant use of colour – a combination of
blue, red and rich terracotta.

AJ, 16/5/90, pp. 49–51; *London Docklands*, A Builder
Group Supplement, 3/98, p. 31.

The Circle, Queen Elizabeth Street (1989).
CZWG. This development creates a strong sense
of streetscape and is a focal point in a grid of
streets. It has a mix of uses with shops, offices,
restaurants and a health club, with a swimming
pool on the ground floor (Fig. 2.100). Above are
302 apartments which range from 38–50 sq. m
studios to three-bedroom penthouses of over 100
sq. m. Parking for 400 cars is in two levels of
basement. The residential accommodation is in
four segments, each served by pairs of lifts and
approached by lobbies on either side of the street.
The central circle acts as an approach and set-
down to the entrances. The walls facing the circle
were finished in ultramarine-coloured glazed
bricks which creates the impression of a blue
canyon. Complete with the equestrian statue in

FIGURE 2.100
The Blue Circle: site and dwelling plans.

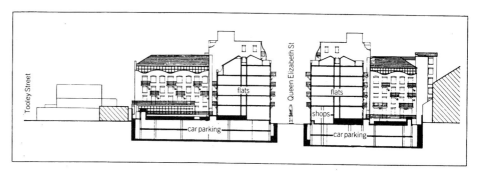

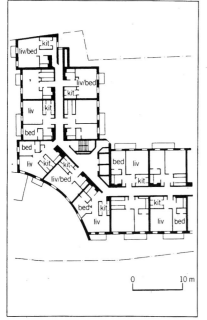

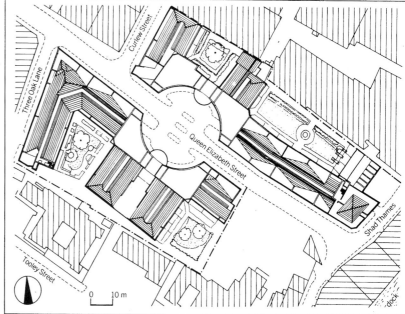

the centre of the space, it is one of London Dockland's special places (Fig. 2.101).

AJ, 17/10/90, pp. 26–40; *Blueprint*, 7/90, pp. 34–37; *London Docklands*, A Builder Group Supplement, 3/98, p. 32.

China Wharf (1988). CZWG. China Wharf reflects the stylish reputation of its architects. The building nestles ingeniously into a tight site amongst a number of sober Victorian warehouses, most of which have been converted into housing. The ground floor contains offices and above are seventeen flats each planned in a scissors form so that every flat has a river view.

The scheme has three elevations, each responding to its immediate location. The facade

FIGURE 2.101
The Blue Circle.

FIGURE 2.102
China Wharf: elevational drawing by CZWG.

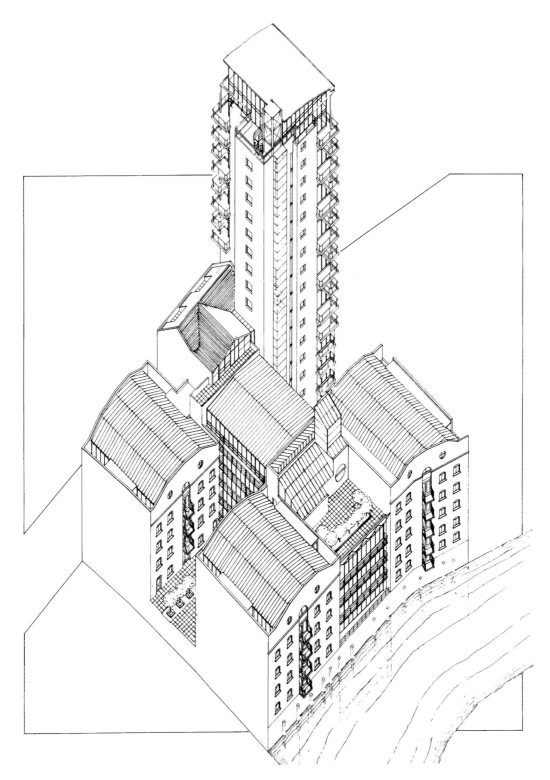

FIGURE 2.103
Vogans Wharf: axonometric drawing by Michael Squire and Partners.

to Mill Street is clad in London stock brick with blue engineering brick details to match its warehouse neighbours. The courtyard facade is designed with small windows turned away from directly looking over New Concordia Wharf. The river facade has large areas of glass and each apartment has its own balcony (Fig. 2.102). To provide privacy the central *in-situ* concrete panel was introduced with wings and flanges, making it read like a ship's construction. The whole of this was then painted in red B.S. 04 E 51.
AR, 4/89, pp. 28–37.

Vogans Mill, Mill Street (1989). Michael Squire and Partners. Vogans Mill rises like a beacon up to its sixteenth storey penthouse. The tower replaces an existing grain mill built in 1813; it combines with Grade II listed former warehousing to provide sixty-five two- and three-bedroom luxury flats. The slim tower contains one flat per floor and is best viewed from the river where the whiteness of its modernity, with its cut-away corners and curving roof, makes it stand out above the darkness of the old warehouses (Fig. 2.103).
AJ, 16/5/90, pp. 38–41.

Gainsford Street Halls of Residence (1990). Conran Roche. Designed for the London School of Economics, this modest six-storey building is built in pale yellow brick but enlivened on the Gainsford Street frontage by the inclusion of nautically inspired balconies. The building accommodates 280 students in a series of six-bedroom flats planned around a basic core of kitchen and bathroom facilities.
AJ, 16/5/90, pp. 25–26.

The Anchor Brewhouse (1990). Pollard Thomas and Edwards. This is one of London's most picturesque sites next to Tower Bridge, which has been beautifully transformed into housing and offices. Originally built in 1789 and rebuilt in 1891 after a fire, the building was a Courage brewery. It now provides a variety of dwellings inside, ranging from tiny studio flats with bedrooms at mezzanine level to an enormous multi-level apartment under the cupola. The

external appearance has been sensitively restored to its former condition. New levels have been inserted which give some rooms truly exciting views.

The major change to the outside of the building was the provision of a vertical glass bay which has been put into the previously blank west end of the complex overlooking Tower Bridge. This adds to the spatial quality, giving wonderful views out through the bridge.
AR, 10/90, pp. 81–84.

New Concordia Wharf, Mill Street, EC2 (1981–3). Pollard Thomas and Edwards in succession to Nicholas Lacey and Partners. This project pioneered the conversion of the warehouses in this part of Docklands. The courtyard of buildings was formerly part of St Saviour's Flour Mill established in 1882, and rebuilt in 1894–98 after a fire. The mill complex is specially known for its water tower and chimney.

The conversion into mixed-use development, principally housing, has carefully preserved the existing fabric of the buildings. The long facade to St Saviour's Dock has deeply recessed new windows, in keeping with the character of the building, and metal balconies were fixed across the former loading bays. The timber jetty was renewed to its original pattern and crossing the entrance to the dock there is a delightful new footbridge designed by Whitby and Bird and Nicholas Lacey and Partners (1995).
AJ, 12/2/98, pp. 27–28.

Wolfe Crescent, Surrey Quays, SE16.
1989. CZWG Architects. U. Surrey Quays.

The majority of Surrey Quays is suburban but with a very high quality landscape infrastructure which can be best appreciated from the top of Stave Hill. Wolfe Crescent is one of the few exceptions to this. Built on a 0.8 hectare (2 acre) site fronting Albion Channel, which is all that remains of the extensive former Surrey Docks, the development contains fifty-three apartments and twenty-six houses. It has two principal

FIGURE 2.104
Wolfe Crescent, Surrey Quays.

elements – a large crescent of houses terminated by four-storey apartment buildings and five small free-standing octagonal blocks of apartments (Fig. 2.104). Four of these stand on the channel front enclosed by the crescent. The fifth is on the east corner of the site. This arrangement enables most of the flats and houses to have a view of the water course to which the scheme relates. The brick octagonal buildings with their corner windows, basket balconies and domes are best seen from the well landscaped walkways alongside the channel.

B, 11/9/87, pp. 59–61; *RIBAJ*, 7/89, p. 5; *AT*, 1/90, pp. 22–25.

Thames Tunnel Mills, 113 Rotherhithe Street, SE16.
1984. Hunt Thompson Associates. U. Rotherhithe.

Until its conversion by the London and Quadrant Housing Trust this nineteenth century warehouse

and flour mill had stood empty for more than 10 years. Initially the building appeared too deep for housing but the architects produced an imaginative design solution, bringing light into the interior through a glazed top-lit atrium. Built around this are seventy flats and a communal meeting room. The composition of the handsome refurbished building with the eighteenth century St Mary's church behind with its brick and stone tower and spire is one of the focal points along the River Thames (Fig. 2.105).
AR, 1/80, p. 37.

Riverside Apartments (formerly Princes Tower), Rotherhithe Street.
1990. Troughton McAslan and Tim Brennan Architects. U. Rotherhithe.

This eight-storey tower is one of the landmarks along the River Thames. Its design is unashamedly of the modern movement with

FIGURE 2.105
Conversion into housing of Thames Tunnel Mills.

FIGURE 2.106
Riverside Apartments, formerly Princes Tower.

FIGURE 2/107
Boundary Street Estate: one of the earliest LCC housing developments.

reference to the designs of Eric Mendelsohn and Serg Chermayeff in the inter-war years. The bow windows, horizontal strip windows and white cladding are supported on a steel frame which is an update of the experimental concrete and steel of early modernism. The client required a two-storey penthouse at the top of the building which included a sun terrace and glass observation room on the roof. The building is best viewed from across the river (Fig. 2.106).

AJ, 16/7/86, pp. 20–23; *AJ*, 12/2/98, p. 39.

TOWER HAMLETS

Boundary Street Estate, Arnold Circus E2.
1896–1902. LCC Department of Architecture. U. Shoreditch.

The Boundary Street estate is the oldest surviving development of rented housing built by a local authority. The estate of 1002 flats was built in twenty tenement blocks on slum clearance land and the streets were laid out as tree-lined avenues radiating from a small circus with parades and a bandstand (Fig. 2.107). The radical development also included schools, workshops, and community facilities on the site, following the principles of the arts and crafts movement, of which some of the LCC architects were members. The scheme was co-ordinated by Owen Fleming and six different architects worked on the design of the buildings.

The scheme was first occupied mostly by white collar workers as the rent was too high for poorer people, but this changed in later years. It is now subject to wholesale improvement including stock transfer to a housing association. English Heritage has recommended the buildings worthy of Grade II* listing.

B, 3/1/86, pp. 20–21; *AJ*, 8/5/97, p. 12.

FIGURE 2.108
Lansbury Estate: 1951 perspective of four-storey flats by G.A. Jellicoe. [AJ, 3/7/74, p. 38.]

Lansbury Estate, East India Dock Road, Poplar, E14.
1951. LCC Department of Architecture.
DLR All Saints.

The concept of millennium villages is not a new phenomenon, for one of the features of the 1951 Festival of Britain was the live model of architecture and planning – the new Lansbury Estate. The site was a 'comprehensive development area' of 50 hectares (124 acres) which had suffered severe bomb damage during the war. The development was conceived as a neighbourhood of 9500 people, complete with schools, shops, churches and all the facilities necessary to create a community. The brief called for low rise housing of human scale in not more than six storeys (Fig. 2.108), designed to a maximum overall density of 136 persons per acre (336/ha). The buildings were to be built in yellow brick, preferably London stocks, and were to have slate roofs to carry on the local tradition of London's East End.

Many prominent architectural practices were involved in its design (Fig. 2.108). This included Frederick Gibberd who designed the shopping centre and market place with its famous landmark tower – the first new post-war pedestrian shopping precinct in London.

The Lansbury live exhibition was not a success. Architects and architectural writers were not impressed with the quasi-vernacular architecture which was described as worthy, but dull and somewhat skimpy' [1].

AJ, 6/9/51, pp. 275–304; *AJ*, 3/7/74, pp. 23–42; [1] Ibid., p. 40

Cluster Blocks at Usk Street, 1952, and Claredale Street, 1960, Bethnal Green.
Sir Denys Lasdun & Partners. R. Bethnal Green.

Sir Denys Lasdun is a 20th century British architect of great distinction and his housing at Claredale Street is an architectural landmark which English Heritage has listed Grade II* listing.

Lasdun's aim was to improve on the housing that was being built by local authorities. He was interested in Smithson's concept of cluster housing (p. 14) and during the 1950s he designed two schemes. His intention was to create a 'vertical street' in a core structure connected by

FIGURE 2.109
Cluster blocks at Claredale Street.

bridges to four towers set at angles to each other
(Fig. 2.109). The core contained the services of
the building and the communal amenities, clothes
drying platforms, lifts, stairs and refuse chutes,
which are all noisy elements. The dwellings
themselves were akin to semi-detached houses but
placed on top of each other. They were seen to
be very private and quiet with only their entrance
halls, WCs and internal stairs and bathrooms
facing on to the access balconies. The fifteen-
storey Keeling House at Claredale Street contains
fourteen maisonettes and two flats in each of the
four blocks forming the tower.

   Both cluster blocks have deteriorated considerably but Keeling House hopefully will be
restored, when it will be let at a higher rent to
pre-selected tenants.

AR, 5/60, pp. 305–312; *AJ*, 6/12/61, p. 1090; *AR*,
1/77, pp. 52–58; *AJ*, 6/7/95, p. 8.

Ferry Street, Riverside Housing, Millwall, E14.
1982. Levitt Bernstein Associates. DLR Island Gardens.

Circle 33 Housing Trust built this scheme on a
spectacular riverside site. The brief, which took
account of local opinion, was for an equal mix of
houses, maisonettes and flats, of which some 20
per cent were to be occupied by elderly people.
It also required all dwellings to have a view of
the river and family dwellings to have gardens.

   The design solution incorporated narrow
frontage, dual-aspect houses into two cranked
terraces which enclosed south-facing private
gardens. A central pathway, on the axis of the
Cutty Sark across the river, allowed public and
emergency vehicle access to the riverside walk.

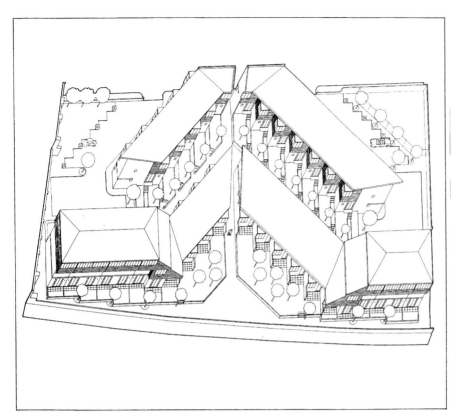

FIGURE 2.110
Ferry Street.

Coloured, corrugated aluminium roof sheeting on metal purlins was used to allow the low roof pitches necessary for the rear terraces to have the river views (Fig. 2.110).
AJ, 25/9/85, pp. 68–79.

Roy Square, Narrow Street, E14.
1988. Ian Ritchie Architects. DLR Limehouse.

Narrow Street is one of Docklands most historic streets on the north bank of the Thames. Roy Square is one of the finest of the new developments in the area and makes a genuine attempt to create private housing of urban quality. The housing is grouped around a rectangular court which is entered from a flight of stairs off Narrow Street. The form of this central space and the large rectangular metal bay windows on the dwellings are reminiscent of courtyards in Berlin's 1984 (IBA) housing exhibition, although the pools at each end linked by a narrow channel and the lush planting give the court a decidedly Moorish flavour (Fig. 2.111).

The external face of the scheme presents a lively frontage to the surrounding streets. The architects sought to respect the Georgian character of the area by designing the housing as pavilions, linked by recessed lower blocks containing stairs and lifts. This is a familiar pattern for housing in London Docklands which clearly succeeds in this scheme.

AJ, 5/89, pp. 35–36; *AR*, 4/89, p. 46; *AJ*, 8/2/89, pp. 24–29; *L'Architecture d'Aujourd'hui*, 12/89, p. 114; *BB*, Autumn/92, p. 8.

FIGURE 2.111
Roy Square: internal courtyard.

Shadwell Basin, Wapping Wall, E1.
1988. MacCormac, Jamieson Pritchard & Wright.
DLR and U. Shadwell.

New Shadwell Basin dates from 1854–58 and it is overlooked by St Paul's Church built in 1820–21 by John Walters. The 169 dwelling units built on three sides of the Basin represent, in style and density, one of Britain's finest attempts at a contemporary dockside housing form.

The design reflects the imagery of industrial docklands but in a very different way to other LDDC schemes (Fig. 2.112). The terraces and flats are not single blocks like warehouses but a series of linked pavilions with Venetian colon-

nades. Unfortunately, during the design-and-build operations changes were made to the colours, notably the London Dockland colours of Venetian red and dark blue were replaced with a bright red which is somewhat uncompromising. *AR*, 2/87, pp. 51–54; *AR*, 4/89, pp. 47–49; *RIBAJ*, 3/89. pp. 38–41.

Cascades, Westferry Road, E14.
1988. CZWG. DLR Heron Quays.

The Cascades stands on a prominent 2.3 acre (0.93 ha) site, bounded on two sides by water, close to the West India Dock and Canary Wharf.

FIGURE 2.112
Shadwell Basin.

The complex, built by Heron Homes, comprises a twenty-storey apartment building and a complementary six-storey apartment building with three shops on the ground floor. Building upwards instead of outwards provided space for landscaped gardens and a health centre/swimming pool. The building offers spectacular views and many benefits of luxury high rise living.

The 168 apartment scheme is most distinctive with its great 45 degree slope (Fig. 2.113) incorporating the fire escape beneath a canopy of corrugated steel and glass which extends over the swimming pool to form a skylight. The cladding is a stock brick with blue engineering brick bands. The architects claimed to have respected the location through incorporating in the design a whole range of portholes, funnels, lighthouse balconies and a tower. The building is very much of its time and is enjoyed by its residents for this.

FIGURE 2.113
Cascades.

FIGURE 2.114
Compass Point: looking towards the River Thames.

AR, 2/89, pp. 30–33; *L'Architecture d'Aujourd'hui*, 12/89, p. 112; *RIBAJ*, 10/88, pp. 30–33; *RIBAJ*, 3/89, pp. 38–41; *RIBAJ*, 12/89, pp. 28–33.

Compass Point, Sextant Avenue, Manchester Road, E14.
1986. Jeremy Dixon. DLR Island Gardens.

Compass Point was built during the boom period for London Docklands. Its design reinterprets many traditional building forms, some of which Jeremy Dixon uses elsewhere in London. The stepped gables are distinctively Flemish whilst the white bow windows reflect nineteenth century English sea-front housing. Behind the riverfront housing are a number of paired villas and terraces of high urban quality, built on an axis at right-angles to the river. The main street, Sextant Avenue, contains the largest villas and culminates at the far end in a crescent with a small gap through to give access to Manchester Road. At the other end the views of the river are framed by two gateway buildings (Fig. 2.114). The spaces created in the scheme – streets, mews, crescents – are enhanced by the care taken with the design of the landscaping.

AR, 2/87, p. 33; *AR*, 4/89, p. 46.

Winterton House, tower block refurbishment, Watney Market Estate, E1.
1996. Hunt Thompson Associates. DLR Limehouse.

It is well worth taking a stop at Limehouse on the Docklands Light Railway to view in one direction the Limehouse Basin (Fig. 1.18) and in the other the twenty-five-storey Winterton House newly clad in brick (Fig. 2.115). The building's original steel frame had been developed by British Steel in the 1960s to be as economic as possible. The former cladding was of lightweight GRP, and the floor was of hollow pots. On its own the frame could not support available cladding systems and the heavier concrete floors which were required to improve the sound insulation. In addition, the block had many of the typical problems of 1960s high rise housing. The jointing between the cladding panels was poor, the windows could only be replaced externally and there were asbestos problems.

The proposal to clad the building in brick came from the brief which required a 50-year life before the first major maintenance. Consequently, the building was stripped back to its frame and concrete core. A new external wall of brickwork was built, which, along with 150 mm of quilt and high performance double-glazed windows, was designed to be highly energy efficient. The brickwork strengthens the existing steel frame to which it is connected by a steel jacking structure at roof level.

The tower has now become the focus of the neighbourhood. At the base is the new housing office serving the local area. There is also a tenants' common room on the ground floor and an office and other facilities to house a tenants' management co-operative, from where the tower is run by its residents.

Hunt Thompson were architects for a second tower block overclad in brick – the **Northwood Tower**, Wood Street, Walthamstow, E17 (R. Wood Street, Walthamstow) – which was renovated for the London Borough of Waltham Forest in 1992.

AJ, 7/11/96, pp. 46–47; *AJ*, 7/11/96, pp. 46–47; *AJ* (Supplement), 12/6/97, pp. 12–14; *BD*, 22/8/97, p. 12; *B* (Brick Awards), 28/11/97, p. 48; Northwood Tower: *AJ*, 5/2/92, pp. 39–41.

Burrell's Wharf, Westferry Road, E14.
1995. Jestico + Whiles. DLR Island Gardens.

The planning brief in 1987 from the LDDC for this spectacular riverside site called for the preservation of the Grade II listed shipyard buildings built by Brunel in 1830 which had been owned for a hundred years by Burrells, the paint manufacturers. The complex now comprises new residential apartments, retail shops, workspace and a large leisure facility with a swimming pool, squash court,

LIVERPOOL JOHN MOORES UNIVERSITY
Aldham Roberts L.R.C.
TEL. 0151 231 3701/3634

FIGURE 2.115
Winterton Tower refurbishment.

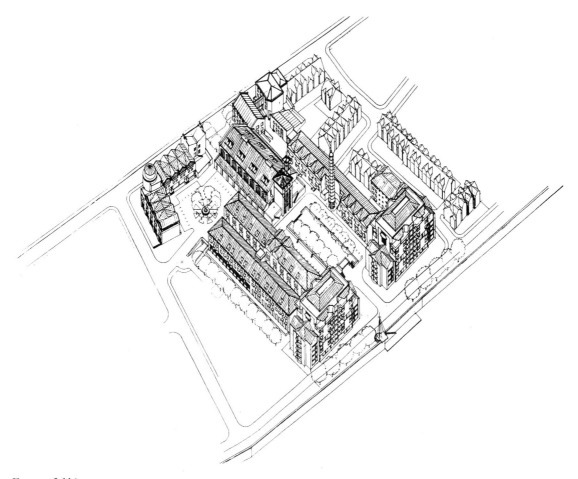

FIGURE 2.116
Burrell's Wharf: axonometric drawing.

indoor running track, gymnasia, library, pool room, restaurant and spa baths (Fig. 2.116).

High density development was necessary to offset the substantial infrastructure costs. The layout took on an axial form with most of the buildings at right angles to the River Thames except for two major riverfront buildings which frame the central square. In this way, most dwellings have a glimpse of the water. Vehicular access to the commercial development is from the north whilst access to the housing and the underground car park beneath the central square is off the riverside drive. The result is a large successful development of fine new buildings integrated with Brunel's workshops within an urban design

framework of considerable strength and integrity.
B (Housing Design Awards), 27/10/95, p. 22; *RIBAJ*, 11/90, pp. 42–43.

Dundee Wharf, Three Colt Street, Limehouse, E14.
1997. CZWG. DLR Westferry.

Considered 'worth a detour' by the assessors of the 1997 Housing Awards, this tall, striking project, built by Ballymore Properties, is a powerful landmark at a bend in the River Thames. A rather extraordinary false oil-rig structure which

FIGURE 2.117
Dundee Wharf.

appears to lean out off the front of the building adds to the variety and sense of fun in the building design (Fig. 2.117). In front is a very fine footbridge designed by YRM/Anthony Hunt Associates and completed in 1995.

B, 28/11/97, p. 52; RIBAJ, 3/98, p. 33.

Queen Mary and Westfield College, student housing, Ifor Evans Place and Westfield Way/Mile End Road, E1.
1995 and 1996. MacCormac Jamieson Pritchard & Wright. U. Mile End.

These two striking projects form part of the expansion of Queen Mary and Westfield College on Mile End Road. The new student housing not only provides much needed student accommodation but contributes to the regeneration of the area. The three-storey housing at Westfield Way stands a storey above the level of the Regent's Canal and enjoys good views across to Mile End Park (Fig. 2.118). The construction of the building opened the canal to the public visually and gave access along a new waterside footpath. The internal plan of the housing was designed around the college principle of individual staircases serving five or six rooms in a three-level house with a dining area/kitchen acting as the social hub. The dining alcoves project out over the canal to gain the views. The rooms have *en suite* shower facilities, now essential for the student accommodation to be used for conferences. The

simple light brick, the bold use of colour in the window panelling and the gabled roofline are all in the best spirit of canal-side architecture.

At the other end of Mile End Road is a very different building for ninety-four students on land previously used for local authority housing. The new development fronts on to a busy road and is flanked by the college's 1960s Maths Tower and a period-style hostel built at the turn of the century. The design comprises two-storey parallel terraces forming a new court. Study bedrooms are grouped into houses which are entered from the courtyard. Each house has six rooms with communal kitchen/dining rooms at ground floor level.

The white modernist architecture makes an excellent transition between the 1960s building and the hostel.

Tower Hamlets Housing Action Trust.
1994+. Director of Development, C. Johnson in succession to June Barnes.

In the early 1990s the government designated six Housing Action Trusts. Tower Hamlets HAT was established in 1993 following a ballot of the residents of three council estates – Lefevre Walk (Parnell Road), Monteith (Old Ford Road) and Tredegar Road – which were built in the late 1960s and early 1970s. These high density estates all displayed the physical problems associated with system-built estates of the time. The master-plan produced in 1994 proposed the demolition of most of the housing and its replacement with over 1100 new low rise dwellings, approximately 50 per cent of which would be houses with gardens.

The master-plan set high development standards and the objectives were to be achieved through extensive participation with the local residents. Of high importance was the intent to produce a sustainable succession strategy, which involved the formation of a Community Based Housing Association (CBHA) and a Community Trust to take over the long-term ownership and management of the community facilities developed by the HAT where this function could not be carried out by the CBHA.

Originally it was envisaged that the development would be totally publicly funded but this proved to be an enormous commitment for the government. Therefore the HAT entered into

FIGURE 2.119
*Cherrywood Close: the first new
housing by Tower Hamlets HAT.*

arrangements with Circle 33, and a newly formed subsidiary, Old Ford Housing Association, for them to take over the development function and to raise private finance to cover the shortfall of government allocation.

Cherrywood Close, Coborn Road, Tower Hamlets HAT, E3.
*1996. Thomas Pollard and Edwards.
U. Bow Road.*

This scheme, comprising eleven two- to four-bedroom houses, twenty-three two- and three-bedroom mews housing and six one-bedroom flats, was the first of new developments to be completed by the Tower Hamlets HAT. The site, which had been a railway station and then a builder's yard, was bought by the HAT to start the process of transferring people and reconstructing their estates. The site was extremely difficult to develop. For much of its length it was little more than a thin slither of land between the railway and the backs of the housing fronting

Antill Road. Noise from the railway was a major problem which was resolved by building a screen wall against the railway line. The narrowness of the site was cleverly overcome by using wide frontage houses with all rooms facing south onto large walled gardens. This enabled the new houses to be built close up to the back boundary of the site. Where the site widened, short terraces of three-storey town houses formed a landscaped square (Fig. 2.119).

The wide frontage houses permitted considerable variety of internal arrangements, and porches, bay windows, verandas and conservatories could be selected by the tenants from a menu of options.

Monteith phase 1, Parnell Road, Tower Hamlets HAT, E3.
1997. AFC Shaw Sprunt. U. Mile End.

Built on a site overlooking the Hertford Union Canal and Victoria Park, this first of five phases in the redevelopment of the Monteith Estate

FIGURE 2.120
*The scheme at 20b Bistern Avenue,
featuring circular balconies at the
entrance.*

comprises terraced housing and a block of flats overlooking the canal. This block is raised slightly to give separation and privacy for ground floor residents living on the canal-front. Its communal areas have been designed to be light and have views of and access through the south-facing courtyard to the canal and park. The low pitched roof has been designed to create the impression of it floating over the structure below (Fig. 1.17). Steel section windows and steel balconies hang from the face of the building to reflect the image of semi-industrial canal detailing. The houses were designed as two terraces and detailed traditionally with London stock bricks, tiles and timber windows.

WALTHAM FOREST

20b Bistern Avenue, E17.
*1990. Wickham and Associates.
R. Wood Street, Walthamstow.*

This scheme of six three-storey local authority flats is quite unexpected for such a quiet, secluded site. The design echoes the modern movement but, unlike the white buildings of the 1930s, the building is painted in dramatic colours – terracotta walls and blue stairwells – which work well in the street scene. Large trees have been retained in front of the flats, almost touching the balconies in places. The flats are on either side of a central covered stairwell in which the rhythm of the circular corner balconies is repeated (Fig. 2.120). The local authority is to be congratulated on commissioning such an interesting scheme.

AR, 10/90, pp. 59–63; *RIBAJ*, 12/91, p. 35; *B* (Housing Design Awards), 11/91, pp. 38–39.

WANDSWORTH

Cottage Estate, Roehampton, Dover House Road.
1922. LCC Architects Department. R. Barnes.

Roehampton is most noted for the 1950s Alton Estate (opposite) but close to it is an LCC cottage

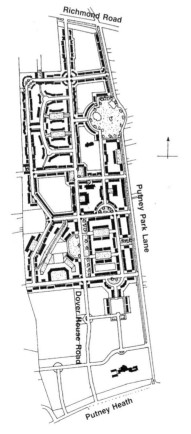

FIGURE 2.121
Cottage Estate, Roehampton. [Redrawn from Swenerton, M., Homes Fit for Heroes, p.170.

estate of some historical significance built as part of its 'Homes Fit for Heroes' programme. Roehampton developed quickly and, as a result, it set the standard for new inter-war LCC housing in general.

The layout placed the houses on either side of tree-lined streets and around greens (Fig. 2.121). Land at the back and between blocks was designated for allotments. The layout achieved a density of 15.8 dwellings per acre (39 dw/ha). As this was higher than the Tudor Walter's maximum, special permission had to be sought from the government. Culs-de-sac were not used for fear that they would cause the housing to degenerate into slums. The appearance of the houses followed the example of Hampstead Garden Suburb. In the early stages the architects used good quality materials, including clay tiles, and inventive detailing – arches, string-courses, decorative brickwork, etc. Regrettably, after the government housing cuts of 1921, these could no longer be afforded which reduced the quality of the later phases.

Swenerton, M., *Homes Fit for Heroes*, pp. 162, 181.

Alton Estate, Roehampton, SW15.
1952–59. LCC Architects Department. R. Barnes.

In the late 1940s and 1950s the LCC seized the opportunity to build large quantities of new housing. It championed mixed development, using a range of houses and flats to suit all ages and household size. Its most ambitious schemes were at Roehampton.

The different design of the two phases, East and West, reflected the liberal attitude of the Architect to the Council, Leslie Martin, who allowed teams to develop a personal style. Roehampton East contained 744 dwellings. The mix of dwellings included ten eleven-storey blocks mixed with four-storey maisonettes and two-storey houses. The site was formerly gardens to a number of Victorian houses and, in order to preserve the mature trees, buildings were placed on the footprint of the former villas. The tower blocks were clad in cream bricks (Fig. 2.122)

FIGURE 2.122
Alton East tower blocks clad in light bricks.

contrasted with the red brick, pitched roofed houses and maisonettes set on the slopes below. The design was the product of a highly sociable approach to housing and it owed its inspiration to 1940s Swedish design.

The later Alton West phase is a larger development comprising 1867 dwellings on a site of nearly 100 acres overlooking Richmond Park. The scheme comprises a mixture of twelve-storey point blocks, five- to six-storey slab blocks, maisonettes, terraced housing and bungalows. The influence of Le Corbusier is easy to see. The five large slab blocks set picturesquely into the slopes of the site are clear descendants of the

FIGURE 2.123
Alton West: unaltered bungalows from the 1950s.

Unité d'Habitation at Marseilles. Most significant was the use of precast elements, which set the agenda for system building for the next 15 years. In total contrast to the rest of the housing are two groups of bungalows for elderly people at Minstead Gardens and Danebury Avenue. These were important to the formula for mixed development in the 1950s and they nestle quietly amongst the trees, virtually untouched and complete with flat roofs and chimneys (Fig. 2.123)

Roehampton has been well cared for by the local authority and the population is settled. Parts of both phases have been recommended for listing by English Heritage.

AR, 7/59, pp. 21–35; *AJ*, 5/11/59, pp. 461–478; *AJ*, 30/3/77, pp. 594–603; Scoffham, E.R., *The Shape of British Housing*, pp. 64–70.

WESTMINSTER

Churchill Gardens Estate, Grosvenor Road, Lupus Street and Claverton Street, SW1.
1949. Powell and Moya. U. Pimlico.

Churchill Gardens was a landmark of early post-war housing which provided much early experience of high density housing. Under the guidance of its Town Clerk, Parker Morris, Westminster City Council in 1946 promoted an architectural competition which was won by Philip Powell and Hidalgo Moya. The site was an area of obsolete terraced houses badly damaged by bombing during the war. The brief called for high density housing appropriate to the site, which resulted in the construction of 1661 dwellings.

The design clearly reflects European modernist thinking of the time. It rejected the traditional form of the Pimlico streets in favour of slabs and terraces set in green spaces (Fig. 2.124). The flats were built in a series of seven- to nine-storey blocks at right angles to the River Thames. Many of the flats were wide frontage to be light and airy. The north–south axial arrangement maximized sunlight penetration, a principle first developed by Walter Gropius for his 1930s Seimensstadt housing in Berlin. Four-storey blocks of flats built between the rows of higher blocks create a series of courts in which there are trees, lawns, gardens and children's play areas. Along the frontage of Grosvenor Road are two terraces of three-storey town houses.

The buildings are concrete-frame structures clad in yellow brick and with glazed staircases and distinctive rooflines. Originally the walls of the recessed balconies were painted with bright colours in the theme of Le Corbusier's Unité. A

FIGURE 2.124
Churchill Gardens Estate.

district heating scheme took surplus heat pumped as hot water through a tunnel beneath the river from the Battersea Power Station. It was then stored in a huge circular glazed heat accumulator (which can still be seen) before distribution to the blocks.

The first phase of the development, won a Festival of Britain Award in 1951 and the whole scheme has been recommended for listing by English Heritage.

AR, 9/53, pp. 176–184; Richards, J.M., *An Introduction to Modern Architecture*, p. 160; Scoffham, E.R., *The Shape of British Housing*, p. 56; *AJ*, 4/7/96, pp. 28–58.

St James's Place, SW1.
1961. Sir Denys Lasdun & Partners.
U. Green Park.

This block of luxury flats reflected all the hopes of the new modernist architecture in the early 1960s, here applied for the first time since 1945 to the top end of the private sector housing market. Lasdun's intention in the design was to produce a building of the time that would link modern architecture with historical tradition. The external architectural treatment is therefore a

FIGURE 2.125
Lillington Gardens, phase 1: a courtyard overlooked by the Church of St James the Less.

direct expression of the internal spatial organization, including the extra-high living rooms. The deep overhanging balconies also have a functional purpose in shading interiors from the summer sun.

AD, 11/61, pp. 510–517.

Lillington Gardens, Vauxhall Bridge Road, Pimlico, SW1.
1968–72. Darbourne and Darke. U. Pimlico.

Lillington Street represented a major shift from the Corbusian image of the 1960s to a brick aesthetic within a high density design framework. Its vibrant red brick matched Street's 1861 Church of St James the Less which overlooks the site (Fig. 2.125). The effect was to influence public sector housing in Britain for the next 10 years.

Built for Westminster City Council, the scheme was the subject of an architectural competition in 1961. The brief required the design to accommodate some 2000 people together with sheltered housing for ninety elderly people, two doctors' surgeries, three public houses, ten shops, a community hall, a public library and a number of ancillary uses. The DOE was anxious to use the first phase of the scheme as an example to set new standards, which resulted in extra funding to achieve the standards of detail and finish.

The first phase of 350 dwellings at Charlwood Street contains three-, six- and eight-storey blocks laid out around the perimeter of the site to form a wall. Wings of housing push out into the central space to create a series of lushly planted interconnecting courts. Access to the dwellings is off decks at two levels. These look on to the courts and continually change direction, opening out into wider spaces at intervals. The partially covered decks are brick-paved and softened with planting on the outer edge. The use of narrow-fronted split-level scissor plans contributed to a high density but this was also made possible by a low car parking ratio of six spaces for every ten dwellings. The dwellings

were smaller than Parker Morris standards but they had large balconies and a high degree of individuality.

The two later phases were both subject to the rigours of the housing cost yardstick and they lost some of the original quality. The third phase was characterized by the use of tile hanging on the upper levels and a reduction in height to three and four-storeys. This enabled more dwellings to be provided at ground floor level with gardens and a higher provision of car parking was achieved. However, the roof streets lacked the landscaped quality of the earlier street decks.

Lillington Street received much praise. The *Times* considered it 'an elegant and exciting environment for young and old' [1]. Phases 1 and 2 have been recommended by English Heritage for Grade II* listing.

[1] *EH*, p. 3; *AR*, 4/69, pp. 281–286; Sheltered housing, *AR*, 5/70, pp. 360–361; *AR*, 9/70, p. 160; *AJ*, 1/12/76, pp. 1031–1039; *AJ*, 12/1/72, pp. 56–58.

Odham's Walk, Long Acre, WC2.
1979. GLC Architects Department.
U. Covent Garden.

Odham's Walk was one of the GLC Architects Department's most successful schemes. It is urban housing at its best, that has continued to be popular with its tenants since it was built in 1979. Set in the heart of Covent Garden, the scheme contains 102 dwellings built at a density of 480 persons per hectare (200/acre) (Fig. 2.126).

The layout reinforces the existing life of the neighbourhood by being built right up to the back edge of the pavement, with shops fronting the main streets. Internally, the housing clusters around a series of pedestrian ways and small squares which relate to the wider network of old alleys in the surrounding streets (Fig. 2.127). These spaces are superbly planted. Located in key positions on principal walkways through the site are shops, a surgery and small business premises. Stairs lead to short upper walkways and to

Figure 2.126
Odham's Walk: a highly popular scheme adjacent to Covent Garden.

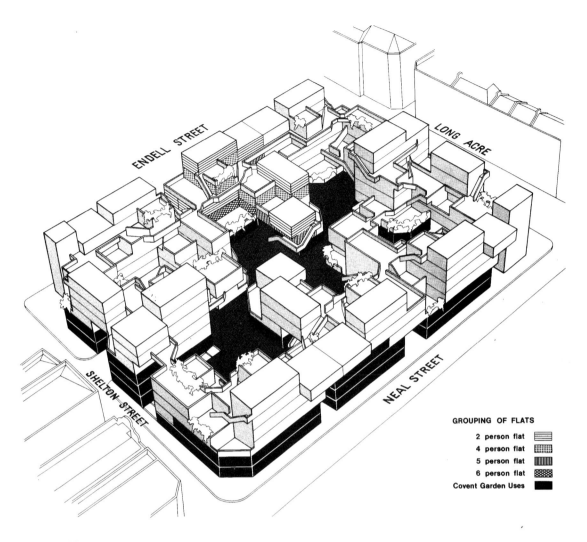

GROUPING OF FLATS

2 person flat
4 person flat
5 person flat
6 person flat
Covent Garden Uses

FIGURE 2.127
Odham's Walk: a view indicating the distribution of dwellings.

individual dwellings which have spacious balconies on the floors above. Car parking was originally provided in the basement but now the demand is so low that only ten spaces are allocated to the tenants whilst the rest are used for commercial car parking purposes. New tenants usually settle for not having a car of their own.

The buildings are concrete-framed, clad in a multi-coloured red/brown stock brick which is festooned with planting at virtually all levels. *AJ*, 29/9/75, p. 887; *BB*, 10/93, pp. 4–9.

171–201 Lanark Road, W9.
1983. Jeremy and Fenella Dixon. U. Maida Vale.

These five Maida Vale villas are deceptive in looking like large individual houses whilst in reality they contain thirty-five starter flats for sale (Fig. 2.128). The scheme was conceived in a very special way. The conditions of the sale of the land set the sales prices to enable the flats to be purchased at a lower price than usual for the

FIGURE 2.128
Lanark Road housing.

area. This presented a challenge to the architect as well as to the developer. Jeremy Dixon therefore designed five separate blocks which could be built and sold separately; the return from the sale of each villa would then be used to construct the next.

Each villa contains two long, narrow-frontage flats on every floor, taking up half of the frontage of the gable. The flats were planned to offer considerable flexibility of use, dependent upon the family circumstances of the occupants. *AR*, 12/83, pp. 54–58.

Ashmill Street, Marylebone, NW1.
1984. Jeremy and Fenella Dixon.
U. Edgware Road.

These fourteen houses, built above seven basement flats, were designed for the same developer who built the villas at Lanark Road. They were also designed to be sold at the bottom end of the private market to people on the council housing waiting list. The simple terrace of houses is most elegantly designed, with a base of white

stucco, red bricks at first floor level and large overhanging eaves above (Fig. 2.129). The facades were cut on each house by a tall, narrow, vertical staircase window to allow a view up and down the street. The steps and railings all relate to the housing design, without any hint of copying any architectural style. Instead, the design is fresh, imaginative and highly appropriate.
AJ, 2/10/85, pp. 20–23.

Crown Head Reach, Grosvenor Road, SW1.
1984. Nicholas Lacey and Partners. U. Pimlico.

This scheme was the subject of an architectural competition in 1977 entered by over 400 architects. It pre-dated the riverside housing that was to follow the establishment of the London Docklands Development Corporation in 1979.

The project developed by the Crown Estates Commissioners (with Wates Developments Ltd) contained fifty-six flats and four detached, two- and three-storey houses, a pub/restaurant and light industry. The housing was designed to form two crescents (Fig. 2.130)

FIGURE 2.129
Ashmill Street.

FIGURE 2.130
Crown Head Reach: early riverside housing.

which Nicholas Lacey considered was a form demanded by the enormous scale of the river and the rigours of nearby, noisy Grosvenor Road. In addition, the crescents shelter two, well planted, open spaces which look on to a public riverside walk.

The flats are clustered around two lift cores and are reached by curving corridors on the road side of the scheme. Dwelling plans vary considerably with hardly any repeat types: the aim was to gain the best possible views up and down the river, dependent upon the location of the flats in the scheme. All have spacious terraces, some of which project over the river. The sculptural play of riverside elevations, clad in rust-brown vitreous enamelled steel panels and glazed tiles, contrasts with the more simple curving roadside elevations of brick.

Sunday Times (colour magazine), 2 April 1977; *AJ*, 6/7/77, pp. 2–4. *Architecture and Urbanism (Japan)*, 7/83; *AJ*, 25/9/85, pp. 68–79.

FIGURE 2.131
New high-rise at Porteus Road.

Nine-Storey tower, Harrow Road/ Porteus Road, Paddington, W2.
*1997. Pollard Thomas and Edwards.
U. Edgware Road.*

No architect could ever have been given a more difficult piece of land to develop than this small triangular site which has a boundary with the A40 flyover at third floor level. The scheme was developed by Network Housing Association but later it was transferred to ARHAG Housing Association which specializes in housing African refugees. In comparison to sites in the surrounding district, the cost of the land was cheap but it was still necessary to design a high density solution.

The architects rose to the challenge of the site with a bold solution which put twenty-six flats into a nine-storey triangular concrete framed tower set against the flyover with six mews houses along the most sheltered side of the site. This contains 3 two-bedroom flats on each floor except at ground floor level where there are 2 three-bedroom apartments. A curved wall

fronting the flyover acts as 'the shield' to the dwellings in the tower which all face away from the noise of the traffic (Fig. 2.131). The other two elevations are very different; they contain larger windows and have an exaggerated parapet. They are built of red bricks to match the surrounding housing in the area.

AJ, 7/11/96, p. 31.

Castle Lane extension, SW1.
1993. CGHP Architects. U. Victoria.

This scheme, designed for the Look Ahead Housing Association, was built on a long, narrow, north-facing site, overlooked from tall buildings around. The constraints that this presented to the design were considerable and it was difficult to persuade the planning authority that anything could be built at all. Yet this challenge has produced a unique piece of architecture that is 'bold, bright, brash, curved, sensuously colourful and exhilarating'*. In Jonathan Glancey's words 'they are the nicest flats you will ever see' [1] (Fig. 2.132).

The scheme comprises twenty flats on two floors, occupied by people with physical disabilities and psychiatric problems. Two flats share one front door which always ensures that the tenants have a neighbour on hand. The flat plans incor-porate various levels of shared facilities. Some share bathrooms and kitchens, some only kitchens, while other flats consist of two totally self-contained bedsits but always with a shared front door and hall. In this way differing levels of mutual support were incorporated into the plans so that the residents could achieve a level of independence by helping each other (Fig. 2.133).

The staircases and glazed canopies all lead to the roof garden – the feature which persuaded the planners to give consent – but no car parking provision was provided.

[1] Glancey, J., The nicest flats you will ever see, *The Independent*, 17/11/93, p. 22; *B* (Housing Design Awards), 11/93, pp. 8–9; *B*, 21/1/94, pp. 35–42.

FIGURE 2.132
Castle Lane extension: 'the nicest flats you will ever see'.

Bruce House, Drury Lane, WC2.
1995. Levitt Bernstein Associates.
U. Covent Garden.

Bruce House was designed in 1907 in the arts and crafts free style by W.E. Riley of the LCC Architects Department. Despite its status as a Grade II listed building it had significantly deteriorated and by 1991 it could only accommodate thirty-five single working men as most of the dormitories had been closed. The Peabody Trust purchased the building from Westminster City Council in 1992 and set about in partnership with Centrepoint and Look Ahead Housing Associations, to improve the building.

Peabody's contribution, through the Rough Sleepers Initiative, was thirty-five one-bedroom Housing Association flats for people with a history of street homelessness. Centrepoint's accommodation for sixty-nine single, homeless young people offered them a place to live for periods between 6 and 18 months while they experience independent living and take part in training. Look Ahead's thirty-one bedsits offered permanent homes in the community for people with enduring mental health problems. In addition the Local Enterprise Agency funded a skills development centre aimed at skills identification, confidence building and support. Also, part of the building was intended for use as a shell-and-core restaurant space and a shop.

Bruce House was originally E-shaped with narrow central corridors. The design solution demolished the centre wing and wrapped a new built layer around the inner rear elevations which

FIGURE 2.133
Castle Lane extension: floor plans.

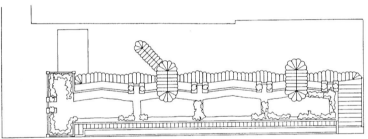

Roof Garden

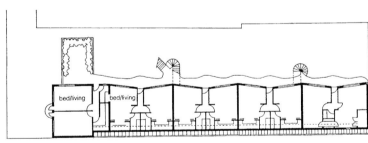

First Floor Plan

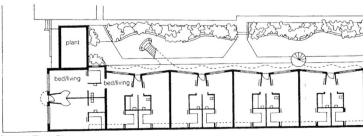

Ground Floor Plan

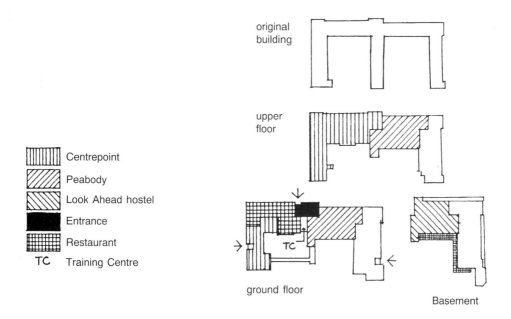

original
building

upper
floor

ground floor

Basement

Centrepoint

Peabody

Look Ahead hostel

Entrance

Restaurant

TC   Training Centre

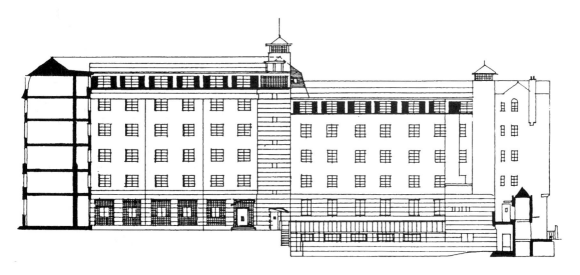

FIGURE 2.134
Bruce House: principles of the redevelopment and new courtyard elevations.

effectively doubled the width of the building (Fig. 2.134). Where the demolished wing once stood, a new lift tower was constructed. The new elevations, which overlook a courtyard and parking square, are sensitively designed to match the quality of the original arts and crafts building. They have glass block screens at ground level and red brickwork above to match the original elevation and other facades. The attic storey is built in glazed bricks and decorative stonework. The interiors have been beautifully refurbished and, wherever possible, the original details such as glazed wall tiling have been carefully restored. *AJ*, 29/95, pp. 24–26; *RIBAJ*, 8/95, p. 54.

FIGURE 3.1
The Dutch Quarter, Colchester.

CHAPTER THREE

The English Regions

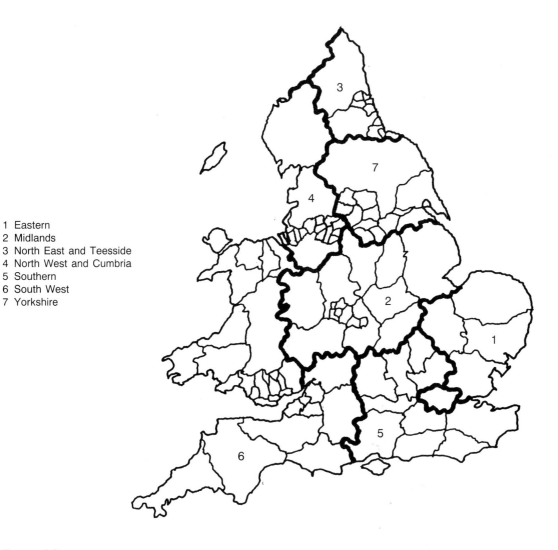

1 Eastern
2 Midlands
3 North East and Teesside
4 North West and Cumbria
5 Southern
6 South West
7 Yorkshire

FIGURE 3.2
The English Regions

EASTERN ENGLAND

CAMBRIDGESHIRE

Highsett, Cambridge.
1960. Eric Lyons and Partners. R. Cambridge.

This Span development contains three distinctively different groups of housing. The 'quad' which fronts the main road, combines flats, maisonettes and garages within a single courtyard of housing (Fig. 3.3). The architectural treatment of the building, with its flat roof and deep, white-painted fascia and tile hanging, set a trend which was extensively copied in both private and public sector housing design in the 1960s.

Behind the quad housing is an L-shaped group of simple two-storey terraces of flat-roofed houses with porches, designed in typical Span style with panels of brickwork alternating with areas of white-painted timber and glass. The third group comprises three-storey town houses built in a pale yellow brick. These face the street or are built at right angles with footpath access (Fig. 1.1).

EH, p. 10; *AR*, 1/58, pp. 74–75; *AJ*, 29/9/65, pp. 4 and 10.

Sudbury Court, Stonald Road, Whittlesey, Peterborough.
1977. Matthew Robotham & Quinn. R. Peterborough.

This scheme of thirty-two single-person flats and bungalows, a warden's house and a common room was built for elderly people by the Nene Housing Association in a suburb of Peterborough. In addition, five family houses were included to provide variety and to help overcome any institutional feeling. The East Anglian vernacular with its mixture of roof heights, dormers, low eaves and traditional materials created a village quality. The

FIGURE 3.3
Highsett: 'quad' courtyard housing by Span in Cambridge.

detailing of the traditional materials, especially the brickwork, is particularly outstanding.
AJ, 2/11/79, pp. 1096–1097.

Tuckers Court sheltered housing, South Street, Stanground, Peterborough.
1988. Matthew Robotham Associates.
R. Peterborough.

This sheltered housing scheme for elderly people built by the Minster Housing Association provides a real uplift to the area. The masterly integration of organization and elevation, carried through to the smallest detail, has produced a building of the highest architectural and spatial quality.

Most flats are accessed off a linear internal street set with paviors and covered by a pitched roof with exposed trusses. The upper floor flats have their own staircase which can accommodate a stair-lift. A delightful feature of the street is how, at intervals, it looks out onto small garden courts. The white rendered walls with diagonal and stained-wood feature windows and contrasting stained balcony timber, together with the

FIGURE 3.4
Tuckers Court sheltered housing.

natural clay tiles, produces a colourful way of relating to the vernacular tradition of the English Fenlands (Fig. 3.4).
Housing Design Awards 1989, A *Building* Publication, pp. 50–51; Colquhoun, I. and Fauset, P.G., *Housing Design, An International Perspective*, pp. 180–183.

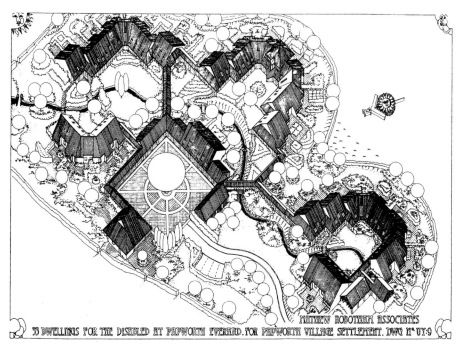

53 DWELLINGS FOR THE DISABLED AT PAPWORTH EVERARD. FOR PAPWORTH VILLAGE SETTLEMENT. DWG N° UY·9

MATTHEW ROBOTHAM ASSOCIATES

FIGURE 3.5
Papworth Village Settlement for people with physical disabilities.

Southbrook Field, Church Lane, Papworth Everard.
1987. Matthew Robotham Associates. R. Huntingdon.

Papworth Village Settlement is a charity and housing association whose objectives are the rehabilitation, training, employment and housing of physically handicapped people and their families. Established in the 1920s it has grown into a thriving community where physically disabled people are fully integrated into the village.

The scheme was designed to offer independence and privacy for thirty-three physically disabled people who may be confined to wheelchairs. The housing is grouped around three courts (Fig. 3.5) with a common room and warden's office, kitchen, laundry and guest bedroom sited centrally. Sixteen car-ports have been provided with covered access to the dwellings through 'cloisters'. The main dwelling type is a self-contained single-person flat with separate sitting room, bathroom and bedroom.

AR, 1/86, p. 65; Colquhoun, I. and Fauset, P.G., *Housing Design: An International Perspective*, pp. 209–210.

ESSEX

The Lawns, Mark Hall North, Harlow.
1950. Frederick Gibberd. R. Harlow Mill.

This ten-storey block was the first high rise flats built in Britain. It was a selected exhibit in the 1951 Festival of Britain and, almost 50 years later, English Heritage now recommend both the block and the accompanying three-storey terrace for Grade II listing.

The block contains two bed-sitting rooms with their own kitchen and bathroom and two one-bedroom flats on every floor except for the

FIGURE 3.6
The Lawn, Harlow: Britain's first tower block.

FIGURE 3.7
Part of Mark Hall
neighbourhood,
Harlow (from
Design in Town
and Village,
HMSO, 1953,
p.30).

KEY

A. Shops.

B. Service Industry.

C. Service Garage.

D. Methodist
    Church.

E. Health Centre.

F. Community
    Group.

G. Public House.

H. Car Park.

J. Central Recrea-
    tion Area.

K. Cricket Field
    with Sports
    Pavilion.

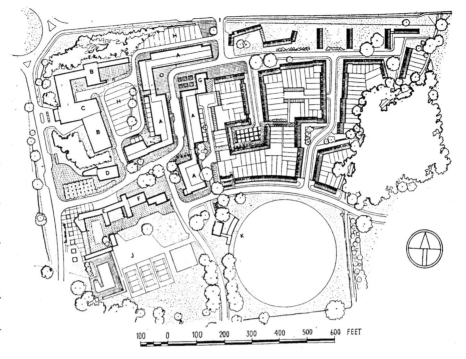

ground floor which has four bed-sitting rooms. It has a very individual butterfly shape with no right angles. This ensured that living rooms and their balcony would have a southerly aspect. The flat roof contained a roof garden, with shelter against the wind and the rain. The curved, patterned red-brick walls reflected the Swedish influence upon housing design in the years immediately after the war (Fig. 3.6).

AR, 9/51, pp. 82–84; MoHLG, *Design in Town and Village*, HMSO, 1953, p. 30; Glendinning, M. and Muthesius, S., *Tower Block*, p. 54; *EH*, p. 6.

Town houses, Harlow New Town, 3–12 Orchard Croft, 3–12 Mardyke Road and 161–165 Mardyke Road, Mark Hall North, Harlow.
1951–53. Frederick Gibberd. R. Harlow Mill.

These houses were an important part of Gibberd's urban design concept for the Mark Hall neighbourhood. His plans emphasized the need for a compact and urban type of building

(e.g. the town house) around the large green in the centre of the neighbourhood (Fig. 3.7). The houses have integral garages with living rooms and kitchens at first floor level (Fig. 3.8). The living room windows were emphasized externally by a projecting concrete surround, a motive used

FIGURE 3.8
Town houses overlooking the village green, Mark Hall, Harlow.

FIGURE 3.9
Bishopfield, Harlow.

by Lubetkin at Genesta Road, and by Goldfinger at Willow Road. The scheme won a MoHLG Housing Design Award in 1953. Currently it is being considered for Grade II listing.
AR, 5/55, pp. 311–315; EH, *Something Worth Keeping? New Town Housing*, p. 7.

Bishopfield and Charter Cross, Harlow New Town.
1963. Neylan and Unglass. R. Harlow Town.

The design of this scheme was based on research into courtyard housing undertaken at Cambridge University by Leslie Martin and Lionel March (p. 18). It was the subject of an architectural competition in 1961 won by Michael Neylan who adopted the L-shaped patio houses as the basis for his design. This form of house had been successfully used by Jørn Utzon in his 1960 Kingohusene estate at Helsingør in Denmark and it was thought to offer a high degree of privacy. At Bishopfield it was combined with narrow pedestrian lanes similar to those in traditional Turkish villages – hence the name by which the estate was known – 'The Casbah' (Fig. 3.9).

The brief set three principal design criteria – a density of twenty dwellings per acre (45 dw/ha), 100 per cent car parking and the layout

had to take account of the site which was a hill isolated by roads from neighbouring developments. The scheme provided 239 houses, flats and maisonettes. At the top of the hill was the 'podium' – a platform beneath which was garaging for cars. Its roof was a pedestrian concourse around which was a ring of flats. Stepping down the hill were fingers of patio houses which were separated by wedges of open space.

In its early days Bishopfield was well liked and there was a strong sense of community spirit. This was somewhat affected by problems with the original electric under-floor heating, and dampness and condensation. Today the occupants feel threatened in the lanes and in the garaging beneath the podium. Its form is alien to newcomers.
AJ, 25/5/61, pp. 765–772; *AJ*, 3/11/71, pp. 967–968; *AR*, 7/66, pp. 39–42.

Basildon New Town, Felmore.
1980. Basildon Development Corporation and Ahrends Burton and Koralek. R. Pitsea.

New Towns were important in the 1970s as places to experiment with new ideas in housing design. Basildon produced a number of high density/low rise schemes which are interesting in the way that the designs endeavoured to break

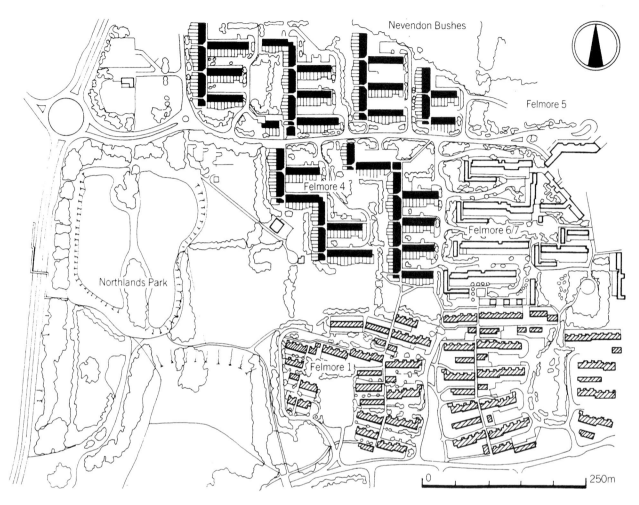

FIGURE 3.10
Felmore neighbourhood, Basildon New Town: hatched housing by ABK Architects, other by Basildon D.C. architects.

down the scale of large numbers of housing built in one single scheme. This was achieved by establishing identifiable groupings of housing, detailed design and landscaping.

Felmore contains two large but distinctively different schemes (Fig. 3.10). The 418 dwellings designed by ABK Architects was the first major project in Britain to develop techniques of passive solar energy (Fig. 3.11). The single- and two-storey houses all face south and are organized in three main identifiable groups separated by wide greens. The house designs incorporated high standards of insulation, draught-proofing and carefully considered natural ventilation systems

FIGURE 3.11
Felmore: housing by ABK Architects.

LIVERPOOL JOHN MOORES UNIVERSITY
Aldham Robarts L.R.C.
TEL. 0151 231 3701/3634

which ensured that a reduction of 30–40 per cent in energy use was possible.

The second scheme, Felmore 4, designed by the Corporation's architects, was timber-framed with dark stained timber walls and clay pantiled roofs. The layout was a rectilinear pattern of terraces with gardens facing south or east. The houses were two and three storeys in height, designed with a stepped section to offer more space on the ground floor than a conventional house. This could be used for sleeping, study or as additional living space. The external materials have retained their freshness and natural colours extremely well whilst other schemes in Basildon have not weathered so well and are looking somewhat drab.
AJ, 24 and 31/8/88, pp. 52–59.

Noak Bridge, Basildon.
1995+.

In stark contrast to the two schemes in Felmore is the recently developed private housing at Noak Bridge. In an attempt to create individuality, every house is a one-off country cottage or town house of many styles and materials. To establish a village image they are grouped along lanes and around small squares. The design is unashamedly pastiche but nevertheless popular.

Dutch Quarter, West Stockwell Street, Colchester.
1977. Colchester Borough Architects Department. R. Colchester.

The Dutch Quarter in Colchester received its name from sixteenth century Huguenot refugees. They left behind a tightly knit area of splendid timber-frame cottages, pressed close together amongst the winding lanes in the centre of Colchester. In the 1950s some of these cottages were demolished by the council but fortunately in the mid-1970s the remainder were renovated and the vacant sites developed with forty-seven houses and flats for rent.

The layout took its cue from the existing street pattern with the buildings kept close to the pavement. Development built on the backlands of the site were grouped around landscaped courts connected to the main streets by alleys. The form of the housing reflects the existing buildings, with projecting upper floors, steeply pitched roofs and white plastered walls (Fig. 3.1). The scheme was very important to the early promotion of the Essex Design Guide.
AJ, 26/10/77, pp. 780–781.

Brentwood Place, Sawyers Hall Lane, Brentwood.
1975–79. David Ruffle Associates. R. Brentwood.

This scheme of sixty-four private houses is close to the centre of Brentwood. It was a forerunner of the Essex Design Guide and, as such, it is now possible to see the success of the original concepts. The houses are grouped in a series of courts, mews and private drives, with access off a single spine road (Fig. 3.12). The design seeks to reflect the character of an historic Essex townscape, and it employs a wide range of external materials and colours which have mellowed with time. Groups of houses are linked by garages and screen walls which are covered with overhanging planting.

Figure 3.12
Brentwood Place: Essex Design Guide housing.

FIGURE 3.13
South Woodham Ferrers: entrance to a shared access loop.

South Woodham Ferrers.
Started 1974. Master plan by Essex County Council. R. South Woodham Ferrers.

The decision to build South Woodham Ferrers, with a projected population of 18 000, was taken in 1974. Responsibility for its coordination has been entirely in the hands of Essex County Council Planning Department. Over 4500 houses have now been built, together with schools, public houses, churches and other communal facilities and its town centre. Most controversial is the 'period look' of the centre, which was implemented in line with the Essex Design Guide principles, but the housing development has given opportunity to experiment with the design of roads and footpaths (Fig. 3.13). The lack of Housing Association rented housing (a mere 7 per cent) is most concerning.

NORFOLK

Rural housing at Ditchingham and Loddon.
1947–63. Tayler and Green. (Private transport essential.)

The recent proposed listing of post-war housing by English Heritage has drawn attention to a number of almost forgotten rural housing developments built for the former Loddon Rural District Council in south Norfolk, from the late 1940s to the early 1960s, by architects Herbert Tayler and David Green. A number of the schemes were illustrated in the early government Housing Manuals issued after the war. They were widely admired and copied and have remained popular with their tenants, a few of whom have lived in them since they were built.

The schemes were small, simple groups of houses and bungalows. At a detailed level they are full of delightful brick pattern-work and detailing. Some brickwork is colour-washed; elsewhere it is covered with trellising which has retained its original freshness. Frequently the schemes are dated in decorative brickwork. The use of pantiles and 'crinkle-crankle' walls all came from the architects' understanding of the local vernacular.

The schemes selected by English Heritage for listing are as follows:

1–30 Windmill Green, Ditchingham (1947–49). A scheme with simple colourwashed terraces of houses around three sides of a green.

25–39 (odd) Hollow Hill Road, Ditchingham (1951) and 1–28 Scudamore Place with 12–20 (even) Thwaite Road, Ditchingham (1956–65). This scheme comprises two groups of housing for

FIGURE 3.14
Tayler and Green development at Davy Place, Loddon.

elderly people located across the road from each other. The earlier scheme is a simple terrace. The later has parallel rows of bungalows linked by crinkle-crankle walls and with a prominently designed corner where there is a day centre and warden's house.

7–18 Church Road, Bergh Apton (1956). Housing around three sides of a small green built in subtle pink and black colour-washed brickwork with barge-boards and diaper patterns.

1–6 and **10–20 Davy Place** (Fig. 3.14), 5, 7 and 9 High Bungay Road, 3–13 (odd) and 6, 8 and 10 Low Bungay Road, Loddon. This is a small

development of elderly people's bungalows with a day room and a warden's house. It contains fretted barge-boards, bottle-ends and contrasting brick patterns.

EH, *Something Worth Keeping?*, *Housing and Houses*, *Rural Housing*, pp. 8–9; *Masters of Brickwork*, *AJ* Supplement, 12/12/84, pp. 28–31.

Friar's Quay, Norwich.
1975. Feilden and Mawson. R. Norwich.

The potential for attractive urban living in a compact city is no better illustrated than at

FIGURE 3.15
Friar's Quay, Norwich.

Friar's Quay in Norwich. The development, on
a prominent site overlooking the River Wensum
and close to the Cathedral, consists of forty
houses (plus nine granny flats), twenty-five with
integral garages, and forty parking spaces. The
houses are in tall, three- and four-storey terraces
grouped in a tight, high density urban form (Fig.
3.15). The layout creates a fine sequence of
spaces which wind through the scheme to culmi-
nate in steps down to the riverside (Fig. 3.16).
The landscape reflects traditional features of the
locality – notably gravel and raised lawns – all

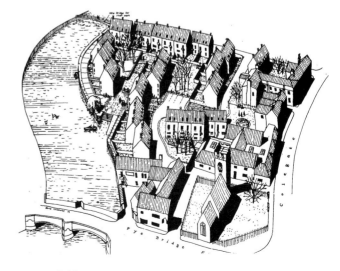

FIGURE 3.16
Friar's Quay: axonometric drawing.

softened by slender silver birch trees and white-beam.

All houses have four bedrooms. Nine houses originally contained granny flats on the ground floor but these have been sold as self-contained units. The rear gardens are walled and very private. The steep roof pitch of 55 degrees was chosen to reduce the eaves height without compromising living space. The decision has made a bold but sympathetic contribution to the already dramatic roofscape of the area.

AR, 11/75, pp. 311–315; *Baumeister*, 2/80, pp. 158–161.

Queen Elizabeth Close, Palace Plain, Ferry Road, Norwich.

1973. Feilden and Mawson. R. Norwich.

The site of this lovely scheme, once the orchard of the Old Bishop's Palace, was surrounded on three sides by massive random flint walls with sloping tile copings. Within these walls is a sheltered housing scheme for elderly people of great distinction comprising eighteen flats, six three-person houses and accommodation for a warden.

The flats were positioned in a two-storey strip on the north side of the site, close up to the existing wall, which made them effectively single aspect, but with a superb view of the Cathedral. Most of the houses were located on the east and west sides of the site, so that a large open courtyard could be provided in the centre of the scheme (Fig. 3.17). A single house and the warden's house were located here, linked to the flats by a pergola which breaks the courtyard into two areas. The design had to carefully relate the entrance of the scheme to the mediaeval Bishop's Great Gateway nearby. This was achieved through linking two of the houses to the existing flint-faced Victorian vicarage, which created an arched pedestrian entrance into the courtyard and a narrow vehicular access point to car parking.

The flats are one bedroom, single person and one bedroom, two person in size. The smaller flats are placed on top of the larger flats with an access corridor at the rear on the first floor. The relationship between the flats and the old flint wall is extremely well handled. The

FIGURE 3.17
Queen Elizabeth Close: the courtyard.

stone courtyard is a delightful space. All of the flats, including those on the first floor, have a raised flower-bed so that the residents can play a part in maintaining the open space. The houses have small courtyard gardens. There is a common laundry/drying room but it was the client's experience that for a scheme of this size neither a common room nor a guest bedroom would be sufficiently used to justify the cost.

AJ, 15/5/74, pp. 1056–1058; *AJ*, 4/6/75, pp. 1181–1191.

SUFFOLK

Estate Cottages, Rushbrooke, Suffolk.
1952–55, 1956–59, 1960–63. Richard Llewellyn Davies and John Weeks. R. Bury St Edmunds (Rushbrooke is to the south-east).

This little scheme of white-washed brick housing linked with high walls in a small village near Bury St Edmunds, built by Lord Rothschild, stimulated considerable interest at the time in simple vernacular forms of housing (Fig. 3.18). In the early 1950s the village had a small number of cottages and a church but no public house. Many of the cottages occupied by farm workers were too small and did not lend themselves to conversion. The social focus of the village life was a club run by a local committee which was also in need of replacement.

The new village was built in three phases. A pilot scheme of two two-bedroom houses was built first on vacant land on the edge of the village. These have identical plans but are reversed and linked by a high wall at the front. The second phase included the demolition and rebuilding of four houses on the north side of the village street and the construction of the village club. The success of the design comes from the continuous linking of the buildings and the use of walls to form an enclosure (Fig. 3.19). The houses varied in size from one bedroom for a single person to

FIGURE 3.18
Rushbrooke: a new village in the heart of the Suffolk countryside.

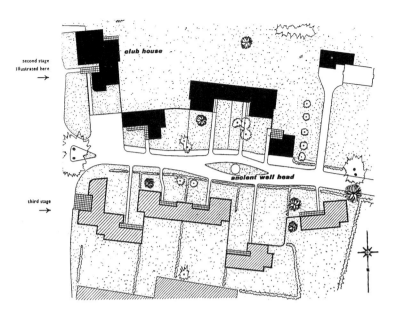

FIGURE 3.19
Rushbrooke: site layout plan of phase 2 and 3 redevelopment.

two and three bedroom types. The third phase on the south of the village road comprised three bedroom houses which completed the scheme. Each house has a storage shed enclosed by the main walls and a large room in the roof intended for further storage or to be used as a children's playroom. The original distinctive two-rail timber fencing has been replaced with hedging but otherwise the scheme remains completely unspoilt.

EH, Something Worth Keeping? Rural Housing, p. 8; *AR*, 8/57, pp. 99–102; *AR*, 2/60, pp. 118–120.

Martlesham Village, near Ipswich.
Master plan + housing, Clifford Culpin & Partners Housing and (1982–88) Feilden and Mawson. R. Woodbridge (via Ipswich).

Anyone interested in new settlements in the countryside would benefit from a visit to Martlesham Heath. The village was conceived in the early 1970s as a balanced community of a finite size consisting of approximately 1000 dwellings. It has its own primary and secondary schools, sheltered housing for elderly people and a somewhat inadequate shopping centre with a community building and a public house, named after Douglas Bader the Second World War RAF

pilot who flew from the air-field on the site. The principal elements of the master plan were twelve 'hamlets' clustered around the village green or set in the landscape and existing woodland (Fig. 3.20). These vary in size from fewer than sixty to over a hundred houses. A primary footpath network runs through the open space providing traffic-free routes to the village centre from the outer housing neighbourhoods. The client's brief required a high degree of individuality – 'coherent chaos' – through the use of different bricks, colour-wash, roof tiles, various porch detailing, chimneys, etc.

The first houses in the village, designed by Clifford Culpin & Partners in 1976, curved along the eastern edge of the village green hamlets. Amongst the last to be developed in the early 1980s were two in the south of the village designed by Fielden and Mawson (Heathfield and York Road/Lancaster Drive). Both hamlets focus on a village green. At Heathfield (Fig. 3.21) the green is larger and the housing around it is in terraced form with the car parking at the front hidden from view by timber palisade fencing. The design of the housing attempted to reflect the essential qualities and details of the traditional Suffolk village character.

BB, 5/77, pp. 3–8; *AJ*, 5/9/79, pp. 485–503; *BD*, 9/3/84, pp. 14–15; *RIBAJ*, 8/88, pp. 42–45; *B*, 25/11/88. pp. 43–54.

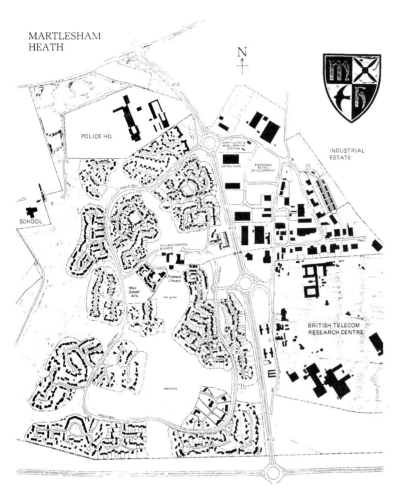

MARTLESHAM
HEATH

POLICE HQ

SCHOOL

HAPPY EATER &
MOBIL SERVICE
STATION

RETAIL PARK

PROPOSED
RETAIL
DEVELOPMENT

INDUSTRIAL
ESTATE

VILLAGE CENTRE
& SHOPS

Proposed
Church

New
School
Site

the green

woodland

BRITISH TELECOM
RESEARCH CENTRE

EAGLE WAY

FIGURE 3.20
Martlesham Heath: plan of village.

FIGURE 3.21
Martlesham Heath: the green,
Heathfield Hamlet.

FIGURE 3.22
Sherborne Wharf, city centre, Birmingham (p. 173).

THE MIDLANDS

BIRMINGHAM

Post-war prefabs, Wake Green Road.
1945. Birmingham City Council. R. Birmingham New Street + local transport

The temporary emergency housing manufactured in redundant aircraft factories between 1944 and 1948 proved to be exceptional value. Around a dozen different types were developed. This little group of sixteen prefabs in Birmingham are of the 'Phoenix' variety which English Heritage have recommended for Grade II listing (Fig. 3.23). Ravetz, A., *The Place of Home*, pp. 96–98; EH, p. 4.

Enveloping of pre-1919 housing, Balsall Heath Road and other locations, Birmingham.
1978–91. Birmingham City Architects Department. R. Birmingham New Street.

In 1978 Birmingham City Council embarked on a most ambitious programme to improve the fabric of its pre-1919 bylaw street housing (p.

28). By 1981, the council had enveloped 1700 dwellings and the programme continued at a high level until the introduction of means testing in the 1989 Local Government and Housing Act. Whilst there was a tendency for enveloping to over-unify the appearance of the housing, it nevertheless gave a huge environmental uplift to many parts of the inner-city in Birmingham (Fig. 3.24). The programme proved that enveloping costs less than clearance and redevelopment and it avoids unsettling the community. It therefore made economic and social sense as well as being good for the physical environment.

Goodchild, B., *Housing and the Urban Environment*, Blackwell Science, 1997, pp 158–161; Housing Design Awards 1983, A *Building* Publication, p. 60.

Stevens Terrace, 45 St Paul's Square.
1983. Associated Architects. R. Birmingham New Street.

Set in the St Paul's Square Conservation Area this seven-storey development by the Trident Housing Association made very good use of a narrow strip of land fronting on to St Paul's Square and in so doing covered the front of the

FIGURE 3.23
*Post-war prefabs: 'little palaces',
Birmingham.*

FIGURE 3.24
Enveloping of pre-1919 housing,
Balsall Heath, Birmingham.

FIGURE 3.25
Stevens Terrace, St Paul's Square,
Birmingham.

multi-storey car park which used to face the square. The accommodation was designed for single people in the form of twenty-three one-bedroom flats and fifteen bedsits.

All dwellings are single aspect, with living rooms and kitchens looking into St Paul's Square and with bathrooms, corridors and, in some instances, kitchens at the back. There is a common room with a kitchen area, laundry, guest room and extensive storage space on the ground floor.

The facade overlooking the square was very simply conceived in brick (Fig. 3.25). Its design is functional and modern yet it blends admirably with the Victorian architecture of St Paul's Square.

RIBA/NFHA, *Housing Association Design*, 1984; Housing Design Awards 1983, A *Building* Publication, pp. 32–33.

Belgrave Middleway Category II sheltered housing, 47 Belgrave Middleway/ Pershore Road.
1987. W. Reed, Birmingham City Architects Department. R. Birmingham New Street.

This two-storey category II sheltered housing, sited at a major road intersection within a short distance of Birmingham City Centre, is a model of skilful design for elderly people. The building is grouped around two superbly landscaped cloistered courtyards. In feel, the scheme is non-institutional and deceptively small but in reality it contains seventy sheltered flats.

The planning of the building is immaculate. The building makes use of every part of the site and even awkward corners have been turned to advantage by using the additional space to provide generous flats for wheelchair-bound residents. The peace and tranquillity of the courts with their pergolas and trellises covered with planting is contrasted beautifully with the views of the bustling city life which many of the flats enjoy.

Housing Design Awards 1987, A *Building* Publication, p. 62.

Brindley Place urban regeneration.
Various Architects and designers.
R. Birmingham New Street.

Brindley Place is part of Birmingham City Council's drive in recent years to regenerate the central area and give the city international status. Situated close to the new International Convention Centre, Symphony Hall and other recently completed cultural buildings and public spaces that now form the heart of the city, Brindley Place is the first mixed-use canal-side city development of its type in the United Kingdom. The design of the new housing relies too heavily on historical references but it has successfully brought people back to live in the city centre. Most memorable is the conversion into housing of the former Fellows Morton and Clayton building at Sherborne Wharf (design by Complete Design Partnership). Situated on a bend of one of the canals, the former factory was given a lightweight 'loft' structure on the roof which provides a most effective 'cap' to the top of the building (Fig. 3.22). The developments are best seen by taking a canal cruise.

Castle Vale Housing Action Trust, Tangmere Drive/Farnborough Road (housing at Abbingdon Drive).
1994–2005. Master plan, Hunt Thompson Associates. R. Birmingham New Street + local transport.

Castle Vale, comprising almost 5000 dwellings, two shopping centres, schools, churches and other social and community facilities, was built between 1964 and 1969 on 200 hectares (600 acres) of land on the north-east edge of Birmingham near the junction of the M6 and M42 motorways. Some 2000 dwellings were high rise flats and much of its low rise housing was of concrete panel construction. Almost 1500 dwellings had been purchased by their owners under the right-to-buy legislation introduced after 1979. From the 1970s, social and economic decline set in with high

FIGURE 3.26
Castle Vale HAT: new housing at Cosford Crescent.

levels of unemployment, which was aggravated by physical and design problems with the housing.

The Housing Action Trust was set up in 1993 following a ballot of the tenants in which gave 93 per cent support. The master plan recommended the demolition of some 1416 dwellings comprising seventeen (of the thirty-four) high rise blocks and twenty-four (of the twenty-seven) four-storey maisonette blocks. These are being replaced by some 1100 new, low rise dwellings on three principal sites in the centre of the development (Fig. 3.26), at Cadbury Drive in the south-west corner and Park Lane in the north-east corner. The remaining high rise blocks are to be refurbished. The plan recommended exploring the possibility of self-build housing and housing ·for sale and shared ownership to create a more diverse tenure. The regeneration of the estate is

being accompanied by a series of economic and social regeneration objectives.

Castle Vale HAT, *Master Plan: Written Statement, 1995*; Castle Vale HAT, *4th Annual Report and Accounts 1996–1997.*

COVENTRY

Six houses at Sheriff Avenue and Mayor's Croft
*1941. Coventry City Architects Department.
R. Coventry + local transport*

Coventry was able to continue to build a small number of new houses during the Second World War to accommodate the thousands made homeless by the bombing and the many more people who came to work in the wartime factories. The schemes were imaginative, making the most of the limited materials available. These six houses are the sole survivors in original condition and have been recommended for listing by English Heritage in recognition of their architectural and historic significance.

EH, p. 4.

LINCOLNSHIRE

Student housing, University of Lincolnshire and Humberside Campus, Lincoln.
1996. Crogan Culling. R. Lincoln.

This striking housing for students is located at the bottom of a hill adjoining the ancient Brayford Pool which now divides the historic city from a new 'tin-shed' retail and commercial area. The siting of the project on a long, narrow site parallel to the Foss Dyke waterway presented

an opportunity to design the 322 units in a series of seven courtyard buildings. Each court is made up of an 'L' of four- and two-storey blocks arranged around a mainly hard space which is enclosed on the south side by a high wall. The student rooms are grouped into families of six with a shared living/kitchen/ dining room.

The architectural appearance is outstanding. The mixture of buff brickwork and render, low pitched roofs and window composition is expertly handled to create a most successful modern image (Fig. 3.27).

AT, 12/96, pp. 10–12.

Elderly people's housing, Vicarage Court, Riverside Close, 1981, and Woodside, Woodside Avenue, 1982, Sleaford.
South Kesteven District Council. R. Sleaford.

These two schemes in the market town of Sleaford are representative of the quality of

FIGURE 3.27
Student housing at the University of Lincolnshire and Humberside, Lincoln.

FIGURE 3.28
Vicarage Court, Sleaford: quality housing by a small (rural) District Council.

design achieved in the early 1980s by a number of small, in-house architectural teams in rural District Councils.

Vicarage Court comprises thirty-two flats and bungalows. The site fronts the River Slea and is crossed by a major pedestrian route leading from the town centre to a large supermarket and car park. As it passes beneath an archway to a footbridge over the river, the route has been carefully integrated into the design to ensure minimal disturbance to the dwellings on either side. This part of the site (Fig. 3.28) contains the two-storey flats which terminate with a three-storey block, providing a focal point to the scheme. The bungalows are grouped around an access-way

on the southern part of the site. The natural clay tiles are a dominant feature of the design, both on the roofs and capping on the garden walls, and represent a detail indigenous to the area.

Woodside. The second scheme of twenty-four passive solar energy bungalows at Woodside Close was designed to reduce energy costs. The short terraces were positioned on a north–south axis to maximize orientation. The entrance porches on the south side are conservatories which act as storage heaters from autumn to spring, dispersing heat to the living room and main bedroom during the evening.

Housing Design Awards 1985, A *Building* Publication, pp. 94 and 96.

FIGURE 3.29
Halifax Place, Nottingham. [From RIBA/NFHA, Housing Association Design, 1984.]

NOTTINGHAM

Halifax Place, Lace Market.
1984. Cullen Carter and Hill. R. Nottingham

Halifax Place was an important part of the regeneration of the old textile manufacturing area in the centre of Nottingham. Commissioned by the Bridge Housing Society, it is a four-storey scheme of maisonettes and bedsits for single people and couples built on an extraordinary labyrinth of caves and cellars. The flats are divided into six clearly defined blocks with a maximum of eight flats in a block.

The urban design requirement was to reconstruct the old street pattern, which led to the scheme being grouped around two private and secure inner courtyards. For the new housing to blend and harmonize with the surrounding Victorian warehouses and their distinctive window pattern, brick colonnades were built on the street elevations to support the internal corridors. The

timber-framed construction supported by these columns gave a vertical scale and created a visual balance of glazing with the existing buildings (Fig. 3.29).

Hockerton Earth sheltered housing.
1998. Newark and Sherwood District Council and Robert and Brenda Vale. R. Newark.

These five houses are Britain's first earth sheltered, autonomous ecological housing. They were constructed by a self-build co-operative and designed as a south-facing terrace, covered with 500 tonnes of earth. Behind the open-plan conservatory and entrance are the living, sleeping and kitchen areas, with bathrooms, study areas and storage space at the back (Fig. 3.30).

The design maximized the use of local materials and the requirements of self-build construction. The pre-cast concrete beam-and-block roof is topped by 300 mm expanded

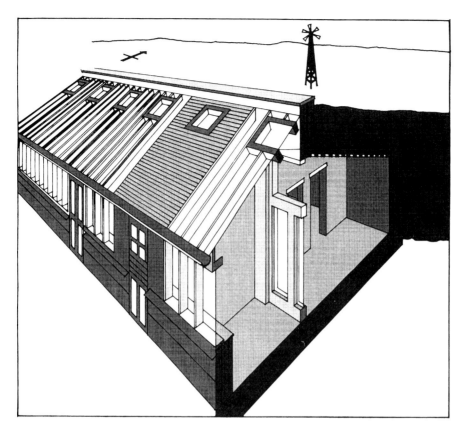

FIGURE 3.30
Hockerton earth sheltered housing: principles of the design.

polystyrene insulation, as well as a 400 mm layer of earth. The high level of insulation results in the houses requiring only minimum heating. Energy is self-generated by a wind turbine and photovoltaic cells, a system which also provides mechanical ventilation. Water for drinking is collected from the conservatory roofs and filtered through sand and ultraviolet units. Grey water is harvested from land drainage, nearby workshop roofs and the access road, and sand filtered. A septic tank and reed bed deal with black waste, discharging it into the aquiculture lake. Compost toilets are installed and waste is recycled on the site. The co-operative intends to grow its own food on the 10 hectare (24 acre) site which is large enough to achieve total self-sufficiency.

For a small District Council to have supported such a project is a remarkable achieve-

ment. The problem is how the ideas can become more relevant to the mass housing market. *Building Homes*, 3/98, p. 6.

WORCESTERSHIRE

Steel houses, Henwick Street, Worcester.
1998. John Edwards. R. Worcester.

These four detached, steel-framed and clad houses are most refreshing in the use of modern technology for speculative housing. They are located in an area of Georgian housing and look down on to the dramatic view of the Severn flood planin (Fig. 3.31).

The design takes advantage of the framed structure to cleverly perch the houses over the

FIGURE 3.31
Steel houses viewed from across the river.

edge of the river's bank with the steel columns standing on piles half-way down the bank. At street level a continuous parking deck has been constructed and at the front there is an entrance lobby at this level with stairs leading up to the two floors of housing above. The roofs and wall panels match the traditional materials of the surrounding neighbourhood. Roofs are ribbed profile steel sheeting, coloured dark grey, and wall panels are faced with British Steel Colorcoat HP200 in a plank profile running vertically and finished in a very pale colour.

AJ (Supplement), *Steel Design*, 25/6/98, pp. 1 and 6–9.

FIGURE 3.32
The Byker Wall, Newcastle upon Tyne (p. 183).

NORTH-EAST ENGLAND

MIDDLESBROUGH

St Hilda's, Cleveland Street.
1984. The Byker Group. R. Middlesbrough.

St Hilda's is close to the centre of Middlesbrough in an area that requires any built structure to be robust. This small scheme of forty-eight dwellings has successfully achieved this.

Developed by Middlesbrough Borough Council, the scheme comprises a mixture of flats, houses and bungalows with a meeting room. The housing was designed around two well landscaped pedestrian courts. Car parking is located at the rear which allows the option of an on-curtilage parking space for most dwellings. At Byker the group had gained considerable experience of timber-framed housing which they put to good advantage. The plywood clad elevations express the timber structure and add colour to the area (Fig. 3.33).

AR, 1/92, p. 51; RIBA Northern Region, *Housing North*, p. 10.

Central area housing, Grange Road/Hartington Road.
1986. Dixon Del Pozzo. R. Middlesbrough.

Situated close to the centre of Middlesbrough, this scheme was developed jointly by Middlesbrough Borough Council, Sanctuary Housing Association and North Housing Association. It is an excellent model of high density housing that is well suited for its urban location.

The scheme comprises a mixture of two- and three-storey housing incorporating flats, houses and shops. The layout was designed in the form of curved terraces which neatly create a series of interwoven streets, courts and pedestrian spaces (Fig. 3.34). Vehicular penetration is very high with car parking organized in small groups amongst the excellent landscaping. Despite its location, there are few signs of vandalism. The buildings are all robustly designed with a good balance between brickwork and painted timber panelling. The external works have stout railings, walls and fences (Fig. 3.35).

RIBA Northern Region, *Housing North*, p. 12.

FIGURE 3.33
*St Hilda's,
Cleveland Street,
Middlesbrough.*

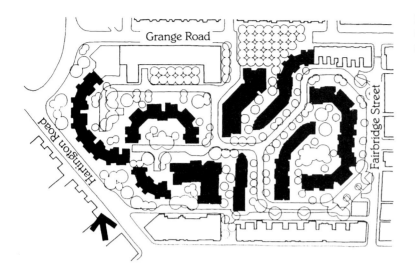

FIGURE 3.34
Grange Road, Middlesbrough: site layout.

FIGURE 3.35
Central area housing, Grange Road, Middlesbrough.

NEWCASTLE UPON TYNE

The Byker Redevelopment.
Completed in stages from 1971 to 1982. Ralph Erskine, Vernon Gracie & Associates.
R. Newcastle Central Station. +Metro (M.) Byker.

Byker, which was one of the last large local authority schemes to be built, has a special place in British housing. Located one mile east of the centre of Newcastle, the scheme comprises 2200 dwellings built on a south-westerly slope and has excellent views across Newcastle and the Tyne Valley (Fig. 3.36).

A small pilot group of forty-eight houses at Janet Square provided the architects with essential feedback from the tenants. A substantial part of the 'Wall' on the northern perimeter of the site followed. It contained small units which were intended for households without children, mainly elderly people. The outer face of the Wall is a masterly design of brick whilst the inner face is an abundance of colourful covered timber balconies. The Wall was to shelter the courts of low rise family housing with gardens from the noise that was expected to be generated by a proposed motorway which was ultimately not built. Car parking provision of 1.25 spaces per dwelling was required and extensive tree and shrub planting took place in the early years to conceal it. Within the pedestrian areas children's play areas, seats and tables were provided (Fig. 3.37).

No-one visiting Byker will come away without sensing the thrill of Newcastle City Council's brave commitment. Generally the fabric of the estate is still good and it is well cared for except for some neglect of communal spaces and the closure of the shops.

Ralph Erskine also designed timber-constructed houses for sale at Lakeshore (completed in 1970) at Killingworth, north of Newcastle (R. Newcastle Central Station + M. Four Lanes End).

AJ, 16/5/79, pp. 1011–1021; *AR*, 12/74, pp. 346–362; *AR*, 7/97, p. 23; *AJ*, 4/4/76, pp. 731–742; *AJ*, 9/5/79, pp. 961–969; *AR*, 12/81, pp. 334–343.

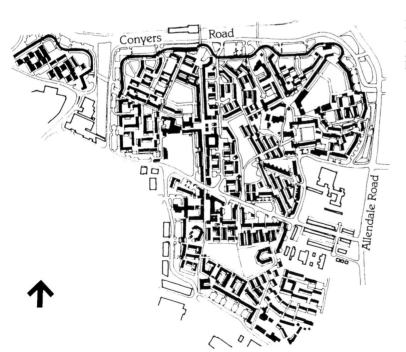

FIGURE 3.36
Byker redevelopment: site layout.
[From RIBA Northern Region,
Housing North, *p. 25.]*

FIGURE 3.37
Byker: family housing and high rise sheltered housing.

Private housing, Jesmond and North Newcastle.
(1962–70). R. Newcastle Central Station + M.

Newcastle possesses a number of private housing schemes built in the 1960s in the northern suburbs developed by A. Cragie and Son Ltd which are outstanding. Their design was influenced by the Span developments and, in the same way, the appearance has not been altered by a succession of house purchasers. Unlike Span, however, no maintenance company was ever established and there is no commitment except an annual payment for grounds maintenance.

FIGURE 3.38
Fenwick Close, Jesmond: high quality private housing.

FIGURE 3.39
Wyncote Court/Jesmond Park Court.

Fenwick Close, Buston Terrace, Jesmond (1962–4). Brian Robson. M. Jesmond. The existing Victorian house on the site was converted to provide two large family houses with five two-storey family houses and two smaller, single-storey units being built in the grounds. The houses are remarkable for their copper-covered hyperbolic paraboloid roofs, which give clerestory lighting within the deep house plan. English Heritage has recommended that this scheme be listed.

Avondale and Ferndale, Rectory Road, Gosforth (1968). Waring and Netts Partnership. M. Milford Road. These houses were built on the adjoining gardens of two large detached Victorian villas. The double courtyard evolved from the separate acquisition and development of the two sites (Fig. 3.38).

Wyncote Court/Jesmond Park Court, Jesmond Park East (1970). Waring and Netts Partnership. M. Jesmond. This scheme, which comprises thirty-five houses and fifty flats, consists of two-storey terraces cleverly arranged to retain and set the existing trees within a series of well landscaped courts. The design accommodates the motor car in small groups within garage courts and ensures a quiet and pleasant pedestrian environment (Fig. 3.39).

EH, 1987, p. 10; RIBA Northern Region, *Housing North*, pp. 6 and 23.

Clayton Street West.
1982. Barnett Winskell. R. or M. Newcastle Central Station.

This scheme, situated in an outstanding conservation area close to Newcastle's Central Station, has transformed a run-down part of the city into a desirable place in which to live. It was developed for households without children by the North British Housing Association and it contains 216 one-, two- and three-bedroom flats and forty-four bedsits. Funding from the Historic Building Council and Newcastle City Council supported

FIGURE 3.40
Clayton Street West.

the normal Housing Corporation allocation, and enabled the stone Clayton Street West facade to be refurbished and incorporated into the scheme. Within the development the red engineering brick facades with the tall oriel windows of black solar glass has created a distinctively urban image (Fig. 3.40). The central landscaped courtyard has communal tennis courts and car parking.

RIBA Northern Region, *Housing North*, 1987, p. 15.

NORTHUMBERLAND

Collingwood Court, Oldgate, Morpeth.
1988. Jane Darbyshire & David Kendall Ltd (formerly Jane Darbyshire Associates). R. Morpeth.

Located on a most attractive riverside site in the Morpeth Conservation Area, this private sheltered

FIGURE 3.41
Collingwood Court, Morpeth.

housing scheme for elderly people was the subject of a designer/developer competition promoted by Castle Morpeth District Council. The brief insisted on the retention of the existing trees and the leafy river bank.

The scheme is approached through an elegant high archway (Fig. 3.41) which opens on to a series of interlocking courtyards with two-storey buildings and landscaped gardens (Fig. 3.42). Each dwelling is independent and most have south-facing living rooms which look into the courtyards. In common with other private sheltered housing schemes, there is little demand for community provision and as a result only one small room and ancillary accommodation have been provided next to the warden's office.

The building materials were chosen to blend with the character of Morpeth – a blend of slop-moulded facing bricks, with reconstructed stone dressings and second-hand slate roof coverings, complemented with good detailing and external joinery.

The part of the site closest to the town centre contains a small local authority scheme,

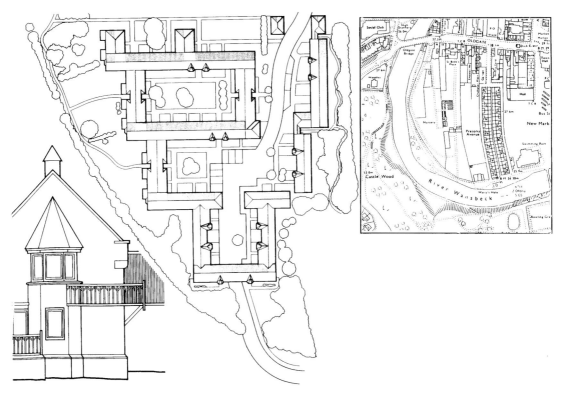

FIGURE 3.42
Collingwood Court: site layout and location plan.

Old Gate Court, designed by the District Council's in-house architects and completed in the late 1980s.

Housing Design Awards 1989, A *Building* Publication, pp. 14–17; *RIBAJ*, 12/89, p. 9.

Northumberland Village, Monkseaton, North Tyneside (between Percy Avenue and Beech Grove).

1990. Jane Darbyshire & David Kendall Ltd (formerly Jane Darbyshire Associates). M. Monkseaton.

Northumberland Village, built in 1880 as a children's home and hospital, is close to the centre of Monkseaton. It was purchased in 1986 by the District Council to prevent commercial development and sold on to Wimpey Homes for housing development. The scheme contains ninety-nine flats of which fifty-four are sheltered dwellings for elderly people (Fig. 3.43).

There were five Victorian villas on the site with large front gardens; four were converted into large semi-detached houses and one was demolished. The rear extensions were removed and new double garages with bedrooms above in steeply pitched roofs were added. These provided a new attractive road elevation for the houses and maintained the scale of the existing architecture. A large administration block, built in 1938, was converted into sheltered flats, a small block of 1960s flats was upgraded and seventy-six new flats were built on the vacant land. To enhance the entrance to the site, the existing Davis Court flats were given a face-lift with a change of colours and balconies.

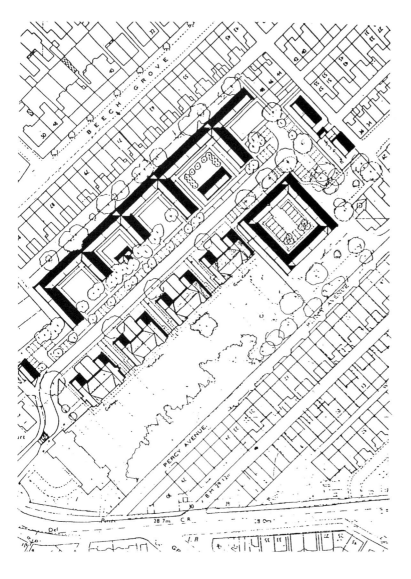

FIGURE 3.43
Northumberland Village: site layout.

FIGURE 3.44
Northumberland Village: superb use of tiling.

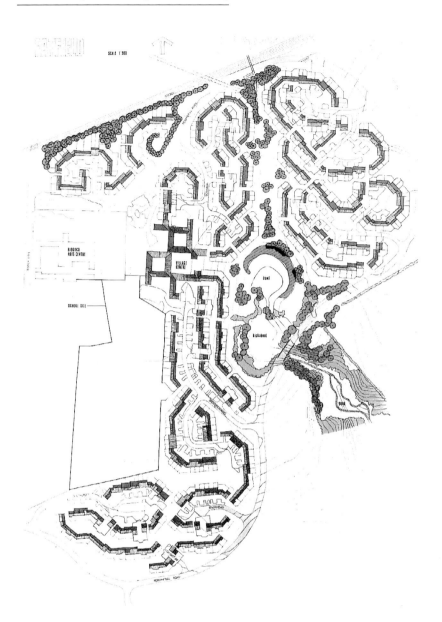

FIGURE 3.45
*Fatfield Village: site layout
showing the Washington
style of housing layout.*

The new and the old buildings blend well into a series of open and enclosed courtyards off the central spine road. Existing trees have been retained and car parking is located in small, well camouflaged groups. Most impressive is the retention and additional use of red/orange wall tile hanging in delightful traditional English patterns (Fig. 3.44).

Housing Design Awards 1991, A *Building* Publication, pp. 11–13; *RIBAJ*, 12/91, p. 33.

SUNDERLAND

Washington New Town.
1964–1989. Chief Architect, Eric Watson. (Private transport necessary.)

During the period 1970–1990 the Development Corporation received numerous RIBA, Housing and Civic Trust Awards for their housing design. Whilst Runcorn and Telford New Towns

FIGURE 3.46
Fatfield Village, Washington New Town.

pioneered the first shared access ways, Washington's architects were interested in 'mews' and 'mixer courts'. These incorporated the car very successfully into high density, low rise layouts and were frequently designed into schemes with long, continuously curving terraces of varying heights, ranging from single to three storeys (Fig. 3.45).

Fatfield Village (Malvern Road), completed 1980, contains over 500 houses, flats and bungalows for rent. On the steeper slopes the houses take on a split-level form. The painted, roughcast rendering and red and brown pantiles are not of the area but they were intended to give the effect of a hillside village, which is best appreciated by viewing the scheme from the top of the nearby Lambton Worm Hill (Fig. 3.46).
DOE Housing Awards publication, 1978, p. 19.

Lambton Village (Fallowfield Way), completed 1982, contains 812 dwellings for rent, designed on Washington design principles. The centre contains a meeting hall, shops, a public house and a clock tower. A sheltered housing scheme for elderly people is designed around covered cloisters.

West and East Bridge Streets, 14 Mount Pleasant, completed 1980. This scheme improved terraces of miners cottages built in the form of 'Tyneside' flats with front doors of ground and first floor flats alongside each other. Included with the development were extensive improvements to the external environment and the banks of the River Wear.
DOE Housing Awards publication, 1980, p. 50; RIBA Northern Region, *Housing North*, pp. 37 and 39.

FIGURE 3.47
Bonsall Street, Hulme redevelopment (p. 204).

NORTH-WEST ENGLAND

CHESHIRE

Hamilton Close, Parkgate, Wirral.
1960. Nelson and Parker. R. Neston.

Located in a leafy suburb, this cul-de-sac contains five exquisitely designed detached houses with pyramidal copper roofs and oversailing cedar-clad upper floors. The appearance of the houses has changed very little and the quality of the design can easily be seen (Fig. 3.48). English Heritage has recommended that the houses be listed.
EH, p. 10.

Black Road, self-build housing improvement, Macclesfield.
1974–75. Rod Hackney Associates. R. Macclesfield.

The old terraced houses on Black Road were built in 1815 to accommodate textile mill workers. By the 1960s they were in poor condition, having outside privies, damp walls and rotting stairs; demolition appeared inevitable. The residents, many over 65 years of age, were actively opposed to moving out of the neighbourhood. They asked Rod Hackney, then living at 222 Black Road, to speak for them.

His first task was to get Black Road reclassified as a General Improvement Area by proving the cost of improvement would be less than demolition and rehousing the occupants. To qualify for a housing improvement grant, the tenants would have to buy their houses and raise the money to do so. The tenants were agreeable to keep the costs down by undertaking some of the building work themselves. This gave a clear advantage to refurbishment but considerable political campaigning was still required before consent and funding were given by the local authority.

Subsequently, fifty-five families began the hard task of reconstructing their homes to suit individual requirements (Fig. 3.49), building out single- or two-storey extensions for kitchens and bathrooms. The back yards were converted into a mixture of well planted communal and private areas.

FIGURE 3.48
Hamilton Close.

FIGURE 3.49
Black Road: the early years of community architecture.

A second scheme at Black Road quickly followed, after which Rod Hackney developed schemes in many places throughout the country. His experience suggests that housing rehabilitation is not so much an architectural problem but one of organization, management and financing, requiring a large measure of goodwill and trust between all the parties.

AJ, 20/2/85, pp. 995–1002; *AJ*, 5/10/77, p. 630; *AJ*, 29/10/75, p. 876; *AJ*, 12/11/75, pp. 995–1002; *AR*, 4/85, pp. 57–61; *Architecture and Design*, 1–2/91, pp. 73–75; DOE Housing Awards, 1975, p. 21 and 1980, p. 51.

informally shaped parking courts located on either sides of the culs-de-sac. A separate footpath system leading to children's play areas and open space was built into the design (Fig. 3.50).

After completion, the design was thoroughly researched and it proved to be as safe as a conventional layout. Its principles were ultimately embodied in *Design Bulletin 32* published in 1977 and numerous local authority planning and design guides.

AJ, 21/3/79, pp. 385–596; *AJ*, 14/10/70, pp. 889–902; Colquhoun, I. and Fauset, P., *Housing Design in Practice*, pp. 63–64; DOE Housing Awards 1969, pp. 23, 33–34.

The Brow, Halton Brow, Brow Road, Runcorn New Town.
1969. Runcorn Development Corporation.
R. Runcorn.

Halton Brow was the first scheme to draw public attention to the concept of curtailing traffic speed in housing areas through the integrated design of residential buildings and environment. Its long culs-de-sac took on the appearance of winding country lanes, varying in width and set in an environment of dense tree and shrub planting. The houses were randomly arranged around small,

Warrington New Town.
1979–86. Warrington and Runcorn Development Corporation Architects Department or as stated.
R. Birchwood unless indicated.

In the early 1980s Warrington and Runcorn Development Corporation's architects and consultants produced housing that perfected the concept of a highly landscaped, pedestrian orientated environment (Fig. 3.51).

Admirals Road/Curlew Grove, Birchwood (1979). The layout of this scheme of 120

Plan of the Estate

FIGURE 3.50
Halton Brow: site layout. [From: Colquhoun, I. and Fauset, P.G., Housing Design in Practice, *Longman UK, p. 64.]*

houses affords views of interest and variety upon every turn. The housing is set in superb landscaping and the colourful cream brickwork on the housing with red brick bandings and quoins make it quite exceptional.

Gorse Covert Road/Stainmore Close and Darnaway Close (1984). The semi-detached houses and bungalows in this scheme,

designed for first-time buyers, set a good standard for private sector housing. The wide-frontage houses are grouped informally around two culs-de-sac with an open space in the centre.

Cromwell Avenue/Gregory Close and **Cavendish Close, Old Hall** (1984). R. Sankey/Warrington. This scheme of almost 300 houses, made up of one- to three-storey housing,

LIVERPOOL JOHN MOORES UNIVERSITY
Aldham Robarts L.R.C.
TEL 0151 231 3701/3634

FIGURE 3.51
Landscape-dominated environment typical of schemes in the Birchwood/Oakwood area of Warrington New Town.

was planned to emphasize the central tree-lined pedestrian route which focuses on a 'gateway' leading to the local centre. The spine road is a tree-lined avenue with frontage housing and a flowing alignment to limit traffic speeds. It gives access to a series of pedestrian/vehicular courts of housing.

Old Hall Road/Nansen Close (1986). R. Sankey or Warrington. These 115 two-storey houses are grouped around two large culs-de-sac. Most are semi-detached but houses in visually key places in the culs-de-sac are grouped as L-shaped terraces to create a greater sense of enclosure.

Redshank Lane, Oakwood (1984). MacCormac Jamieson & Prichard. R. Birchwood.

In its construction and appearance this project of 360 houses and flats reflects Cheshire's traditional half-timbered housing. The layout groups between eight and eighteen dwellings around mews courts which are linked by a footpath system. A strong edge is given to the development by locating the flats which peak to four-storeys along Redshank Lane.

Admirals Road, Oakwood (1984). Farrell/Grimshaw. This scheme is located adjacent to Birchwood Brook and woodland and was planned to have three distinct areas. Separated by green spaces, these groups of thirty to thirty-five dwellings built along village lanes were conceived by the architects as 'places'. The houses were designed to be flexible with a 'universal core' common to each dwelling containing the services, stairs, kitchen and bathroom.

AJ, 13/9/78, pp. 471–485; *AJ*, 8/12/82, pp. 37–41; *AR*, 10/85, pp. 46–55.

Sunningdale Community Project, Chapelhill Road/Hopfield Road, Wirral.
1988. Brock Carmichael Associates. R. Birkenhead.

In the mid-1960s when these four towers on the Sandbrook Lane Estate in Moreton were proposed, the local newspaper commented that they would 'bring a touch of Manhattan to the West End' [1]. By the mid-1980s, the blocks had degenerated and drastic measures were required.

The solution reached for the fifteen-storey Wheatfield Heights was to overclad and convert its eighty-five flats into sheltered housing for elderly people. The nearby maisonettes were demolished and replaced with twenty-four, two-storey flats and four new shops facing the street. They were grouped to create a large, landscaped courtyard which accommodates car parking and pleasant, well used communal gardens and a summerhouse. First floor flats have balconies overlooking the courtyard, from where intruders are instantly noticed (Fig. 3.52). There is a

FIGURE 3.52
Sunningdale Community Project.

communal meeting hall at the entrance to the courtyard which is controlled by a 24-hour watch. *AJ*, 3/8/88, pp. 33–47; [1] Ibid., p. 34.

CUMBRIA

New Village, Harriston, Aspatria, Allerdale.
1978. Napper Errington Collerton Partnership.
R. Aspatria.

With the exception of a few buildings, this scheme completely replaced a former mining village. The new houses, built by Allerdale

FIGURE 3.54
Harriston New Village.

District Council, comprised seventy three- and four-bedroom houses, six flats and twenty mobility standard bungalows. These are in the form of simple cottages, grouped around a large green to give the feel of a Lakeland village (Fig. 3.53). Its white, rough-cast blockwork walls, Welsh slate roofs and window and door detailing are all common to the area (Fig. 3.54). Although a shop (just) exists, the village has no church, school or community centre, or any other social and visual focus.
AJ, 9/1/80, pp. 78–89.

Regeneration of George Street and Queen Street, Whitehaven.
1975–1984. Barnett Winskell. SRB Dockland Project. 1992–2002. R. Whitehaven.

The centre of Whitehaven represents a unique piece of urban history, for it survives as England's first Renaissance planned town conceived in the seventeenth century and mainly built in the eighteenth. Laid out by Sir John Lowther, a friend of Sir Christopher Wren, as a coaling port for his mines, Whitehaven became a fashionable town with streets of fine Georgian housing.

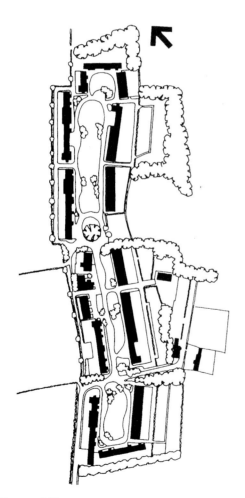

FIGURE 3.53
New Village, Harriston: site layout.

FIGURE 3.55
Urban regeneration, Whitehaven.

By 1960 the centre of Whitehaven had become a picture of decay and dereliction as the local economy declined. In the mid-1970s the Old Town Centre was designated an outstanding conservation area which enabled Copeland District Council to seek funding from the Department of the Environment for improvement. It then made 75 per cent grants available to stimulate housing improvement and initiated the redevelopment of cleared sites. The new housing in Queen Street/George Street, completed in 1975, retained the essential architectural character of the eighteenth century housing; colour-washed rendering, stone architraves around windows, and shallow-pitched slate roofs (Fig. 3.55). Further phases followed in the 1980s in George Street/Scotch Street, and in Duke Street/Queen Street.

In 1992 the Whitehaven Development Company Limited (WDC). was established. This was a public/private partnership of British Nuclear Fuels, English Partnerships, Copeland Borough Council, Cumbria County Council and the Whitehaven Harbour Commissioners. A 10-year programme was launched via a successful single regeneration bid (SRB) to regenerate the old harbour area with housing and commercial development and to create training and employment opportunities for local people.

AJ, 1/10/70, pp. 658–661; *Housing and Planning Review*, pp. 24–25.

FIGURE 3.56
Webster's Yard, Kendal

Webster's Yard, Highgate, Kendal.
1989. Hanson Walford Marston. R. Kendal.

This scheme shows how new sheltered housing (in this instance for sale) for elderly people can be woven into the fabric of old towns, producing an exceptional living environment (Fig. 3.56). Fortunately, a 25 per cent car parking level was acceptable to the local authority which enabled a dense scheme appropriate to the site to be achieved.

Entered from Highgate, where existing four-storey buildings were restored and converted into shops with flats above, the new Webster's Yard has a central pedestrian route passing through a series of courtyards and steps up a steep slope to the lane at the rear of the site. The first courtyard is New Inn Yard, which is a long, narrow stone paved space containing thirty-six sheltered dwellings designed in the form of three-storey stepped-back flats and maisonettes. A conservatory divides New Inn Yard into two parts and gives access to communal facilities and a lift. Beyond this is the small Lower Yard, around which are eight sheltered flats, and the Upper Yard, containing four houses fronting on to the rear lane and eight flats. The scheme included the relocation of the Dowker Arch, originally built in 1833.

The materials – second-hand Welsh roofing slates and rendered blockwork which is now the substitute for stone in Cumbrian housing – reflect the Lakeland tradition.
AJ, 24/5/89, pp. 34–45.

New build co-operative housing, Liverpool.
From 1978. Innes Wilkin Ainsley Gommon, The Wilkinson Hindle Halsall Lloyd Partnership, Brock Carmichael Associates, McDonnell Hughes. R. Liverpool Lime Street.

The co-operative housing movement began in Liverpool during the early 1970s with tenant management buy-outs from private landlords in order to seek improvement grants. The co-ops grew in strength in the early 1980s out of opposition to the militant City Council's housing policies. A number of tenants' groups were not prepared to wait to be rehoused by the City Council. Instead, they formed housing co-operatives to procure their own new housing. In June 1983 they held a protest march to the City Council and successfully secured support and building sites at no cost. The government seized the opportunity to demonstrate its own new-found housing philosophy and support came from Michael Heseltine the then Secretary of State for the Environment.

The co-ops ranged in size from twenty to sixty family units. Supported by one of Liverpool's co-operative development agencies, they registered as a non-equity housing co-operative with limited liability. When the houses were completed the co-op members became tenants, paying standard fair rents, but they were also, collectively, the landlord, responsible for management and maintenance. Three of the most innovative co-ops were those at Weller Street, Hesketh Street and the Eldonian Village.

The **Weller Street** co-operative, established in 1977, pioneered the participative approach in the design of its new housing which is simple, two-storey and grouped around small landscaped courts. The process involved in designing the scheme is most significant. The co-operative organized itself into subcommittees to consider design, education, social events etc. Design decisions evolved through a process of education, involving visits to schemes, slide shows and 'planning for real' participation at weekly design meetings. The procurement process for the Weller Street project took two and a half years – a long time to maintain people's interests.

Newland Court, Hesketh Street. Innes Wilkin Ainsley Gommon. Development began in 1979 as a consequence of the clearance of housing in Liverpool 8, from where tenants joined with families who had once lived at Hesketh Street to form a co-operative based on Hesketh Street. The scheme comprised a range of dwelling sizes, from two to seven bedrooms, designed around landscaped courts. The co-op was anxious to avoid the 'corpy' image which included avoiding an over landscaped look.

FIGURE 3.57
Eldonian Village.

The Eldonians were particularly fortunate, as Michael Heseltine directly intervened to ensure that funding would be available for their scheme. The architecture has a traditional private sector image with a high degree of individuality (Fig. 3.57).

AJ, 8/9/82, pp. 51–58; *AJ*, 18/7/84, pp. 35–39; *AJ*, 8/8/84, pp. 18–19; *AR*, 4/85, pp. 57–61. RIBA/CIOH, *Tenant Participation*, pp. 48–49.

railings, limiting entrance to a single point where 24-hour security was located. This created an internal courtyard from which the dwellings were entered. Access to upper floor flats was by newly constructed, brightly lit, glazed staircase 'towers' which served a limited number of dwellings on each floor. A new roof, paintwork and street lighting all added to the appearance of the scheme.

DOE Housing Design Awards 1985, p. 58.

Minster Court, Crown Street, Liverpool 7.
1984. Kingham Knight Associates.
R. Liverpool Lime Street.

Minster Court was built by Liverpool City Council in the 1930s but by the 1960s the flats had degenerated and demolition appeared to be the only solution. Barratt Urban Renewal (Northern) Ltd purchased the blocks for a peppercorn amount and converted them into private housing for sale in Minster Court.

They enclosed the court by blocking off the former archways and constructing new walls and

MANCHESTER

Hulme Redevelopment.
1991–98. R. Manchester (Deansgate).

The redevelopment of Hulme is one of Britain's most significant urban regeneration projects of the 1990s. It is seen as a model for the sustainable urban neighbourhood of the future. The main housing developers are Bellway Urban Renewal Division and a consortium of housing associations led by the Guinness Trust and North British.

FIGURE 3.58
St Wilfred's, Hulme: finely curving terraces following the street pattern.

In 1991 a successful City Challenge bid of £37.5 million pump-primed a 5-year programme of housing renewal and economic and social regeneration, with major infrastructure and environmental works. The total capital investment was expected to exceed £200 million. The scheme involved the demolition of over 2500 deck access dwellings, including the notorious 'Hulme Flats'. Ultimately there will be over 1250 new rented dwellings and Bellways are proposing to build 2000 houses for sale.

The planning approach was to produce an Urban Design Guide to characterize the vision for the area and the principles for the massing and positioning of the buildings. These points are as follows:

• Development of streets which promote sociability, community and natural surveillance, all designed to limit traffic speeds to 20 mph.
• Permeability, i.e. a neighbourhood with strong

FIGURE 3.59
Homes for change: internal courtyard.

links to surrounding areas, which is easy to move around in.

- A sufficient density to support a wide range of shops and services.
- Development which is sustainable environmentally, socially and economically by encouraging energy efficiency, recycling, public transport and urban ecology and allowing the area to adapt to future change.
- A street hierarchy using three-storey housing along the principal routes and two-storey on residential streets.
- A careful treatment of corners, vistas and landmarks – the traditional points of reference in the city.
- Dwellings to achieve a National Housing Energy rating of 9.

So far these principles have been successfully incorporated into the designs. The schemes are varied, colourful and full of life, and have been achieved with tenant involvement.

Aquarius, Aquarius Street (1995). Ainsley Gommon Wood for Guiness Trust. This development contains sixty-eight houses and ninety-seven flats for rent, designed in three-storey form around courtyards but closely relating to the street pattern. The glass-fronted circular staircases to the flats are distinctive.

St Wilfrid's, Mary France Street (1994). NBHA's in-house architects for NBHA. The curved facades of the two- and three-storey terraces flow with the street grid and are punctuated at corners by a range of features such as communal entrances, balconies and special windows (Fig. 3.58). The public square at Mary France Street is a green space with railings in the form of a London square.

Boundary Lane/Bonsall Street (1995). OMI Architects for Guinness Trust. This scheme

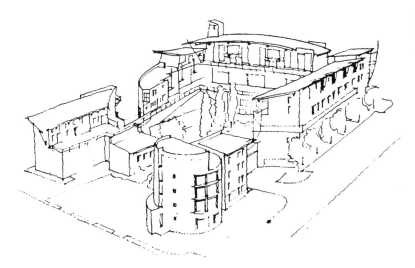

FIGURE 3.60
Homes for change: architects' concept drawing.

is in the form of three- and four-storey rectangular blocks with a five-storey circular tower marking the entrance to the scheme on Boundary Road. A second phase includes forty-one dwellings and two shops.

Mallow Street. NBHA in-house architects for NBHA. This scheme contains eighty-three dwellings. These are built in streets with a multi-coloured brick aesthetic. The corners are strongly emphasized with three-/four-storey towers.

Chichester Road (1994). PRP and Triangle for North British Housing Association. The development comprises fifty-five houses and eighty-three flats. The family housing is in two- and

FIGURE 3.61
Rolls Crescent.

three-storey form whilst in the south-east corner of the site, flats with balconies form a prominent gateway to the whole of the Hulme area.

Homes for Change, Old Birley Street (1996). Mills Beaumont Leavey Channon for Homes for Change. Planning began in 1991 when the Guinness Trust was approached by Hulme residents and small businesses to develop a mixed-use scheme. The result is one of the most exciting schemes built in recent years (Fig. 3.59). It comprises fifty flats and maisonettes and 1500 sq. m (16 000 sq. ft) of managed workspace – including shops, offices, studios, a small performance area which doubles up as a meeting room,

and a cafe – in a four- to six-storey urban building. The workspace, built in a shell-and-core format to allow varying sizes and configurations of units, is confined to the two first floors and has external entrances. The dwellings above are reached through a secured courtyard via open access decks (Fig. 3.60).

Rolls Crescent/Halston Street (1997). ECD Architects. Commissioned by North British Housing Association, this scheme contains sixty-seven dwellings designed in a traditional low-rise street pattern with brightly coloured towers punctuating the corners and intersections of Rolls Crescent (Fig. 3.61). All houses have private

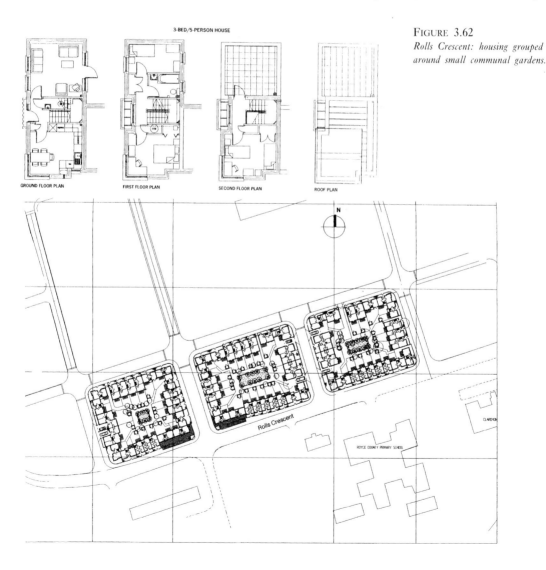

3-BED/5-PERSON HOUSE

GROUND FLOOR PLAN　　FIRST FLOOR PLAN　　SECOND FLOOR PLAN　　ROOF PLAN

FIGURE 3.62
Rolls Crescent: housing grouped around small communal gardens.

Rolls Crescent

ROYCE COUNTY PRIMARY SCHOOL

CLAREMON

gardens with a communal space in the enclosed central courtyards (Fig. 3.62). The unusual roofs are covered in silver aluminium standing-seamed cladding.

URBED, *21st Century Homes, Building to Last*, p. 57; *Building Homes*, 1/97, pp. 30–31; *AJ*, 20/4/94, pp. 16–17; *B*, 6/9/96, pp. 38–43; *AJ*, 12/3/98, pp. 27–37; *B*, 3/10/97, p. 11; *RIBAJ*, 11/96, pp. 6–7; *RIBAJ*, 2/96, pp. 16–17.

FIGURE 3.63
Whitworth Street corridor: conversion into housing.

Conversion of Victorian Commercial Buildings into Housing, Granby Village/Whitworth Street.
1983–98. Various architects. Conversion of Smithfield Buildings. 1998. Stephenson Bell. R. Manchester Piccadilly.

The centre of Manchester contains a wealth of fine Victorian and later buildings, many of which during the 1980s and 1990s were successfully converted into housing (Fig. 3.63). The Central Manchester Development Corporation promoted, with the support of large Urban Development Grant, a programme of conversions and new development along the Whitworth Street corridor. The first scheme, completed in 1983 by Northern Counties Housing Association (NCHA),

was the conversion of the six-storey Granby House into seventy flats for sale. This was followed by a further hundred in India House with a new-build, mixed development scheme of commercial offices and housing for rent at Princess House, built in association with Tung Sing (Orient) Housing Association which caters for the large Chinese community in Manchester (architects Provin & Makin). Between 1990 and 1994, three old warehouses (Bombay House, Velvet House and 55–57 Whitworth Street) were also converted into housing for sale, with the construction by Wimpey Homes of two new blocks of flats at Venice and Velvet Courts [1].

In 1998, **Smithfield Buildings**, the former Affleck and Brown departmental store, a full city block in the 'northern quarter' of the centre of Manchester, was converted into eighty apart-

FIGURE 3.64
Boarhurst Farm: high quality rural housing.

ments. The design has re-created the original central atrium, carved out another nearby, and turned both into a brilliant winter garden. The project was a 1998 Housing Award winner and, in the description of the scheme, the awards publication commented that the project is 'what Unité d'Habitation might have looked like if Le Corbusier supported Manchester United'.

[1] URBED, *21st Century Homes, Building to Last*, p. 34; Housing Awards Publication 1998, pp. 20–23.

Boarhurst Farm, Boarshurst Lane, Greenfield.
1991. Stevenson Architecture. R. Greenfield.

This small cluster of houses is at the edge of the Pennine village of Greenfield. Easily reached from Manchester, the village has become a desirable place to live. Boarhurst Farm consisted of a group of five derelict farm and weavers' cottages, all Grade II listed buildings.

The derelict cottages have been refurbished and three new houses have been built on the old site by a local developer/builder (Fig. 3.64). Two of the new houses, together with a pair of garages,

are placed in conjunction with existing buildings to form a square at the road junction. Buildings are at random angles to each other as they follow contour lines and create a variety of spaces which are in character with the area. The new houses are constructed in traditional stone and, with well detailed slate roofs and small windows, reflect the essential proportions of the existing houses.

AJ, 14/8/91, pp. 24–31; Housing Design Awards 1991, A *Building* Publication, pp. 44–45.

PRESTON

Princes Reach, Preston Docks.
1995. Brock Carmichael. R. Preston.

This scheme forms part of Preston's redevelopment of the former 140 ha dock, which aims to create a new quarter of 1650 dwellings. This first phase of 160 dwellings has been designed to exploit its waterfront location, with varying roof heights and large balconies. It provides a pleasant backdrop to the lock gates, boats and cranes nearby (Fig. 3.65).

Housing Design Awards 1989, A *Building* publication, p. 108.

FIGURE 3.65
Princes Reach: dockyard structures create a maritime environment.

FIGURE 3.66
The Ryde, Hatfield: one of the great schemes of the century (p. 233).

SOUTHERN ENGLAND

BERKSHIRE

Point Royal, The Green, Rectory Lane, Easthampstead, Bracknell.
1961–64. Philip Dowson and Derek Sugden of Arup Associates. R. Bracknell.

The early point blocks were often designed as landmark features. This eighteen-storey block in Bracknell has a striking polygonal form with one convex and one concave side, all suspended by dramatic thrusting cantilevers from a narrow, ground floor podium. English Heritage are proposing that the building should be listed (Fig. 3.67).
EH, p. 7.

The Liberty of Earley House, Lower Earley, Reading,
1996C. PRP Architects, R. Earley.

This scheme is typical of the many sheltered housing developments that have been built in recent years by housing associations to meet the needs of the growing numbers of elderly and frail elderly people who are often in their eighties.

FIGURE 3.67
Point Royal, Bracknell: a landmark feature in the new town.

LIVERPOOL JOHN MOORES UNIVERSITY
Aldham Roberts L.R.C.
TEL. 0151 231 3701/3634

FIGURE 3.68
Liberty of Earley sheltered housing for frail elderly people: morning coffee in the lounge.

This project caters for all needs from low to high dependency where a 24-hour caring service is required. It was designed as a category 2½ sheltered housing project (with extra care) but is run as a registered care home.

It contains thirty, unfurnished two-person, self-contained flats and six bedsits. The provision of communal and ancillary accommodation, including assisted bathrooms, lounge, central catering kitchen and dining room, enables special care registration to be sought in the future on a flat by flat basis, or for the whole project. The attractive lounge has a high sloping ceiling (Fig. 3.68) and large windows looking into the central garden (Fig. 1.19). Each floor has its own common areas and facilities and there is a guest bedroom for use by relatives.

The building is U-shaped and the planning of the circulation avoids central corridors (Fig. 3.69), which allows seating areas to be provided in bay windows from which the beautifully planted central garden can be fully appreciated.

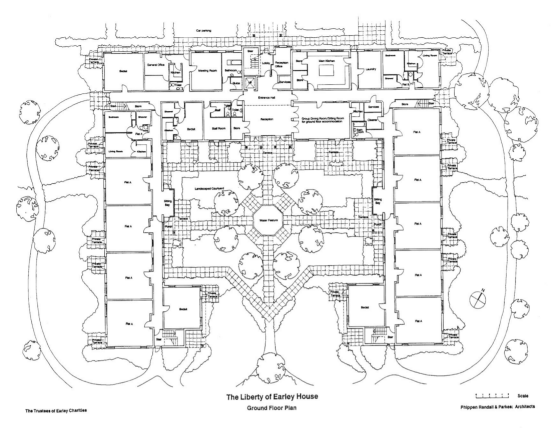

The Liberty of Earley House
Ground Floor Plan

The Trustees of Earley Charities

Scale

Phippen Randall & Parkes: Architects

FIGURE 3.69
Liberty of Earley sheltered housing: designed around a well planted courtyard garden.

BUCKINGHAMSHIRE

Turn End, Haddenham.
1968. Peter Aldington. R. Haddenham.

This small group of three houses had a profound influence in the late 1960s as architects looked for a natural design aesthetic in contrast with modernism. Peter Aldington was keen that the housing should be sympathetic to and enhance the village without resort to pastiche. His design was sensitive and most appropriate.

The interplay of roofs, the use of clay tiles and white walls, and simple stained timber openings particularly caught the imagination (Fig. 3.70). To obtain south and west sunlight and privacy the houses were planned around court-

yards. The spatial quality of the interiors is superb, with high sloping ceilings, changes of level and a wealth of colour from the materials used in the construction. Mud-brick, tile-capped walls around the perimeter of the site were integrated into the design.

The garden to Peter Aldington's own house is a secret delight and its relationship to the house is superb (Fig. 3.71). During warm weather the glazed walls around the courtyard open to create an extra living space. In recommending Grade II* listing, English Heritage commented on the design, 'it is an exceptional and influential example of the reworking of local vernacular precedent and plan forms to create modern village housing'.

AR, 8/68, pp. 102–105; *AR*, 9/89, pp. 71–76; *AH*, 2/9/70, pp. 532–536; *EH*, p. 12; *RIBAJ*, 10/96, pp. 56–62.

FIGURE 3.70
Turn End, Haddenham: the forecourt to the three houses.

Lyde End, Bledlow.

1977. Aldington & Craig; project architect Paul Collinge. (Private transport required.)

The site for these five houses is owned by Lord Carrington, the former Foreign Secretary, who personally set the brief for the development. He wished to provide high quality housing to rent for village residents, which would make a contribution to and form part of the village. However, he considered it best to rely upon the architect to determine the sizes of the dwellings and how many would fit on the site.

The houses, single-storey except for the two-storey house at the entrance, are closely linked around an internal courtyard (Fig. 3.72). Their plans are similar but adjusted according to their position in the layout. The curved walls which enclose the gardens add to the sculptural quality of the grouping of the houses (Fig. 3.73). The lean-to effect of the roofs is a strong feature of the practice's work. The houses are small – around 60 sq. m (600 sq. ft), but the quality of the interior creates the illusion of space and the sloping roof gives extra height. The effect is increased by ground to ceiling windows at each end of the living space which offer a strong link between the interiors and the gardens.

AR, 12/78, pp. 377–380; *AJ* (Brickwork Supplement), 12/84, pp. 32–38.

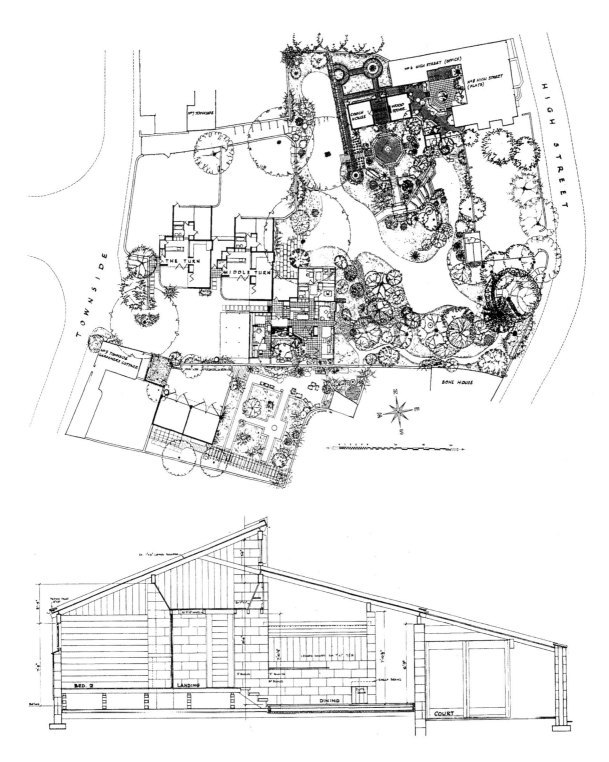

FIGURE 3.71
Turn End: plan of the houses and P. Aldington's garden.
Section through the dining room of P. Aldington's house.

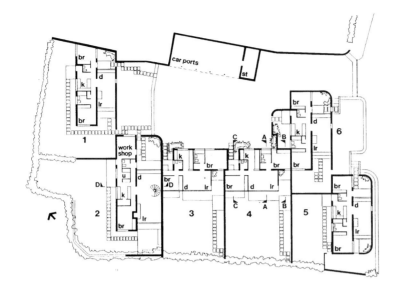

FIGURE 3.72
Lyde End, Bledlow: housing around a small courtyard.

FIGURE 3.73
Lyde End, Bledlow: superb detailing of walls, roofs and windows.

Milton Keynes.
1970–97. Milton Keynes Development Corporation (MKDC) Architects and Consultants. R. Milton Keynes.

Milton Keynes (Fig. 3.74) was the last of the English new towns and contains many inter-

esting housing schemes. There were three main approaches to housing design, reflecting the change of emphasis as the new town developed.

In the early years, housing for rent, designed by the Development Corporation's in-house architects, was mostly large schemes of several hundred dwellings. These had highly structured, formal layouts with flat roofed or mono-pitched

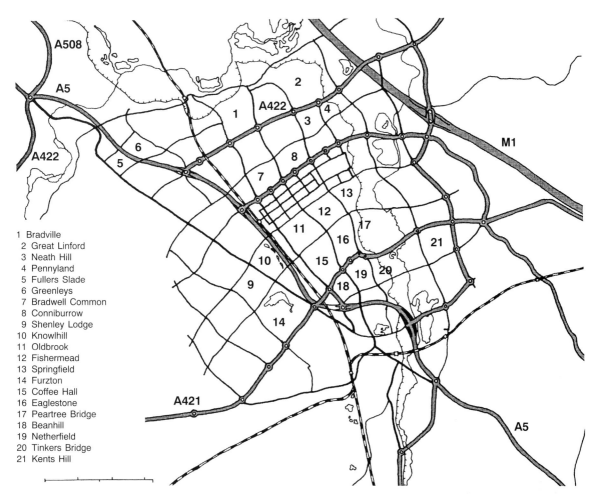

1 Bradville
2 Great Linford
3 Neath Hill
4 Pennyland
5 Fullers Slade
6 Greenleys
7 Bradwell Common
8 Conniburrow
9 Shenley Lodge
10 Knowlhill
11 Oldbrook
12 Fishermead
13 Springfield
14 Furzton
15 Coffee Hall
16 Eaglestone
17 Peartree Bridge
18 Beanhill
19 Netherfield
20 Tinkers Bridge
21 Kents Hill

FIGURE 3.74
Milton Keynes: place names and main roads.

houses built in parallel rows of one-, two- and three-storey terraces (Fig. 3.75). Alternatively, houses were grouped around large landscaped squares. Most had a high level of curtilage parking with extensive tree and shrub planting at the front to reduce the impact of parked cars (Fig. 3.76) (*AD*, 6/73; *AD*, 8/74).

The standardization of dwelling and layout made possible the development of system building and prefabrication, which enabled the Corporation to achieve its building programme of 2500–3000 dwellings per year in an area where there was a shortage of traditional building skills.

The principle projects of this period were **Coffee Hall** and **Bradville** (*AJ*, 25/9/74, pp. 735–777 and *RIBAJ*, 8/84, p. 31), **Greenleys, Lanhall, Fishermead** (*AJ*, 11/5/77, pp. 877–890 and *AR*, 10/81, pp. 233–235), **Fullers Slade** (*AJ*, 10/9/75, pp. 515–526), **Conniburrow, Springfield, Netherfield** (*AJ*, 10/12/75, pp. 1247–1260), **Tinkers Bridge** and **Bean Hill** (Foster Associates).

Other schemes of note from the same period were:

Waterside, Peartree Bridge (1977). MKDC Architects. This scheme comprises a long terrace of 176 three-storey housing that snakes

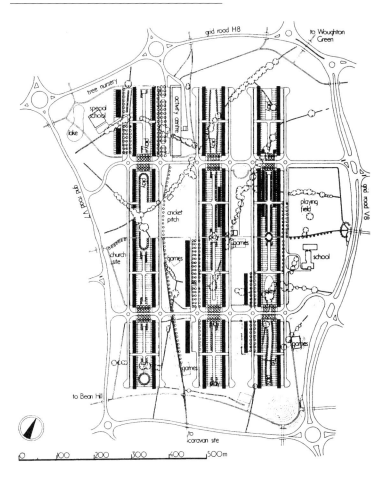

FIGURE 3.75
*Milton Keynes: layout of Netherfield
(AJ 10/12/75, p. 1250).*

FIGURE 3.76
*Early terraced housing with its
mature planting.*

FIGURE 3.77
Waterside, Peartree Bridge.

alongside and overlooks the Grand Union Canal (*AJ*, 4/2/76, pp. 232–234) (Fig. 3.77).

Chapter House, Coffee Hall (1977). MacCormac Jamieson & Pritchard. This was designed for young, single people on a difficult triangular site. It contained a community room, bar, laundrette and WC's and a flat for a caretaker (*AJ*, 10/8/77, p. 249).

Eaglestone (1974). Ralph Erskine. This was built as a mixed scheme of houses for sale and rent and the layout was more irregular than others designed at that time. The houses are clustered in small 'gossip groups' of around thirty to fifty dwellings to increase social contact between the families. There was considerable elevational variety, heralding Erskine's later work at Byker (*AJ*, 10/12/75, pp. 1247–1260).

A change in approach came about following the design by MKDC Architects for **Neath Hill** (1980) (Fig. 3.78). The project presented new concepts, marking a desire for more traditional dwellings. The main roads follow the contours in large curves, off which two- and three-storey brick dwellings with pitched roofs are grouped around short brick-paved mews courts (Fig. 3.79) (*AJ*, 4/2/76, pp. 229–233).

Martin Richardson's design for **Hartley**, Great Linford (1976) contained a mixture of spaces and simple traditional building forms which he described as an 'enjoyable combination of ordinariness and surprise' (*AJ*, 3/9/80, pp. 451–459). His design for 175 dwellings for rent at **Bradwell Common** (1981) was based on the elements of a typical Victorian terrace, as reflected in the orange, buff and white banding of brickwork (*AR*, 10/81, pp. 233–236).

Hazelwood, Great Linford (1977). MKDC Architects. Here a village scale is created in two loose, concentric rings of housing (Fig. 3.80) which cluster around a vehicular court in the centre where the cars are parked under tiled car ports (*AR*, 10/9/78, pp. 243–246).

France Furlong, Great Linford (1979). MacCormac and Jamieson. This development

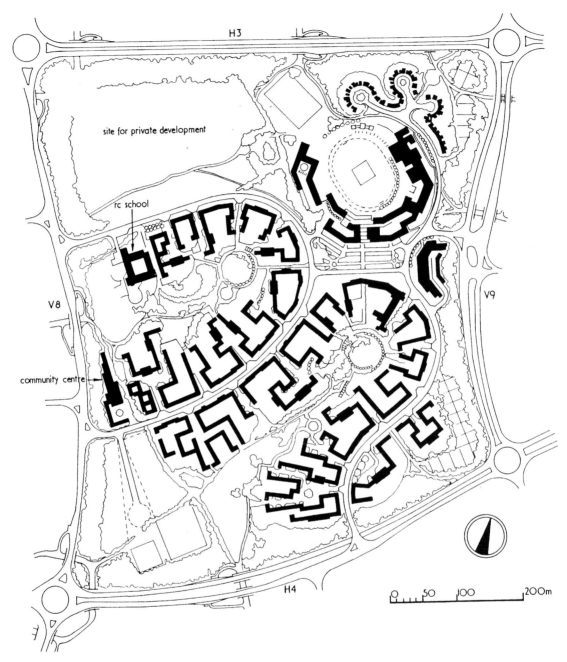

FIGURE 3.78
Neath Hill forecasted a new design approach (AJ, 4/2/76, p. 230).

reflected Richard MacCormac's interest in subur-
bia as the residential convention of the 20th
century (*AR*, 10/85, pp. 53–54). It is a cosily
familiar scheme, built in brick and tiles with

timber windows, but with a relatively structured
layout. The setting-back of pairs of semi-detached
houses along the curving main street to create
parking courts is an effective way of minimizing

FIGURE 3.79
Mews court at Neath Hill.

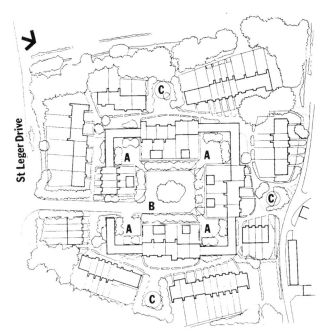

FIGURE 3.80
*Informality at Hazelwood
(AR, 10/78, p. 244).*

A. car court
B. hardstandings and
parking
C. children's play
area

FIGURE 3.81
Oldbrook 2: successful high density housing in a central area neighbourhood.

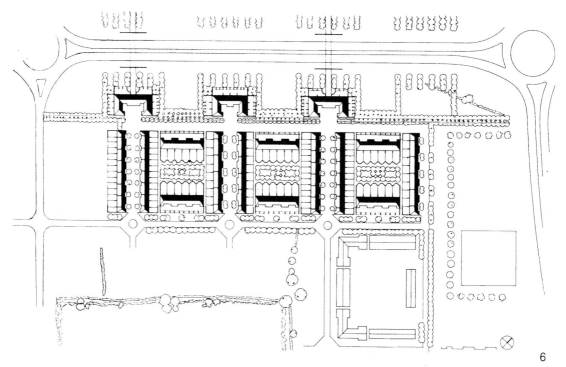

6

FIGURE 3.82
Oldbrook 2: mews court town housing.

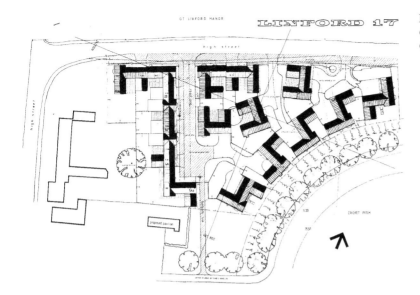

FIGURE 3.83
Clustering of housing at Deerfern Close.

the impact of parked cars on the street (*AJ*, 1/10/80, pp. 627–629).

Colquhoun and Miller's **Oldbrook 2** (1982) has a formal layout, with the 250 dwellings grouped around well detailed and planted block-paved courts. The 'floating' roof over the bedroom loggia is a generous feature giving a useful external space at the top of the houses (Figs 3.81 and 3.82) (*AR*, 4/83, pp. 30–35).

During the last years of the Development Corporation's existence most new housing was for sale. The best schemes took their cue from the

FIGURE 3.84
Waterside housing at Skeats Wharf, Pennyland.

FIGURE 3.85
*Earth sheltered Round House,
Rutherford Gate, Shenley Lodge.*

local context, e.g. an old village, or a major landscape element. **Deerfern Close**, Great Linford (David Tuckley Associates, 1983) comprises fifteen large two-bedroom houses, clustered around tight mews courts in which every house has distinct individuality and personality (Fig. 3.83). At **Skeates Wharf** (Pennyland) (Fig. 3.84) and **Woodley Headland** (Peartree Bridge) the housing takes full advantage of the waterside sites.

A key aim of Milton Keynes Development Corporation from 1972 was to encourage innovation in the efficient use of energy resources. Early experiments included the Bradville Solar House.

The **Homeworld 81 exhibition** at Coleshill Place, Bradwell Common, attracted large numbers of people to the thirty-six houses which demonstrated the latest ideas in design and low-energy technology. In 1985, the Development Corporation designated a 300 acre (121 ha) **Energy Park**

FIGURE 3.86
Midsummer Cottages: Future-world housing at Crowborough Lane, Kents Hill.

at Shenley Lodge, Knowlhill and the northern part of the Furzton. This was launched in 1986 with a show village of forty-eight houses called **Energy World** built at Farraday Drive, Shenley Lodge (*RIBAJ*, 6/92, pp. 52–55). One development used a wind turbine to generate electricity but it proved to be too noisy. The most unusual house was the earth sheltered **Round House** at Rutherford Gate, Shenley Lodge (Fig. 3.85).

The last initiative came in 1994 with **Futureworld**, based on a site at Crowborough Lane, Kents Hill. The simplest houses in the group were **Midsummer Cottages** (Levitt Bernstein Associates) (Fig. 3.86). These were low-tech timber houses incorporating the five themes of energy efficiency – minimizing environmental impact, flexibility in use, cost

effectiveness in construction, and economic to run. The houses have a thermal mass of dense concrete blockwork and 160 mm insulation and triple glazing to retain the heat (*RIBAJ*, 9/93, pp. 30–31; Rudkin, D. and Falk, N., *21st Century Homes*, pp. 72–73).

HAMPSHIRE

Castle House, Southampton.
1963. Eric Lyons. R. Southampton.

In the late 1950s Southampton City Council had an imaginative policy of commissioning private architects to support their in-house department

FIGURE 3.87
Eric Lyons' 1960s Castle Hill housing, Southampton, overlooks 1990s low rise housing.

led by Leon Burger. Just as Eric Lyons was gaining widespread recognition for his housing at Blackheath in 1958, he was invited to design this high density scheme. The block stands on the site of the keep of Southampton's long demolished mediaeval castle. Rising from its brick podium, the building is uncompromisingly of its time and it contrasts sharply with its old and new neighbours (Fig. 3.87). The upper parts are stylishly detailed with a curious broken rhythm of piers to its generous balconies. English Heritage have recommended that it be listed. EH, p. 6.

Wyndham Court, Southampton.
1969. Lyons Israel Ellis. R. Southampton.

This second scheme in Southampton which English Heritage have proposed should be

FIGURE 3.88
Wyndham Court, Southampton, designed to match the Civic Centre.

listed is a most ambitious block of flats, maisonettes and shops built on a prestigious city centre site. It was originally intended to be let at above-average rents to professionals and its level of finish is very high. The design matched the nearby 1930s Civic Centre which was the most dominant building in the city centre. It is therefore an uncompromising concrete structure but its powerful, sculptured form has offset the fears normally associated with too much exposed external concrete (Fig. 3.88).

EH, p. 6

West Downs Village, King Alfred's College, Winchester.
1997. Fielden Clegg Architects.
R. Winchester.

One of the most active areas of development in the 1990s was student housing as the expanding universities and colleges of higher education looked for high quality design in their new buildings as a means of raising their image to students. Some projects contribute to the regeneration of the town or city in which they are located and others help raise the general economic well-being of an area. The architects for this project in Winchester have achieved this with great conviction.

The scheme focuses on a spectacular street which serves as a north–south spine (Fig. 3.89). Seven rooms are grouped in maisonettes with shared dining/kitchen and bathroom accommodation. By stacking the maisonettes in four-storey blocks and providing external steel stairways to upper maisonettes, the architects have minimized internal circulation. They have created opportunities for the street to become a lively social space, particularly during the summer when the students use the staircases as verandahs. The upper maisonettes have further contact with the street as the dining/kitchen area projects out in the form of a conservatory.

AJ, 17/7/97, p. 51; DOE/RIBA, Housing Design Awards, 1997, pp. 22–24.

FIGURE 3.89
Bright modern housing design for students at King Alfred's College, Winchester.

John Darling Mall, Housing for Handicapped People, Eastleigh.
1985. Hampshire County Council Architects. R. Eastleigh.

Hampshire County Council Architects Department is best known for its school buildings, but this project contains all the same qualities. It was built for people who require intensive care to help develop their skills sufficiently for independent living. The building is completely sheltered by a single, covered translucent roof which means that the residents are able to move around, regardless of the weather, what appears to be an external environment (Fig. 3.90).

The accommodation provides twenty-four bedsitting rooms, six sheltered flats and shared common space with sitting areas and a large room which can be used for concerts and games (Fig. 3.91). The bedsits, which were intended for short stay use, are grouped in fives or sixes with shared dining and sitting rooms. The sheltered flats cater for potentially permanent occupation with a

FIGURE 3.90
John Darling Mall: a peaceful internal garden.

generous kitchen/living room, bedroom and bathroom which can be specifically tailored to suit the needs of the individual resident. All dwellings have their own front doors and milk and post is delivered daily. Brickwork is light coloured and the planting was chosen for its all-year quality.

AR, 6/85, pp. 58–61; *BB*, 9/92, pp. 22–23.

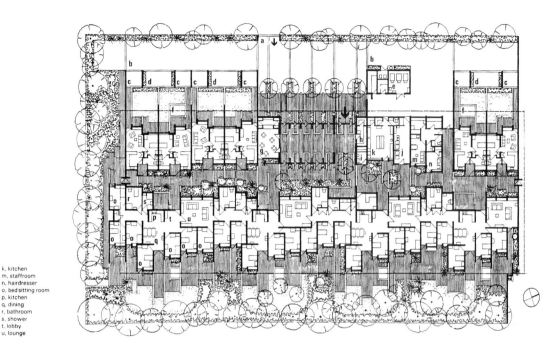

k, kitchen
m, staffroom
n, hairdresser
o, bed sitting room
p, kitchen
q, dining
r, bathroom
s, shower
t, lobby
u, lounge

FIGURE 3.91
John Darling Mall: layout plan.

Letchworth Garden City.
Started 1903. Parker and Unwin. R. Letchworth.

Letchworth (Fig. 3.92), with its boulevards of housing and mature public gardens, is a superb place in which to live. Barry Parker and Raymond Unwin set high standards for the design of the new housing which were pursued with an idealist zeal (Fig. 3.93). Their housing at **Westholm** (Fig. 1.2) (1) and **Birds Hill** (2), designed in 1906, is an early example of workers cottages grouped around greens and culs-de-sac. These groups, with their rough-cast walls, prominent tiled roofs and picturesque groups of dormer windows and chimneys, show the full variety of Parker and Unwin's early housing design. Other architects involved in designing housing were M.H. Baillie Scott, C.M. Crickmer, and Parker's assistants, Cecil Hignett, Robert Bennett and Wilson Bidwell.

The most significant pre-1914 housing in Letchworth is **Rushy Mead** (3). **Lytton Avenue** contains the major part of the 1907 **Urban Cottages exhibition** entries in the section between **Gernon Road** and **Pixmore Avenue** (4). The cottages are in pairs or groups, facing a small green and pedestrian cul-de-sac to the west and east of the road.

The **Cheap Cottages exhibition** of 1905 attracted wide publicity. The objective was to build housing for agricultural workers at a cost of £150. Some designs demonstrated new techniques to speed up construction. This included building steel and reinforced concrete framed housing rendered externally. In total, 114 cottages were built between the railway and **Icknield Way** (5).

Information and maps are available at the First Garden City Museum, 269 Norton Way South, which was formerly B. Parker's office. Addresses of housing referred to above:
(1) Westholm: nos 1–24 and 162–176 (even) Wilbury Road.
(2) Birds Hill (South side): nos 9–27 (odd) and nos 2–122 (even) Ridge Road.

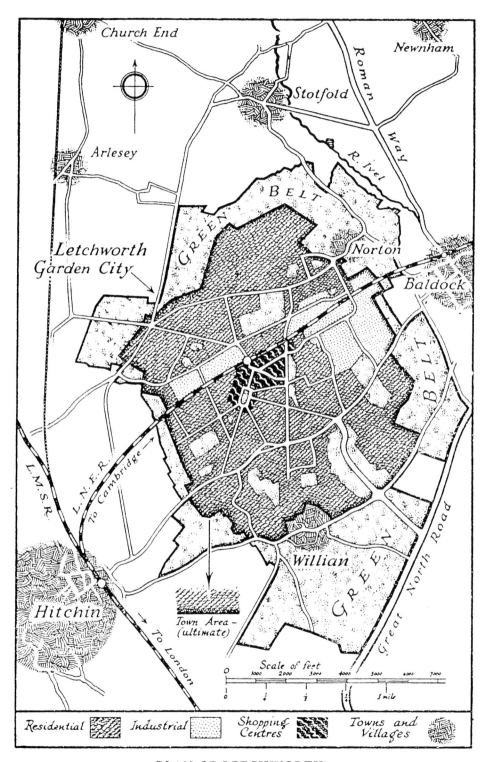

PLAN OF LETCHWORTH

FIGURE 3.92
Letchworth Garden City. [Reproduced by courtesy of the Town and Country Planning Association.]

FIGURE 3.93
7–17 (odd) Lytton Avenue (C.M. Crickmer 1907).

(3) Rushby Mead: nos 2–42 (even) and 44–58 (even) (by Parker and Unwin); nos 60–78 (even), 86–144 (even) and 103–115 (odd) (by Parker and Unwin).

(4) Lytton Avenue: nos 3, 5, 7–17 (odd) and 19–25 (odd).

(5) The principal houses of the Cheap Cottages exhibition, Icknield Way: nos 123 (steel framed), 217, 219, 212 (listed), 241; Nevells Road: nos 203, 205, 206, 208, 212, 216, 220; Norton Way North: nos 7 and 7A (by Baillie Scott and listed); The Quadrant (West Side): nos 1, 6, 8; Wilbury Road: nos 122, 126, 248, 150–156 (even) and 160, 158 (reinforced concrete framed house developed by John Brodie, Liverpool City Engineer).

Welwyn Garden City.
Started 1919. Louis de Soissons. R. Welwyn Garden City.

Ebenezer Howard was determined to seek a second site, which he succeeded in achieving in 1919 just north of Hatfield. Louis de Soissons' master-plan of 1919 (Fig. 3.94), with only minor modification, still works today. It seems remarkably at ease with the motor car despite the absence of the hierarchy

FIGURE 3.94
Welwyn Garden City: plan by Louis de Soissons, 1920. [From Purdom, C.M., The Building of Satellite Towns, 1925 and 1949, reproduced by courtesy of George Weidenfeld and Nicholson Limited.]

FIGURE 3.95
Welwyn: large neo-Georgian houses overlooking the central gardens.

of roads which dominate the later new towns. The central gardens provide a strong focus.

Although not universal, red-brick cottage Georgian style prevails. The houses in **Parkway** (early 1920s) which overlook the central gardens most typify this architectural approach (Fig. 3.95). Much of Welwyn Garden City's housing is grouped around culs-de-sac (e.g. **Handside Close**, early 1920s) to promote the sense of community which Howard wished to achieve. Louis de Soissons' town houses at 82–124 (even) and 83–125 (odd) **Knightsfield** (1955–56) have been recommended for listing by English Heritage. They are three-storey houses, flats and maisonettes, ingeniously designed to mask the complexity of the house types within. The neo-Regency appearance is unusual but carried out with conviction.

In 1948, following the passing of the New Towns Act, Welwyn became a new town and it has now expanded by over 100 000 people, but it still remains a beautiful place in which to live.

AR, 2/27, pp. 175–182; Eserin, A., *Welwyn Garden City*, The Chalford Publishing Company, 1995, pp. 8–9; Girardet, H., *The Gaia Atlas of Cities*, Gaia Books Ltd. pp. 54–55; EH, *Something Worth Keeping?* New Town Housing, p. 7.

The Ryde, Hatfield.
1966. Phippen Randall and Parkes. R. Hatfield.

Established in the early 1960s by Michael Bailey, the Cockaigne Housing Group built twenty-eight single-storey courtyard houses with landscaped gardens, a tennis court and a common room for a day nursery and evening activities, in what was then fields adjacent to the railway in Hatfield New Town. Cockaigne was, and still is, a co-operative housing society and most of the members of the group were gathered through an advertisement in a daily newspaper.

The first tasks of the group were to find a site and raise the funding. Michael Bailey wrote of the difficulties of this in *The Listener*: 'We tried the Building Societies. They were polite too – but we must understand that in the event of their financing us there must be no new-fangled

ideas. The houses must be good, traditional semi-detached, of tile and brick' [1]. The scheme was eventually supported by a small number of officials in the Hatfield Development Corporation and Hatfield Rural Council – because 'they liked the look of us and our ideas' [1]. The group then set about appointing an architect – 'someone youngish and unknown and bursting for a chance to show us his talents. As a result of a chance encounter, a young architect employed in the LCC agreed to set up in practice on the strength of our job' [1].

The outcome was a scheme constructed within 7 m cross-walls (Fig. 3.96) which run the entire length of the houses and the rear gardens. The houses were arranged on an east–west orientation for maximum benefit from the sun (Fig. 3.97); rooms at the front and rear would receive sunshine in the morning and evening, respectively. The quality of light internally was further

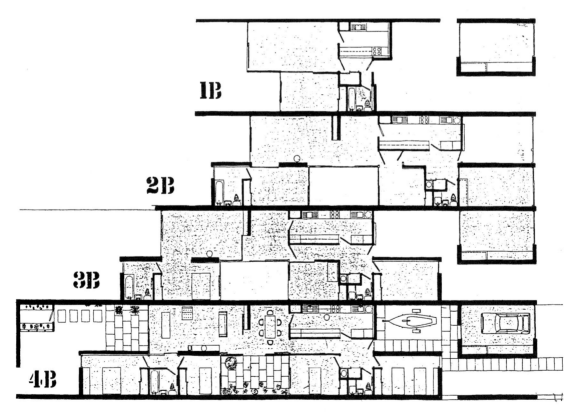

FIGURE 3.96
The Ryde, Hatfield: dwelling plans.

LIVERPOOL JOHN MOORES UNIVERSITY
Aldham Robarts L.R.C.
TEL 0151 231 3701/3634

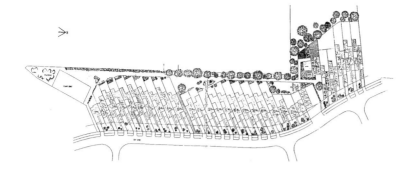

FIGURE 3.97
The Ryde: houses planned on an east–west orientation.

FIGURE 3.98
The Ryde: large windows link the inside with gardens and courtyards.

heightened by the floor to ceiling windows which linked the inside of the houses with the gardens and courts (Fig. 3.98). The design of the interiors attempted to establish an appropriate relationship between areas of common use and private use by parents and by children, i.e. to give members of the family the advantage of community and privacy as described by Serge Chermayeff and Christopher Alexander [2]. Furthermore, the single storey plan and the timber construction within the party walls offered flexibility and adaptability in the use of the space, a principle that has, over 30 years of occupation, been proven to work. The majority of the houses have garages at the front which are large enough to include a workshop space.

The scheme has survived unaltered: (Fig. 3.66) it is a credit to the vision of Michael Bailey, the Cockaigne Housing Company and their architects. *AJ*, 16/11/66, pp. 1207–8; *AJ*, 16/8/72, pp. 365–376; [1] Bailey, M., An experiment in housing, *The Listener*, 6/1/66, pp. 14–15; [2] Chermayeff, S. and Alexander, C., *Community and Privacy: Towards a New Architecture of Humanism; Building Homes*, 6/98, pp. 38–41.

KENT

Span Housing, New Ash Green.
1967–69. Eric Lyons and Partners. R. Longfield.

New Ash Green was the apotheosis of Span's vision, a complete village in the rural countryside

FIGURE 3.99
Unchanged Span housing at New Ash Green.

of Kent. The scheme envisaged a mixture of private housing and housing for rent built by the GLC. Span proceeded to develop the housing for sale and the shopping centre until 1969 when the GLC pulled out of the development, leaving Span in financial difficulties. The plan, approved in 1967, was for a new village with appropriate services and community facilities for between 5000 and 6000 people. The development was divided into a number of small neighbourhoods of around 100 houses. The early Span developments were laid out in a typical Lyons manner with short terraces around landscaped pedestrian spaces with grouped car parking (Fig. 3.99). Today the mono-pitched houses with timber and tiled panels between the party walls remain untouched by time. The benefits of communal maintenance (p. 22) is clearly evident. The landscaping has particularly matured to create a splendid habitat.

The two-level shopping centre clustered around a linear square is thriving, although somewhat in need of the care that Span would have given. After the collapse of Span Developments, the rest of the village was completed by Bovis and Architect/Planners, Barton Wilmore Associates.

AJ, 8/12/71, pp. 1265–1268; *AJ*, 23/7/69, pp. 138–140.

SUSSEX

Diggers and Sea-Saw, Self-build co-operative housing, Brighton.
1995. Architype. R. Brighton.

The Diggers, built by a tenant self-build co-operative on a steeply sloping site, comprises nine detached and semi-detached houses for rent. Housing Association funding came through the South London Family Housing Association (SLFHA) and CHISEL (Co-operative Housing in south-east London). The co-operative became contractors to the developing association, SLFHA, and they earned 'sweat equity' from their labour which could be cashed in when they left, or traded in for additional features in their homes. The Segal method of post-and-frame construction was chosen because of its straightforward design and construction methodology: the breathing walls and the grass roof are developments of the method by Architype.

The houses are grouped around a central green with car parking at the edge of the site. The design exploits the slope of the site with a split-level section which opens out on to south-facing conservatories and balconies (Fig. 3.100 and 3.101). They are extremely well insulated and energy bills in the first year were very low (between £28–58 per year).

FIGURE 3.100
The Diggers: Segal self-build in Brighton.

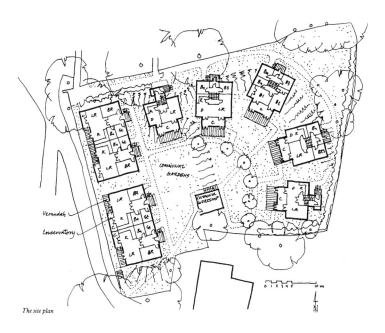

FIGURE 3.101
The Diggers: site layout.

The second scheme, Sea-Saw, is at Kemptown on a site alongside Brighton's racecourse. It comprises twenty-four dwellings which face south across a hill towards the sea. The use of a single type of house was a requirement of the funding housing association, but despite this the conservatories and verandahs offer the tenants ample scope for personalizing their homes.

AJ, 8/6/95, pp. 37–38; *AJ*, 7/11/96, pp. 48–50; *AJ*, 17/7/97, p. 51; *AT*, 2/97, pp. 26–28.

Youthbuild Housing, Diggers Brighton.
1994. Ken Claxton. R. Brighton.

Adjacent to the co-operative housing at the Diggers is a group of single-storey houses built by young people using a similar method of construction (Fig. 3.102). The scheme was created by the Young Builders' Trust (YBT) set up in the early 1990s by Ken Claxton and others. Most participants in YBT's schemes are in the age group 16–18 but the upper limit is 25. Whilst working on the schemes they secure NVQs leading to employment prospects in the building industry and they can obtain a secure home through participating in a project.

The scheme at Diggers was designed to offer a wide range of building skills. The Segal system was used, as this is a relatively simple method of construction which eliminates wet trades. Timber-framed construction also has a psychological benefit in that the early erection of the frame gives the participants the motivation to continue.

Schemes by the YBT in other locations have adopted other approaches including brick masonry construction.

RIBAJ, 12/89, pp. 38–41.

WEST SUSSEX

Broadfield, Crawley New Town.
1982. Phippin Randall & Parkes. R. Crawley.

After 1968 Crawley New Town was expanded by the construction of a new neighbourhood of 5000 people at Broadfield, complete with local shops, library, schools and sports facilities. Within Broadfield, the Guinness Trust developed an 8 hectare (20 acres) site with a mixture of family houses and flats, grouped flats for elderly people and housing for young, single people. The design was based on a highly sophisticated form of sixteen courts of housing (Fig. 3.103) with walls enclosing parking areas. The scheme is served by a road network of four culs-de-sac, tightly designed to give a sense of intimacy and enclosure and to provide public open space at the centre of the scheme. In addition, there is a separate footpath system. The design endeavoured to preserve as many trees as possible, particularly within the courtyards of housing.

RIBA/NFHA, *Housing Association Design*, 1984.

FIGURE 3.102
The Diggers: housing built by young people.

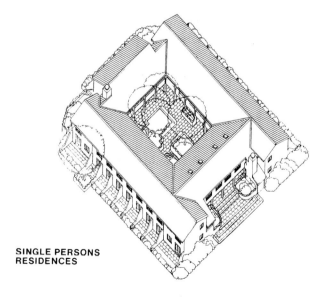

SINGLE PERSONS RESIDENCES

FIGURE 3.103
Broadfield: courtyard of young people's housing.

FIGURE 3.104
Bristol waterfront: WCA warehouse conversion (p. 239).

SOUTH-WEST ENGLAND

BRISTOL

Bristol Docks, conversion of the WCA warehouse, by the Redcliffe Bridge.
1997. Architecton. R. Bristol Temple Meads.

Since the early 1980s Bristol has preserved its waterside heritage through the conversion of former warehouses and other buildings into housing and the construction of related new development on vacant sites.

This Grade II listed warehouse overlooking Bristol's floating harbour was built for the Western Counties Agricultural Co-operative around 1910 and it was one of the first concrete-framed structures built in Bristol (Fig. 3.104). The City Council who owned the building in the 1980s was anxious to see it converted into community housing. The first designs in 1986 were for twenty-eight flats but the scheme built by the Bristol Churches Housing Association increased this to thirty-nine in order to make it viable for a housing association grant. The new design produced twenty-nine one-bedroom flats and ten two-bedroom flats, two of which are for wheelchair use. Four of the additional flats were added through building a lightweight steel and glass structure on the roof, and six more were inserted at dock-side level in space that was previously a public walkway. The diversion of the walkway to a platform over the floating harbour called for considerable perseverance, as the parliamentary order that was required delayed the project by 2 years.

The building had suffered acute problems associated with water penetration, including heavy

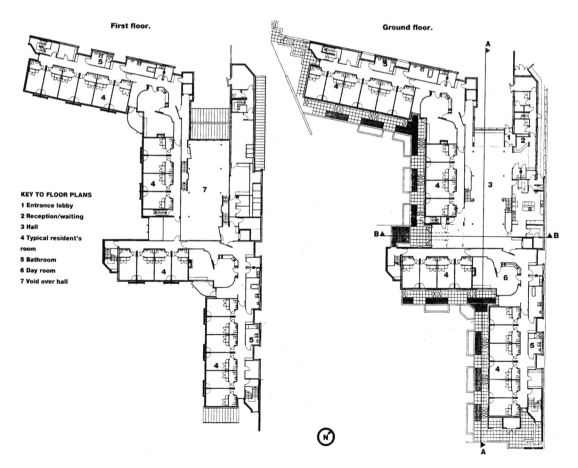

KEY TO FLOOR PLANS
1 Entrance lobby
2 Reception/waiting
3 Hall
4 Typical resident's room
5 Bathroom
6 Day room
7 Void over hall

FIGURE 3.105
Benough's House: floor plans.

carbonization of the internal concrete frame and the distortion of the original cast-iron windows due to severe corrosion. To combat this the structure was extensively repaired and strengthened, and insulated to overcome cold-bridging problems. The building is now a fine illustration of the architectural skill and ingenuity that is required to bring new life to old buildings (*AJ*, 3/7/97, pp. 29–38).

There are interesting groups of housing all round the waterways. An early dockland scheme of merit is **Baltic Wharf**, Cumberland Road (Halliday Meecham Partnership). It is also worth visiting **Ecohome** (1996) at Bristol's Create Centre, Smeaton Road.

Benough's House, Passage Road, Brentry, housing for elderly people.
1996. Fielden Clegg Architects.
R. Bristol Temple Means + local transport

Designed for Orchard Homes, this scheme is a registered nursing and residential home for elderly and frail elderly people, but many residents enjoy a high degree of independence. The most important feature of the design is its plan (Fig. 3.105). As at Bridge Care in Bath, the design focuses on a central dining hall which is a double-height space. Here, however, the forty bed-sitting rooms are grouped in two L-shaped wings, each with its own south-facing day room overlooking the gardens.
RIBAJ, 12/96, pp. 49–54; AJ, *Brick Bulletin*, 6/11/97, pp. 8–9.

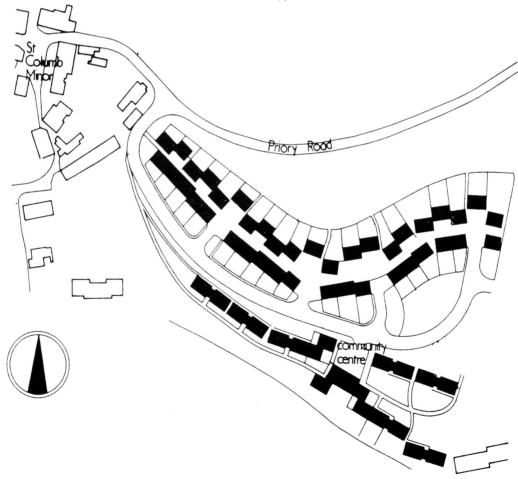

FIGURE 3.106
St Colomb Minor: the site layout reflects the land form and footpath movement.

St Colomb Minor, Priory Road, Newquay.
1977. Feilden and Mawson. R. Newquay.

St Colomb Minor is a small inland Cornish village on rising ground, trapped in the outer fringe of Newquay's suburbs. This local author-ity scheme, comprising a mixture of two- and three-storey houses and flats, was applauded for its strongest and most deliberately designed feature, the pedestrian walkway which re-created the character of a Cornish 'back street' (Fig. 3.106). At some points it is less than 4 m wide and at others it opens out to admit light to courts

FIGURE 3.107
St Colomb Minor: footpath focused on the fourteenth century church.

and access to garages. The new west footpath route frames the splendid pinnacled tower of the fourteenth century church (Fig. 3.107). The concrete block walls are somewhat severe but the overall effect has the feel and the character of the traditional architecture of the area.

AJ, 30/11/77, pp. 1068–69; DOE Housing Design Awards 1978, p. 4.

DORSET

Rural housing, Abbotsbury Glebe, 1992–93, Redlands Farm, Broadwindsor, 1995–96, Corfe, 1997.

Ken Morgan Architects. (Private transport necessary.)

The difficulty of building housing in rural areas has been admirably overcome in a number of recent developments in Dorset villages, notably Abbotsbury, Broadwindsor and Corfe, where schemes with genuine rural quality have been built. In each case the schemes contain a variety of forms and materials that fit well into the village, in marked contrast to so much other residential development that is currently built in the countryside.

The scheme on the eastern edge of the village of **Abbotsbury**, commissioned by the Raglan Housing Association on the Diocesan of Salisbury site, comprises twenty two- and three-bedroom rented and shared-equity houses and eight four-bedroom houses for sale. They were designed to be built in local stone, some finished with render, with a combination of thatch and slate roofs, all with chimneys (Fig. 3.108). At the entrance to the scheme, a terrace built at an angle fronts on to the main village road. Behind this, the rest of the houses are grouped along a new

FIGURE 3.108
Rural housing at Abbotsbury Glebe.

FIGURE 3.109
*Abbotsbury Glebe: axonometric
drawing.*

street and around a village square. The design
and detailing of the roads and footpaths reflect
the typical village wall-to-wall, hard-surfaced
space, an effect which was achieved through
persuading the highway engineers to deviate from
their rule-book (Fig. 3.109).

Cross-subsidy was essential to secure affordable rents. The builder/developer produced the
social elements of the scheme for a price specified
by the housing association and the Diocese. In
return, the land for the freehold element was sold
to the developer for a price at the bottom of the
local market rate. An overriding condition was that
the houses should only be occupied by local people
(*Building Homes*, 14/6/91, pp. 20–22).

The scheme at **Broadwindsor** (Fig. 1.22),
which reflects the local village vernacular of
stone, rendering, thatch and slate, also benefited
from cross-subsidy. It contains fourteen two- and
three-bedroom houses for rent, twenty-six two-,

three- and four-bedroom houses for sale and one
house for the vendor. The scheme links two
existing roads in the village with a new street,
contrary to the highway engineer's preference for
culs-de-sac.

A similar scheme at **Corfe**, built by the
Corfe Castle Charities, received an award from
the Civic Trust in the special rural housing
category.

Poundbury, by Dorchester.
*Started 1993. Developer, Duchy of Cornwall;
master planner, Leon Krier; coordinating architect,
Percy Thomas Partnership, Bristol. R. Dorchester.*

The new housing at Poundbury on the western
edge of Dorchester has been the focus of considerable debate due to the involvement of HRH,

Figure 3.110
Poundbury: a rekindling of the traditional town street.

the Prince of Wales. Leon Krier's master plan is based on a Continental urban grid of boulevards laid out in a classical manner. The total development is projected to contain some 3000 dwellings with neighbourhoods centred on a formal square surrounded by civic buildings designed in the manner of Greek temples and Italian Renaissance towers. A mixed-use settlement of housing, workshops, employment and shopping is envisaged, in which the housing will all be within walking distance of the communal facilities. The village will take 25 years to build which its promoters consider will enable it to grow organically.

The first phase contains 250 dwellings, 50 per cent of which are owned by the Guinness Trust. The design of the housing reflects urban village principles. Fifteen or more architects have been involved, each being responsible for a small area only, to avoid an estate image. Most of them have succeeded in creating authenticity but the design is still condemned as pastiche (Fig. 3.110).

However, the layout is most innovative (Fig. 3.111). An important feature is how the road system 'engages' traffic. Instead of excluding or calming traffic, it is 'civilized' within a permeable layout of urban spaces of human scale which avoid long vistas that allow drivers to accelerate. Junctions have tight

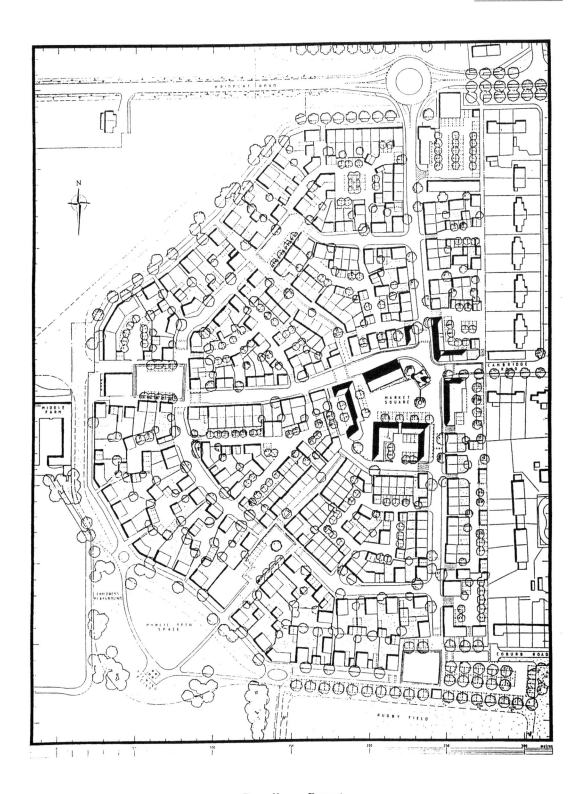

Poundbury, Dorset

Figure 3.111
Poundbury: layout of first phase.

radii to reduce speeds, and limited sight-lines make drivers slow down or stop. Car parking and garages for two spaces per dwelling plus visitor parking is provided by a combination of street parking on wider roads and garages/parking courtyards at the rear of the houses.

RIBAJ, 11/95, pp. 6–11; Ibid., p. 7; *B*, 159/89, issue 37, p. 60; *Building to Last*, p. 36.

Walpole Court, Puddletown, housing for elderly people.
1985. Sidell Gibson Partnership. R. Dorchester.

The inspiration for the English Courtyard Association came in the mid-1970s from Noel Shuttleworth, searching for accommodation for his widowed mother. He could not find a place of reasonable size situated in pleasant surroundings, near to shops and amenities, where she could remain independent, feel secure and receive emergency help, that could be met from a modest fixed income. Walpole Court is one of nineteen developments built by him since that time, many of which have received housing design awards.

The design is based on the traditional courtyard plan of almshouses, consisting of terraces and courts of two-storey cottages and flats. The architecture blends with the traditional local vernacular and materials (Fig. 3.112). The grounds are landscaped to create the atmosphere of a country house garden or college courtyard. These are maintained by a couple employed as warden and caretaker who live in a flat near the entrance to the scheme.

Walpole Court contains twenty-three two- to three-bedroom cottages and flats. The first phase of development is centred on the conversion of a beautiful mellow brick and stone courtyard of

FIGURE 3.112
Walpole Court: traditional almshouse image.

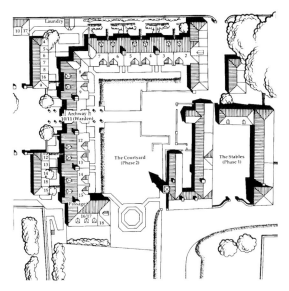

FIGURE 3.113
Walpole Court: site layout.

nineteenth century cottages and stables, with bell tower and spire. Approached from Orford Street, the second phase and main part of the project consists of new two-storey cottages on two sides of a garden (Fig. 3.113); the third side of the court-yard is formed by phase 1. Each of the new cottages offers a high degree of flexibility of use, depending upon the extent of physical disability of the occupant(s). Ground floors have a shower/WC and stairs which accommodate stairlifts, and give several choices of living arrangements as people become more frail; the design also allows for live-in help. All windows are set to lower level to allow a good view out when sitting down.
AR, 10/85, pp. 56–61; *B*, 30/10/87, pp. 30–35.

SOMERSET

Bridge Care, sheltered housing for elderly people, St John's Road, Bath.
1991. Fielden Clegg Architects. R. Bath.

Bridge Care is a residential home for thirty-two frail elderly people, built on a site overlooking the River Avon. The design uses the slope of

the site, with the main entrance at the middle level leading to two storeys above and one below raised on columns above the flood plain on the river side. The bedrooms are in two converging terraces linked to a double-height communal hall/dining area which opens out to a south-facing garden through a conservatory (Fig.

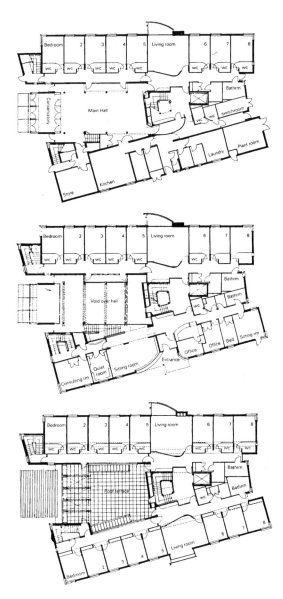

FIGURE 3.114
Bridge Care: floor plans.

FIGURE 3.115
Bridge Care sheltered housing for elderly people: lunch-time in the communal hall/dining area.

3.114). The space of the hall could be likened to a foyer of a hotel or a great hall of a country house. It is spacious but not overwhelming, colourful and full of light. There are eight bedrooms in each residential terrace and a semi-private day room which incorporates a dining area (Fig. 3.115) and kitchenette, a sitting space around a fireplace and a balcony overlooking the river. The accommodation also includes specialist assisted bath/shower rooms, a library, chapel, laundry and kitchen and consulting and treatment facilities.

Most noticeable is the strong sense of caring that exists between the church community who run the building, many on a voluntary basis, and the residents. The building helps create the environment in which this atmosphere can flour-

ish and everyone appreciates the image which the architects have created.

Archetype, 1/94, pp. 35–38; *AJ*, 20/5/92, pp. 30–45.

WILTSHIRE

Town centre regeneration, Calne.
1996. Aaron Evans Associates. R. Chippenham (private transport recommended).

The demolition in 1983 of a large factory in the centre of Calne created a vacant site of 2.5 hectares (6.2 acres). The North Wiltshire District Council, wishing to see the land used for a new town centre, established the Calne Project, a

FIGURE 3.116
Urban regeneration in Calne.

FIGURE 3.117
The Ropewalk blends into its hillside setting.

partnership between the County, District and Town Councils, English Heritage, local businesses and voluntary organizations. ARC Developments, with Aaron Evans, were appointed in 1989 to develop proposals for the bank site and a further two vacant central area sites.

In 1993 funding was eventually secured from the Housing Corporation by a partnership between the District Council, the Knightsbridge Housing Association and Cowlin Developments. The outcome is a delightful scheme of twenty-two houses, six flats, three shop units and a public car park, designed in a simple terraced form fronting the existing streets. It is built with a variety of materials including Bath stone, red stock bricks, slate, leadwork and clay single Roman tiles. Traditional elements of dormers, balconies, string courses, stone and brick head and sill detailing, with a mixture of traditional and sash cottage-style windows, successfully demon-

strates how to incorporate new development into an old town conservation area (Fig. 3.116).
AJ, 7/11/96, pp. 34–35.

The Ropewalk, Newtown, Bradford-on-Avon.
1988. Fielden Clegg Design.
R. Bradford-on-Avon.

The Ropewalk is situated on the hillside near the town centre, immediately above Bradford-on-Avon's ancient Saxon church (Fig. 3.117). Planning permission had been granted for four houses built of local materials, but the architects convinced the planners and Bradford Preservation Trust that their design for a two- and three-storey building with a varied roof-line was preferable. Its mixed stone facades with ashlar stone and clay roof tiles blend into the hillside. The compact form of the building enabled the mature

FIGURE 3.118
*Earls Manor Court:
excellent use of local
building materials.*

trees to be retained and gave space for superbly planted gardens.
RIBAJ, 12/89, p. 9; Housing Design Awards, 1989, A *Building* Publication, pp. 18–22.

Earls Manor Court, Winterbourne Earls, English Courtyard Association.
1992. Sidell Gibson Partnership. R. Salisbury (private transport recommended.)

This delightful scheme consists of eight two-bedroom flats, eight two-bedroom cottages, four three-bedroom cottages and a warden's flat. These are grouped around two courtyard gardens linked by open archways (Fig. 3.118). A village scale is created by the superb use of the long, low roof and dormers, and of local materials including brick, stone, flint decoration and clay tiles.

Earls Manor Court serves the top end of the housing market. Nevertheless, it has many details of design and management which could well be incorporated more widely into housing for elderly people. The dwellings are spacious and attractive to people often moving from larger houses. The space is within the dwellings rather than in communal meeting rooms and the residents clearly prefer to meet their neighbours and entertain in their own homes. The gardens are immaculately cared for by the warden's husband, which has proved preferable to contract maintenance. The sense of care by the warden is clearly evident. Residents receive help until they can no longer look after themselves, when alternative living arrangements are made by the resident's relatives or by the Association.
Housing Design Awards 1993, A *Building* Publication, 11/93, p. 17.

FIGURE 3.119
The Mews, Aldwark; compact housing within York's city walls (p. 263).

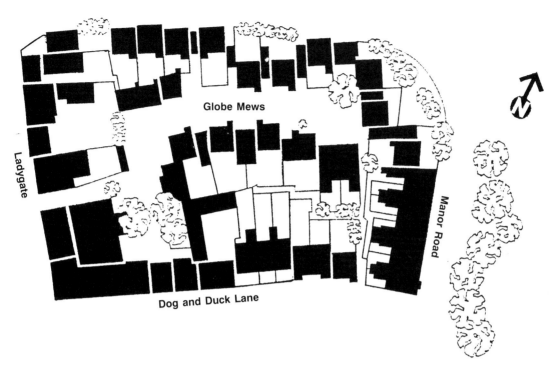

FIGURE 3.120
The Ropewalk nestles comfortably in the hillside above the town centre.

YORKSHIRE AND HUMBERSIDE

BEVERLEY

Globe Mews, Beverley.
1982. David Ruffle Associates. R. Beverley.

The central area of the small market town of Beverley possesses a number of extremely well designed private and housing association developments which contrast markedly with the speculative housebuilders' estates on the periphery. Two schemes are described but there are several more on other sites in the town.

Globe Mews, commissioned by Tallishire Limited, demonstrates that there is sound commercial potential in developing urban sites with compact high density housing for sale (Figs 3.120 and 3.121). The scheme reflects an effective brief prepared by the local Planning Department and the requirements of the developer who

FIGURE 3.121
Beverley: Globe Mews fronting Dog and Duck Lane.

selected the Essex architect after seeing a programme on TV concerning the County's Design Guide. The houses are a mixture of two and three storeys, grouped around a tight mews court. Each house has its own small walled garden at the rear. The massing of the buildings and the varied roof-line, combined with the screen walls and garages, is very much in scale and character with its location. The use of integral garages has enabled a high density of twenty-nine dwellings per acre to be achieved with a car parking provision of two spaces per dwelling.

DOE/RIBA/NHBC, Housing Design Awards 1983, p. 10.

FIGURE 3.122
Beverley: St Andrew Street Co-operative sheltered housing.

St Andrew Street, Beverley, Co-operative sheltered housing.
1987. Crease Strickland Edmunds. R. Beverley.

Faced with the prospect of wholesale clearance of their housing located in streets near to Beverley Minster, the remaining residents of St Andrew Street in 1977 formed themselves into the St Andrew Street Co-operative Ltd Housing Association with the aim of revitalizing their community.

It was eventually decided to improve the best of the existing run down nineteenth century terraces and to demolish the worst to make way for new houses. Land adjacent to the Minster was acquired from the council for additional new building to expand the Association into a viable self-sufficient body and help to further the council's conservation area objectives. New housing was built but only after a fierce contest and a public inquiry on whether it was right to build on the open land in front of Beverley Minster (Fig. 3.122).

The scheme comprises thirty-six two-storey flats, a warden's house and a common room. In addition, there are eleven two- and three-storey houses with five general needs flats located to the east of St Andrew Street. The housing is beautifully designed around block-paved roads, courts and a green at the rear. The use of traditional Yorkshire brick and tile detailing is particularly well handled.

LEEDS

Chapel Allerton town street redevelopment, Leeds 7.
1970. Leeds City Architects.
R. Leeds + local transport.

This small scheme in an old village that was encompassed long ago by the city of Leeds contrasted greatly to much of the other local authority housing built at that time. The houses now appear dated but at the time the scheme was much admired, particularly the layout (Fig. 3.123). The previous houses were cleared as part

of the city's slum clearance programme but several fine buildings remained on the periphery of the site, including the Wesleyan Sunday School, the Nags Head hotel, Leak Cottage and The Old House.

The mix for the thirty-eight houses was typical of the time – 25 per cent one bedroom, 45 per cent two bedroom and 30 per cent three bedroom. Fortunately, the housing cost yardstick allowed garages to be provided on a one for one basis. A key feature of the scheme was the use of the former Town Street for pedestrians only, leading to an existing shopping centre to the west and to the local primary school. This was made possible by the construction of three new roads around the site. An informal layout of dark brick clad houses follows the line of the curved pedestrian route and opens out into well proportioned squares echoing the quiet atmosphere of the former village.
AJ, 1/12/71, pp. 1245–1247.

The Calls, Riverside, Leeds city centre.
Various architects. R. Leeds.

A principal focus of attention for the Leeds Urban Development Corporation during the mid 1990s was the regeneration of the riverside area – the Calls – below the railway. This was achieved through a combination of warehouse refurbishment and conversion into housing, the construction of new housing, and the creation of offices, studios, restaurants, a hotel and the new Armories Museum. The result is a most varied and lively riverside scene (Fig. 1.124).
AJ, 22/5/97, p. 33.

Gledhow Bank Eco-Housing.
1997. Jonathan Lindh. R. Leeds.

The Gledhow Bank Eco-Housing in Chapel Allerton, north Leeds, is a privately funded development comprising a terrace of three self-built houses. Its site is a narrow piece of steeply

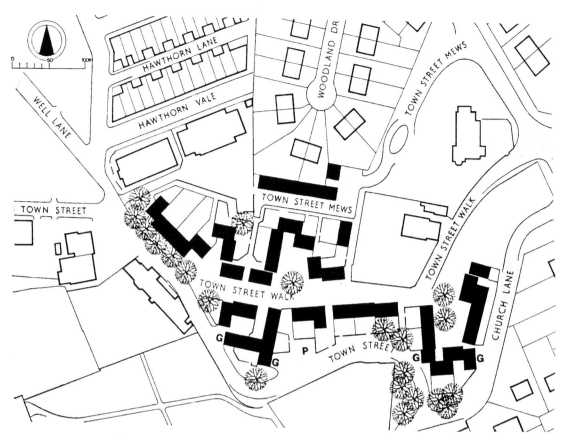

FIGURE 3.123
Chapel Allerton Town Street development.

FIGURE 3.124
The Calls.

sloping land wedged between two large Edwardian villas. The three families who built the houses all knew each other before starting and jointly purchased the site, taking out individual mortgages with the Ecology Building Society.

The houses were designed to maximize energy efficiency and to use recyclable or renewable materials and minimize the use of toxic materials. The Segal system was adopted as the small footprint minimized the impact of the building on ground ecology. Its key feature is that the houses are not connected to the water mains. Instead, each house operates its own autonomous three-pipe system: drinking water is derived from rain collected from the roof; treated grey water is used for bathing and washing; and black waste does not enter the water system, but is treated in the compost toilets. The water system minimizes electricity consumption from pumps and other appliances.

RIBA, *Building Homes as if Tomorrow Mattered*, 1997, p. 30.

KINGSTON UPON HULL

North Hull Housing Action Trust, Greenwood Avenue.

Brown, Smith Baker and Partners (Hull), Hull City Council Technical Services Department, Gammond Evans Crichton Ltd, Hurd Rollands Partnership, The Wilkinson Hindle Halsall and Lloyd Partnership. 1999. R. Hull Paragon.

A most significant achievement for Hull in the 1990s was the designation in 1992 of the first Housing Action Trust in Britain in the North Hull Estate. Its task was to improve 2000 cottage-style, inter-war houses and to develop approaches to social and economic regeneration. Tenants participated extensively in the design process, and the refurbishment of the houses and environment has been implemented to a very high standard (Fig. 3.125). In addition to the mandatory improvements – reroofing, new doors and windows, damp-proof courses, dry-lining internally, etc. – most tenants

FIGURE 3.125
North Hull HAT: transformation of an inter-war cottage estate.

were offered the opportunity to select their own additional improvements from a menu of choices, ranging from rear porches, to french windows, wall lights, higher quality kitchen units, and many more. Each item was valued on a points system and the choice could be made up to an agreed level. A small number of new houses were also built to accommodate young people and families who were living with their parents and could not be housed in existing properties.

The physical improvements were supported by social and economic initiatives to raise the level of personal awareness, health and self-esteem, particularly on the part of women. Training and education to enable people to acquire employment skills and education opportunities were made available. Some local people worked for the contractors or for the HAT itself. The 'exit strategy' includes the establishment of a

Community Development Trust. This is supported by a sinking fund, the interest from which will be used to continue the social/economic development and to ensure the sustainability of the investment.

SHEFFIELD

Park Hill/Hyde Park, Duke Street.
1961. Sheffield City Architects.
R. Sheffield Midland.

Park Hill introduced Britain to deck access flats and to 'streets in the sky' (p. 14). The site was considered suitable for high density, multi-storey housing because it was close to the city centre and the topography allowed scope for planning

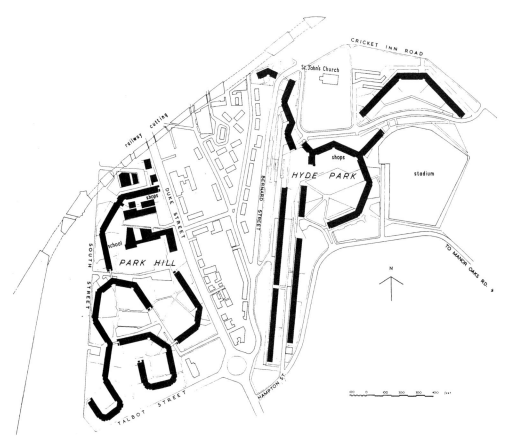

FIGURE 3.126
Park Hill and Hyde Park. [From Sheffield City Council, Ten Years of Housing, p.39.]

high flats with ample light, air and magnificent views. The scheme comprised 495 flats and 500 maisonettes built at an average density (net for housing) of approximately fifty-six dwellings per acre (138 dw/ha) (Fig. 3.126). The terraces of dwellings were arranged to create a series of large interlocking courtyards containing children's play spaces, kick-about areas, seating places etc. At the bottom end of the site is the shopping centre and the primary school.

The community support given to people at the beginning had a long-term benefit. Whole streets of people were transferred from the old to the new housing which meant that everyone knew their neighbours. People were positively helped to settle in and social groups were set up. During its early years, Park Hill was undoubtedly a show-piece of social housing.

A second scheme followed in the mid 1960s – **Hyde Park**, built on the higher ground above Park Hill. This contained 1313 flats and maisonettes at a density of forty-six dwellings per acre (114 dw/ha) (160 persons per acre or 395 per hectare). The development was in two distinct parts, two long terraces of four person flats with six-person maisonettes above which follow the contours, and a deck access scheme up to eighteen storeys. It was likened to an Italian hill town but was never as successful as Park Hill.

During the early 1990s most of Hyde Park was demolished except Castle Court (p. 260). The two long terraces were overclad in colourful brickwork. The council now has plans to refurbish Park Hill which English Heritage propose should be listed Grade II*.

Sheffield City Council, *Ten Years of Housing in Sheffield*, 4/62 p. 38; *B*, 22/4/55, p. 669; *AR*, 12/61, pp. 405; *RIBAJ*, 12/62, no.12, pp. 447–471; *AJ*, 20/8/69, p. 465; *RIBAJ*, 10/95, pp. 52–60; EH, p. 3.

Gleadless Valley, Blackstock Road and others.
Early 1960s. Sheffield City Architects. R. Sheffield Midland.

Gleadless Valley is a complete example of a 1950s/early 1960s mixed development scheme.

Started in 1955, the estate was planned to accommodate some 17 000 people in 4451 dwellings. The site was divided naturally into three neighbourhoods by a large area of woodland but linked by a footpath system. Each neighbourhood was provided with its own junior and infant school and shopping centre and other communal facilities (Fig. 3.127).

The general pattern of development included two-storey houses, a three-storey block of flats, and four- and six-storey maisonettes. Three thirteen-storey tower blocks crowned the hilltop at Herdings and formed the architectural climax of the development. Its layout is a model for hillside housing, demonstrating many ways of building on steep slopes. The form of the housing arranged along contours was determined by the extent of the slope. On very steep slopes, for example Fleury Road, completed in 1962, 'upside-down' houses were built with the living room on the first floor and the bedrooms below. Six-storey maisonettes had bridge access to an intermediate level entrance to reduce the walk up distance. On less severe slopes, houses with entrance at mezzanine level were developed. Where houses were arranged down the contours, they were generally narrow-fronted to minimise the drop between dwellings. On very steep slopes, they were staggered to allow footpaths to run diagonal with the contours.

The estate is now in need of refurbishment but it remains a popular place in which to live.

Fleury Road: *AJ*, 20/8/69, p. 466.

Paxton Court, self-build low energy housing, Gleadless Netherspring, Cedric Green.
Mid-1980s. R. Sheffield Midland.

This group of ten houses clustered round a small, brick-paved court on a steep slope in Gleadless came about as the result of the persistence of a group of people to build themselves their own low energy housing. The research at Sheffield University by architect Cedric Green had led to the construction of the experimental

FIGURE 3.127
Hillside housing at Gleadless Valley, Sheffield.

'shed' which enabled him to prove the viability of solar energy. This was transferred to the site to form a workshop. The construction reflected the skills of the group which included two bricklayers. This enabled the external walls to be of brick but much of the construction is timber framed. The south-facing conservatories were important to the total energy saving system (Fig. 3.128).

The site was developed house by house by the whole group working together. As each house was completed and occupied another mortgage was obtained. In this way they were able to avoid bridging loans during the construction stage.

Castle Court, young people's housing, St John's Road.
1993. DBS Architects. R. Sheffield Midland.

The preparation in the early 1990s for the World Student Games in Sheffield provided a focus for the building of new sports buildings in the city. It also enabled Northern Counties Housing Association to refurbish and convert into housing for young people part of the Hyde Park flats that had not been knocked down.

The new colourful overcladding completely encases the former concrete structure (Fig. 3.129). The 355 flats were reduced to 311 and on the

FIGURE 3.128
Paxton Court: low energy, self-build housing.

FIGURE 3.129
Castle Court: new life for part of the Park Hill flats.

ground floor a small community centre and laundrette were provided. The lifts were made graffiti-proof and the decks became enclosed. Corridors were carpeted from where some spectacular views over Sheffield can be enjoyed during all weathers. A single entrance, supervised 24 hours a day, was created and security cameras and pass-key systems were installed. The site around the block was extensively planted to create semi-private space belonging to the building.

Housing Design Awards 1993, A *Building* Publication, 11/93, no. p. 13.

SKIPTON

Old Bridge Mews, Belmont Wharf, off Belmont Road, Skipton.
Wales, Wales and Rawson. 1997.
R. Skipton.

This National Housing Design Award winning scheme of 1997 overlooks the Leeds to Liverpool Canal in the centre of Skipton. The tallest building by far in the complex is the Victoria Mill, constructed in 1848, which was converted into thirty-one one- and two-bedroom apartments. Around the mill are three clusters of new two- and three-storey town houses built in the same local stone. Cars are parked within the ground floor of the mill, and garages are integral with the houses. In this way, the need to accommodate a high level of car parking has been turned to great advantage by using the fall of the site to create first floor links between the mill and raised internal garden courts amongst the housing. A curving bridge and the balconies are all beautifully detailed to reflect the canal-side location (Fig. 3.130).

The development was undertaken by a small local family firm of developer/builders, Raven Homes of Ilkley, using local craftsmen and suppliers. The work, which has been continuous, started in 1988 and the last house in the whole development was not completed until 9 years later. The scheme is embedded into the urban fabric of the town and it appears timeless. It is surely the kind of development that should be

FIGURE 3.130
Old Bridge Mews, Skipton.

encouraged elsewhere to meet the increasing need for more housing.

AJ, 11/7/97, p. 51; *BD*, 11/7/97, p. 4.

YORK

New Earswick, 1901+ Parker Unwin refurbishment.
1966. The Louis de Soissons Partnership. R. York + local transport.

New Earswick began in 1901 when Joseph Rowntree purchased an estate of 150 acres (60 ha) near his cocoa factory, some 3 miles north of York. Here, he and his architects, Parker and Unwin, built the first stages of a new village which has continued to be developed up to the present day.

Although the site was flat, the planning of the village took full advantage of the natural features on the site. Trees and hedgerows were preserved but the sensitivity of the design is best seen to the south-east of the site where the houses follow the line of the brook. Unwin believed that the layout of the houses should be free from the constraints of the street pattern. Consequently, pedestrian paths weave their way through the housing to the village green, around which are arranged the shops, school, church and the Village Institute (the Folk Hall). The first cottages were full of picturesque interest with long, low, red pantiled roofs overhanging walls finished with rough-cast render. After 1918, the need for severe economies resulted in much simplified designs but despite this the village has a strong sense of identity due in no small part to Parker and Unwin's plan and landscaping treatment which ties the whole village together.

In the late 1960s major refurbishment took place which included bringing the houses up to Parker Morris standards, more easily accommodating the motor car and landscaping the open spaces between the houses. The road and footpath pattern separated pedestrians from vehicles along Radburn lines in order to increase accommodation for motor cars. This considerably enhanced the quality of the village, except that many of the original chimney stacks were removed. Development is continuing at the present day, with recently completed lifetime homes and new groups of elderly people's housing.
AR, 60/78, pp. 327–332.

Lifetime Homes, Alderway, Conifer Close, Spruce Close, Jasmine & Acub Close, New Earswick.
1996. Jane Darbyshire & David Kendall Ltd. R. York + local transport.

Jane Darbyshire's extension to New Earswick was based on a thorough study of both the principles behind the original designs of Parker and Unwin and the improvements made in the late 1960s. The proposals comprised eighty-nine dwellings in a mixture of two-storey houses and flats and bungalows. These are clustered around carefully landscaped, shared open spaces and a linear

village green which creates a focus for the development.

The layout reflects the Radburn principles which had been adopted for the environmental improvements in the 1960s (Fig. 3.131). These resulted in housing fronting on to pedestrian routes but clustered around small, secluded culs-de-sac which give access to the rear of the properties. This separation of pedestrians and vehicles had worked in the case of the 1960s refurbishment. In the new development the houses are generally semi-detached with a gated private outdoor link from front to rear. This, together with the careful location of visitor parking at the interfaces between road and pedestrian routes, avoids any misunderstanding of front and back.

All dwellings are designed to 'Lifetime Homes' standards (p. 31) to be accessible and adaptable to the needs of the occupiers throughout their lifetimes (Fig. 3.132). The houses are simply designed using traditional materials – clay pantiles and Yorkshire slop-moulded bricks – giving an intimate scale with low eaves-lines and sheltering porches.

The Mews, Aldwark, private sector housing on an infill site.
1980. Shepherd Design Group. R. York.

In his report on the planning of York, published in 1971, Lord Esher considered that one of the most important proposals for the future of the city was that it should encourage private housing to return to the historic core, confirming that York was a place in which people wanted to live as well as work and visit. Since then the city has had little difficulty attracting developers, most of whom have risen to the occasion in terms of the quality of the design approach, which has strengthened the urban fabric of the city.

One of the pioneering schemes, and still one of the most successful, is at Aldwark and can best be seen by walking around the city walls (Fig. 3.119). It was built by Shepherds of York and comprises thirty-four two-storey houses grouped

NEW EARSWICK PHASE V

FIGURE 3.131
*Lifetime homes, New Earswick: note
the Radburn layout.*

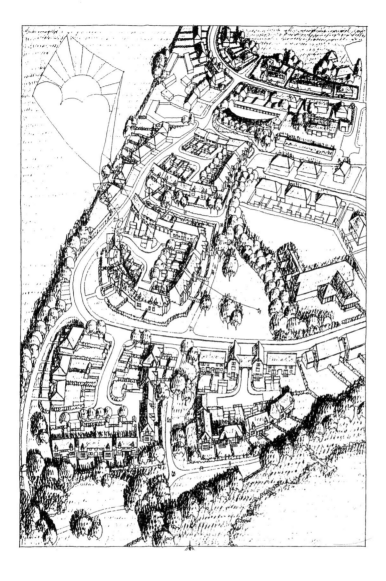

into semi-detached and short terraces around two linked mews courts off Aldwark. The resulting development, with its clay pantiles, red slop-moulded bricks and concrete pavior mews courts, has produced a piece of urban environment of considerable quality, which has been carefully nurtured over the years by the residents' own planting at the front of their houses.
DOE/RIBA/NHBC, Housing Design Awards 1981, pp. 10–11.

Bretgate/Walmgate, infill housing.
1982. York University Design Unit. R. York.

From the 1960s to early 1980s York University's Design Unit produced some excellent housing schemes for the main campus at Heslington and for sites in the city centre. This is one of the finest examples. Commissioned by the York Housing Association Ltd, the fifty-three flats

FIGURE 3.132
*Lifetime homes:
three-bedroom house.*

GROUND FLOOR PLAN

replaced an area of slum housing within the city walls and was designed for elderly and single people.

The housing was built on the street boundaries of the site, which enabled a large, internal, block-paved courtyard to be created. This provides space for car parking but the surface treatment of block paving, which matches the brickwork of the housing, gives the space a very pedestrian feel. This is emphasized by limiting entrance into the court to a few access points only. The now mature trees were very carefully located to avoid overshadowing in the courtyard. These, together with the simple railings around front gardens and other items of street furniture, add up to a most pleasant environment.

The design of the housing exploited the use of the roof-space which extends in some cases above two upper storeys and incorporates inset balconies with a sunny orientation. This adds to

the sense of friendliness in the courtyard and has been a great success (Fig. 3.133).
DOE/RIBA/NHBC, Housing Design Awards 1983, p. 44.

FIGURE 3.133
Bretgate, York: compact housing within the city walls.

FIGURE 4.1
The promenade, Swansea Maritime Village (p. 271).

| CHAPTER FOUR |

Wales

1 Caernarvon and
  Merionethshire
2 Cardiff
3 Gwent
4 Swansea

FIGURE 4.2
Wales: location of schemes

CAERNARVON AND MERIONETHSHIRE

Holiday Housing, Porthmadog.
1974. Philips/Cutler/Philips/Troy. R. Porthmadog.

Whilst this scheme mainly provides second homes, its design was highly influential, particularly the dense grouping of the buildings in the wild natural landscape (Fig. 4.3). Initially the design caused controversy from both the public and the local planning authority, but when built it became accepted and even admired. Clough Williams-Ellis, whose Portmerion is just round the corner, commented that these little harbour houses are 'special' in design....the saw-tooth skyline of their roofs, alternately pitched this way and that in a single span, is fidgety, yes, but becomes interesting and then acceptable as one recovers from the initial shock'.
AJ, 18/9/74, pp. 650–653.

LIVERPOOL JOHN MOORES UNIVERSITY
Aldham Roberts L.R.C.
TEL. 0151 231 3701/3634

FIGURE 4.3
Porthmadog: harbour housing amongst the Welsh Hills. The photo was taken when the houses had just been completed.

CARDIFF

Cardiff Bay regeneration.
*1987. Regeneration strategy, Llewelyn-Davies
Planning; architects as mentioned. R. Cardiff
Central.*

In 1987, the Cardiff Bay Urban Development
Corporation commissioned Llewelyn-Davies
Planning to produce an overall 'regeneration
strategy'. The focus of this was the construction
of a barrage across the entrance to the bay to
create a freshwater lake around which the development would take place. The housing proposals
were for 6000 new houses to be built and 2000
to be refurbished. A substantial proportion of the
25 per cent social housing was to meet special
needs, particularly for single and elderly people
in existing communities, through partnership
arrangements with housing associations.

The first completions were at **Atlantic
Wharf** (Fig. 4.4) where a number of very fine
nineteenth century warehouses were refurbished
and converted into housing (Fig. 4.4). The most
interesting of the recent schemes is **Adventurers'**

FIGURE 4.4
*Cardiff Bay: conversion into housing of the 1893 Spillers &
Bakers Ltd warehouse at Atlantic Wharf.*

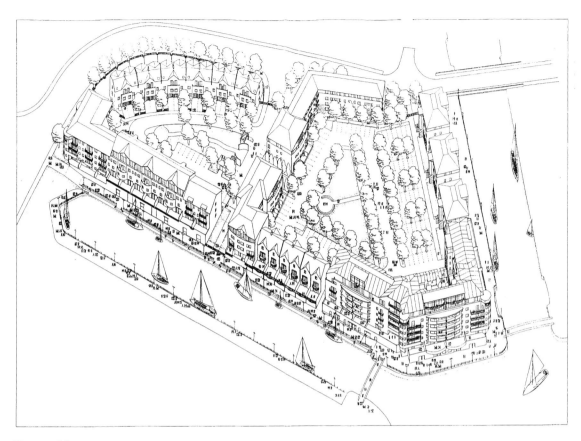

FIGURE 4.5
Adventurers' Quay: design drawings by Richard Reid.

FIGURE 4.6
Penarth Haven.

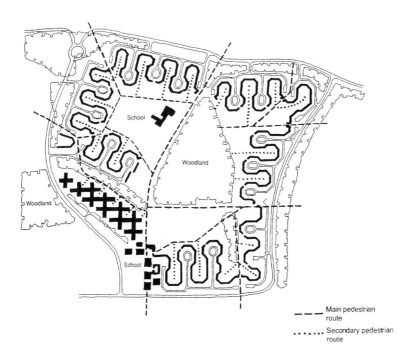

FIGURE 4.7
Duffryn: perimeter housing.
[Drawing from Colquhoun, I. and
Fauset, P.G., Housing Design in
Practice, *p. 53.]*

Quay (design: Richard Reid; second stage, Osborne V. Webb and Partners), a mixture of town houses and flats located on a prominent point at Roath Basin (Pierhead Street) (Fig. 4.5). **Penarth Haven** (Halliday Meecham), across the bay, is a pleasant waterfront scheme of two- and three-storey town houses and flats designed around the former dock system (Fig. 4.6).

GWENT

Duffryn, Lighthouse Road, Newport.
1978. MacCormac & Jamieson.
R. Newport + local transport.

This scheme of some 1000 prefabricated timber-framed dwellings commissioned by Newport Borough Council was significant in that it gave MacCormac and Jamieson the opportunity to further develop their ideas of perimeter housing beyond the scheme at Pollards Hill (p. 110).

At Duffryn, the housing was arranged around the perimeter of the old park of Trede-

gar House (Fig. 4.7). The layout of the wide-fronted house has a strong geometry of 45 degree angles and splayed house plans to utilize the corners. The distributor roads feed the perimeter road, off which short culs-de-sac serve the housing. This arrangement achieved a high density of 175 persons per acre (433/ha) whilst preserving the woodland and enabling land to be available in the centre for a school and open space. The architects used three kinds of brick to provide variety but this does not offset the enormity of the scheme.

AR, 1/76, p. 11; *AJ*, 10/8/77, pp. 247–8; *AR*, 4/80, pp. 205–214.

SWANSEA

Maritime Village, Swansea.
1975+. R. Swansea.

Swansea was the first industrial seaport in the UK to set about solving its problems of dockland and industrial blight in a comprehensive way. It did so without an Urban Development Corporation or any other form of direct government intervention. Maximum benefit was, however, taken of South Wales' special economic status with respect to government aid, but success came entirely from public initiative as the City Council during the 1980s managed to exploit every form of public finance and to seek effective partnership arrangements with the private sector. The scheme also benefited from the City Council ownership of most of the land which simplified the planning process and the phasing of the infrastructure works.

Among the first buildings to be completed in 1975 was a new leisure centre and fifty-four local authority houses. The Marina opened in 1982 and private sector developments quickly followed. Today, in addition to over 1000 new dwellings, the Village has a conference hotel, a food store, offices, shops, restaurants, an art gallery, a hostel, a boat club and a multi-storey car park. The development has created some fine urban townscape and architecture, and what was once a derelict dock and industrial area has been transformed to become a major asset for the city. Colquhoun, I., *Urban Regeneration*, pp. 97–98.

Abernethy Quay/Ferrara Square, off Trawler Road (1986). Burgess Partnership). This group of 256 flats is situated on the southern side of the Maritime Village between South Dock on the west and the Tawe Basin on the east. It was a joint venture between the developers, Kingdomwide, who provided 223 one- and two-bedroom flats for sale and the Family Housing Association who funded thirty-three single-person flats for rent. Built in three- and four-storey blocks, they are grouped to create small, semi-public squares and walkways around the edge of the docks. Steel balconies are juxtaposed with bright blue and red cladding, brick and blockwork. The result is typical but neat dockland architecture.

Ferrara Quay/Marina Walk, off Trawler Road (1988). Halliday Meecham Partnership; craftsmen for the civic artworks: sculptor Philip Chatfield, steel compiler Robert Conybear, potter Martin Williams and wood carver Jack Whitehead.

Overlooking the revitalized sea front and promenade on one side and the south dock marina on the other, Ferrara Quay is one of the most striking of the housing projects. Developed by Lovell Urban Renewal, it comprises 287 dwellings on a site of approximately 5.5 acres (2.2 ha). On the northern boundary the housing, designed to reflect a warehouse silhouette, contains a mixture of one-, two- and three-bedroom flats built into four- and five-storey blocks with basement garaging. In contrast, the dwellings on the south side of the site are three-storey, three- and four-bedroom houses with traditional sea front facades of coloured render (Fig. 4.1).

Two crescents form part of pedestrian links or 'sea gates' between the marina and the sea front. The paved public spaces and walkways are enhanced with contemporary public sculpture. This is a mixture of carved stone panels on the buildings and pieces of individual sculpture which are intended to provide a focus of interest at key points in the development and create a sense of 'genius loci'. The extensive use of timber and metal pergolas and substantial planting have a functional practical purpose in screening the open courtyard car parking.
B, 8/4/88, pp. 54–60.

Penplas Urbanbuild, timber-framed housing, Woodford Road, Penplas.
1991. PCKO Architects.
R. Swansea + local transport.

Swansea City Council provided a site for an American Plywood Association initiative which was intended to demonstrate the benefits of timber-framed housing and to promote its use in urban regeneration. Volume housebuilders were unwilling to support the proposals but Gwalia Housing society agreed to become a co-promoter with the American Plywood Association of an architectural competition.

The winning design produced a modular design solution that allowed for a high degree of repetition in the prefabricated timber frame whilst achieving the potential for considerable

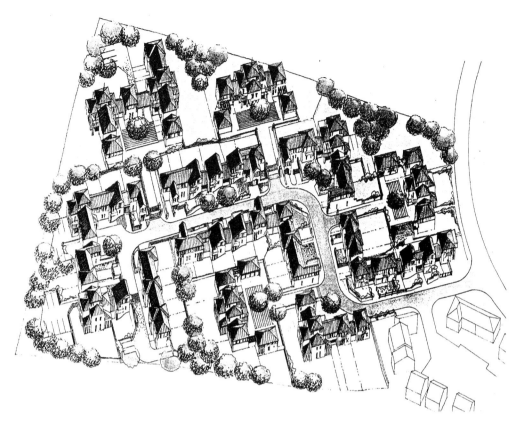

FIGURE 4.8
Penplas Urbanbuild: low energy timber-framed housing.

FIGURE 4.9
Penplas: axonometric drawing of the scheme.

FIGURE 4.9
Honddu Place: passive solar energy housing.

variety of building forms. Family dwellings were developed on a simple generic plan which could produce two- and three-bedroom houses and one- and two-bedroom apartments by simple additions, links, split levels and minor modifications of the basic plan. The system enabled the layout of the dwellings to engage corners, enclose views, create dominant elements, and use sloping site to advantage (Fig. 4.8). The timber construction also gave considerable design freedom in terms of the positioning and shape of the window areas and the lightness of the timber cladding in the upper parts of the dwellings. The lower rendered blockwork, is in common with local masonry tradition, and provides a robust base to the buildings (Fig. 4.9).

AJ, 14/10/92, pp. 43–50; URBED, *21st Century Homes*, p. 42; *AR*, 11/5/90, pp. 103–106.

Honddu Place/Beacons View Road, low energy housing.
1997. Design Partnership Wales.
R. Swansea + local transport.

Honddu Place, comprising fifty-two bungalows, flats and houses, was also developed by the Gwalia Housing Society. The project was included in the research undertaken by URBED between 1991 and 1995 as published in *21st Century Homes* (1995).

Forty bungalows and two-storey flats were developed to high thermal environmental standards, a project which was supported by a European 'Thermie' grant covering 40 per cent of the costs of additional energy features. The remaining dwellings were built to normal standards to allow the project to be audited. The low energy dwellings were built with south-facing living rooms, conservatories and bedrooms arranged around a sun store from where warm air flowed directly to them (Fig. 4.10). Sun blinds are available to prevent overheating in the summer. The north-facing rooms have small windows and receive warm air from a sun store via a ventilation system.

The timber-framed construction allowed for a high degree of off-site prefabrication. Breathing wall construction, substantial insulation, heat recovery ventilation using solar collectors and heating by means of a combined heat and power district heating system make up the high performance specification. URBED's research indicated an estimated 25 per cent reduction in energy consumption and a pay-back period between 5 and 9 years [1].

[1] URBED, *21st Century Homes*, p. 40.

FIGURE 4.11
The atrium in the Swansea Foyer.

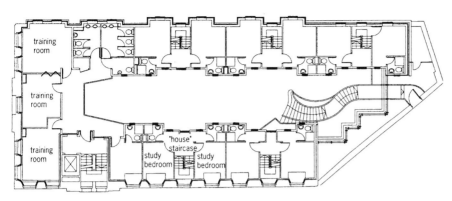

FIRST FLOOR PLAN

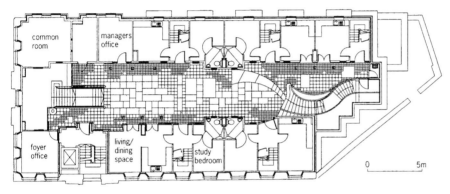

GROUND FLOOR PLAN

FIGURE 4.12
*The Swansea Foyer:
floor plans.*

The Swansea Foyer, Quarry Street.
1997. PCKO Architects. R. Swansea.

In 1994 Gwalia Housing Society decided to help address the problems of homelessness amongst young people in Swansea by providing much needed housing and personal support in a French-style Foyer (p. 35). They were assisted in the project by Swansea City Council, the Welsh Development Agency and Welsh Heritage, but it was still necessary for them to use funds from their own financial reserves.

The brief was to provide a building which created a suitable environment in which integrated work, training and independent living could be offered to the young people. It was important that it did not have an institutional feel. The building envisaged for the project was the former Swansea Working Men's Club, a prominent building constructed in 1885 with listed elevations. In the event only the front facade was preserved as the building was too dilapidated and the new interior was given a splendid glazed atrium (Fig. 4.11). This forms a street off which access is gained at different levels by staircases to individual 'houses' occupied by four or five young people. Within a house each young person has their own bedsit with a WC/shower and there is a shared kitchen/living space.

The accommodation comprises thirty-three bedsits (two suitable for full wheelchair use) and one guest room. There are a number of additional rooms for training and leisure and a residents' coffee area with space for a small cafe (Fig. 4.12). The interior is most striking and the detailing, mosaics and colour scheme create an optimistic and fun environment which young people can enjoy.

AJ, 19/6/97, pp. 33–40.

FIGURE 5.1
Cochrane Street, Irvine: 1990s new town housing for rent.

CHAPTER FIVE

Scotland

1 Aberdeen
2 Berwickshire (Scottish Borders)
3 Cumbermauld
4 Dundee
5 Edinburgh
6 Fife
7 Glasgow
8 Perthshire

FIGURE 5.2
Counties, towns and cities where schemes are located)

Introduction

Scottish housing merits separate consideration for a number of reasons. Whilst there has recently been some merging of design approach with the rest of Britain, there is a tradition of harled and painted walls, crow foot gables, small paned sash windows (often with wide surrounds), steep slate roofs and bold chimneys which gives Scottish housing a national identity. Sir Basil Spence's sketch of proposed fishermen's housing at Dunbar (Fig. 5.3), drawn in 1950, perfectly captured the spirit which has remained a strong influence even on the most modern designs [1].

There is also a wider historical acceptance of tenement living in Scottish towns and cities. By the sixteenth century, flats were well established in market centres in Scotland as the preferred building form for merchants and tradesmen. This closely resembled the experience of continental Europe where urban settlements were often separately administered from their rural hinterlands. Later town expansions in Scotland

FIGURE 5.3
*Fishermen's housing, Dunbar, East
Lothian; sketch by Sir Basil Spence,
1950. [From: Willis, P.,* New
Architecture in Scotland, *Lund
Humphries, London, p. 8.]*

followed this principle and housebuilding was mainly in the form of flats, whilst in England most housing was based on variations of the terraced house. The Scottish Victorian and Edwardian working class tenements are therefore the logical developments of the sixteenth century merchants' flats but in England the minimum sub-division of the terraced house was the 'back-to-back' [2].

The practice of living in flats continued into the 1950s and 1960s when it was translated by local authorities into tenement housing in the peripheral estates and into high rise. Between 1955 and 1975 no other local authority in Britain matched the scale of Glasgow's ambitious programme of public sector house building. Since 1980 there have been remarkable changes in housing policy in Scotland, aimed at stimulating social and economic regeneration of the large council estates. Much was achieved through tenant empowerment, as exemplified in the emergence of the tenant co-operative movement. This is now explained in more detail.

Inter-war policies

By the end of the First World War Scottish towns and cities, particularly Glasgow, had an overwhelming legacy of poor housing and overcrowding left by the Industrial Revolution. By 1919, 700 000 people were packed into the centre of Glasgow in tightly knit housing built in the backlands behind the street buildings with access limited to narrow lanes and closes. Between 1919 and 1939 a third of a million new dwellings were built in Scotland, of which 67 per cent were built by public authorities. However, little of this relieved the slums as the new housing was let to higher wage earners. To overcome this dilemma, the specific task of building 'working class homes' [3] was eventually handed to the Scottish Special Housing Association (SSHA), founded in 1937, but little was achieved until after 1945.

Low rents policy

This policy emerged from the industrial unrest in Glasgow in 1915 and the rent freeze imposed

FIGURE 5.4
Typical peripheral estate tenement. [Photo from Glasgow City Council, Department of Architecture and Related Services.]

by central government. Thereafter, rents in both the public and private sectors continued to be at such a low level that they seldom reached a sufficient amount to support an adequate programme of management and maintenance. Subsidy from the general rates gave some assistance to council housing, but the culture of low rents through custom and practice has remained a feature of Scottish housing.

Cottages or flats

During this period there was considerable tension between the advocates of the garden city ideas from England and the Scottish tenement tradition. Essentially the urgency of its housing problems was causing Glasgow's housing committee to use forms of 'modern' flats familiar in Europe which would give high densities. Their opponents considered that these were unsuitable for Scotland in terms of climate and sunshine [4]. Both types of housing were built but the issues were to become even more vital after 1945.

Non-traditional housing

To build housing more quickly, new construction methods were actively pursued. This appeared to have the benefit of overcoming shortages of skilled craftsmen whilst offering alternative employment to the workers in the declining steel, shipbuilding and coal industries. From 1925, steel-framed houses were built in Glasgow, Edinburgh, Dundee and other locations. These were two-storey in form and traditional in appearance. Timber-framed housing was developed and at the same time the no-fines, poured concrete construction technique was introduced from The Netherlands.

Years of ambition: 1945–1979

Just under half of Scotland's present housing was constructed between 1951 and 1979, mostly by local authorities. In Glasgow, where housing had become a big political issue, the City Council built the greatest number. Until the early 1950s most of the new housing built was of the cottage type, with many local authorities using factory-made steel, timber and concrete systems.

Peripheral estates

The peripheral estates resulted from the concern of the major cities about the flight of their population to new towns. The housing consisted mainly of three- and four-storey tenements (Fig. 5.4). The largest of these estates – Castlemilk, Easterhouse, Drumchapel and Pollock – contained over 10 000 dwellings, with large populations of over 50 000 at Easterhouse and 34 000 at Castlemilk. The estates were a long way from the city centre and the tenants' natural roots, added to which there was an acute lack of local shops and community facilities. This resulted in a concentration of poor people on the estates with low standards of living and poor health.

Non-traditional housing

To build quickly, industrialized systems and standard plans were extensively adopted. Requiring only semi-skilled and unskilled labour, the Scottish Office positively encouraged system building as a way of reducing the impact of manual job losses from the declining heavy industries. The result for the peripheral estates was a drabness of appearance that did little to enhance the lives of the people.

High rise housing

Although the development of the peripheral estates continued after 1955, attention moved towards the replacement of the slums in the centre of Glasgow. The size of the problem called for a new development approach and Roehampton in London was seen as the model to follow. For the politicians in Glasgow, high rise housing also had the virtue of containing the city's population. Slum clearance and redevelopment was concentrated in comprehensive development areas (CDAs). A number of Britain's most distinguished architects were involved in the new

developments, including Sir Basil Spence who designed blocks of twenty-storeys in the Gorbals. In total, 320 tower blocks were built in the city using a variety of systems of prefabrication; no-fines was, however, limited to twelve storeys.

Between 1961 and 1969, approximately one-third of a million new dwellings were constructed throughout Scotland of which three-quarters were high rise flats. The scale of the development was enormous. Right from the start there were serious management problems and by the late 1970s every sizeable town or city had its 'problem' and 'difficult to let' estates.

SLASH

The Scottish Local Authorities Special Housing Group (SLASH) was established in 1963 by Glasgow City Council in order to reduce the impact of high costs and shortages of materials through bulk purchasing. It soon included Edinburgh and some forty other local housing authorities responsible for four-fifths of the national output of new houses. The immediate aim was for the member authorities to use jointly ordered, prefabricated, high rise flats to raise the national output by 10 per cent. To facilitate this SLASH prepared standard house plans and details with a view of reducing construction cost and time. The Scottish Development Department and the SSHA were prime movers in SLASH as was the Scottish National Building Agency. As it developed, SLASH produced some excellent work in promoting good standards. It gained considerable respect throughout Britain for its design and technical publications. When it was finally wound up in the 1980s, regrettably most of its records were lost.

The Scottish Special Housing Association (SSHA)

During the 1960s and 1970s the SSHA developed its own high rise housing and extensively used system building including no-fines. Local Authorities were frequently suspicious of the role of SSHA which they saw as the Scottish Office's building agency. Regardless of this, SSHA played an important role in this period, particularly in the refurbishment of Glasgow tenements. They were also active in the GEAR area and Maryhill Road projects, where they helped to pioneer tenant participation in the design process.

The Scottish new towns

Despite initial opposition from Glasgow City Council, the dispersal of people from the slums was an important part of the Scottish national housing strategy from 1951. Subsidies were available after 1957 from the Scottish Office to support the policy. The first of the Scottish new towns, **East Kilbride**, had been designated in 1947 and **Glenrothes** in 1948. This was followed by **Cumbernauld** in 1956, **Livingston** in 1962 and **Irvine** in 1966 (Fig. 5.5). The outflow of people from Glasgow was so enormous that its population fell from over one million in 1961, to just over 700 000 in 1980. The loss was mainly amongst the middle classes, the skilled and higher waged workers, leaving parts of the city with a concentration of poor people who had the least opportunity to progress. The Scottish new towns made a significant mark in terms of their planning and design, especially Cumbernauld, where a unique master plan and innovative housing design brought international acclaim.

GEAR

The Glasgow Eastern Area Renewal (GEAR), established in 1976, was concerned with the regeneration of 400 acres (160 ha) in the west of the city centre including Bridgeton, Dalmarnock and Shettleston which had suffered intense urban decay and destruction. It contained seven designated Comprehensive Development Areas (CDAs) and had lost two-thirds of its former population. The Scottish Development Agency was given the task of coordinating a multi-agency approach to its regeneration which involved Strathclyde Regional Council, Glasgow District Council, the SSHA, the Health Board, Manpower Services and the local communities.

This project significantly lifted the morale of the remaining people in the area. The quality of

the refurbishment (2049 dwellings in total) and the new housing (1209) built by the SSHA and the housing associations, combined with large amounts of landscaping, transformed the area. Confidence in the locality was demonstrated by the construction of a small amount of private housing (e.g. 134 houses at Dalveen Street, 1979). Less successful were the accompanying social and economic initiatives. Housing investment was not linked to employment and much of the economic benefit was gained at the expense of other parts of the city. However, the experience was invaluable for the later urban regeneration schemes that followed [5].

A new culture

The culture of Scottish housing changed significantly after 1979. Stringent government expenditure cuts caused Glasgow City Council in the winter of 1983/4 to search for ways of attracting alternative funding for the improvement of its estates. From this deliberation, the concept of Community Ownership emerged. Progressively the City Council realized it had to reduce its direct role and transfer some of its stock to co-operatives, housing associations and private sector firms to produce a healthier social mix and to open the way for some genuine choices [6]. In 1986, Glasgow City Council commissioned Professor Sir Robert Grieve to undertake an enquiry which recommended transferring 25 per cent of the council's housing stock, particularly in the peripheral estates. In 1987, the first Community Renewal Partnership programme was implemented using funds raised through a covenant scheme with private investors.

The White Paper 'New Life for Urban Scotland' published in 1988 set out the government's requirements for regeneration in the peripheral and other large estates. Based on the experience of GEAR, a multi-agency, co-operative approach was required which would encourage a variety of forms of tenure including home-ownership. New methods of management and tenant empowerment were important to the process. Consequently, formal 'Partnerships' were

FIGURE 5.5
Braehead, Irvine New Town.

FIGURE 5.6
Castlemilk: successful regeneration of Glasgow's peripheral estate.

established for four of the most problematic estates – **Castlemilk** in Glasgow (Fig. 5.6), Ferguslie Park, Paisley, Whitfield in Dundee and **Wester Hailes** in Edinburgh.

The Partnerships recognized the need to integrate physical, economic and social programmes to establish more sustainable communities. Amongst the major objectives are the following priorities: arresting the population decline and stabilizing the community; providing a range of types of housing and tenure with a mixture of refurbishment and new housing, including homesteading and housing for sale; improving the environment; increasing local economic activity; developing better standards of health, education and community care; and empowering the people to achieve these aims through participation.

Private sector housing

The private sector became involved and many companies worked in partnership with public bodies and agencies in housing and estate regeneration with some degree of success (e.g. **Ingram Square** and **Spiers Wharf**). Further culture change resulted from the expansion of speculative housing for sale in the 1980s. Regrettably the developers introduced the English private house-building vernacular including the predominant use of brick which is not an indigenous material for Scotland. The main reference to Scottish vernacular was 'baronial', and half-timbered housing estates where the housing was small and built to minimum standards with little attention to energy and other environmental issues. The sale of council housing proved popular and in Scotland local authorities were able, until the mid 1990s, to use for development purposes the whole of their capital receipts from sales. This helped avoid some of the bitter central/local relationships that existed elsewhere in Britain.

Tenement refurbishment

The rehabilitation of the pre-1919 tenements in the late 1970s and 1980s encouraged the growth of the community-based housing associations which became key participants in urban housing regeneration. Part of the credit for this can be attributed directly to ASSIST. Formed in 1970 by Raymond Young and Jim Johnston, ASSIST Architects was part of Strathclyde University before separating in 1983 to become the first architectural co-operative in Scotland. The bulk of its early work was community-based refurbishment projects. It specialized in advising the community groups on rehabilitation and renewal and did much to encourage them to campaign to

save areas of the city which the planners wanted to demolish. From the mid 1980s most of ASSIST's work was new housing which it designed with considerable success (pp. 300)

Scottish Homes

From 1979, the SSHA continued its programme of new housing development with a high level of tenant participation in the design process, for example at Kirkland Street (1981–85) and Dalmarnock Road/Summerfield Street (1985–86) (*AJ*, 3/12/86, pp. 37–43). It was merged with the Scottish Housing Corporation in 1989 to form Scottish Homes. This created a single housing development agency which now possesses a wide range of powers. It is required to provide information on housing conditions, to initiate research and to act in an holistic manner on housing policy in Scotland. Similar responsibilities have never been vested in the Housing Corporation in England.

The current housing scene

The architectural quality of the new housing and the refurbishment of the older stock is a physical affirmation of a new vigour. Projects such as Glasgow's Merchant City and **Crown Street** and Canmore Housing Association's Morrison Circus and Crescent (1995–96, R. Edinburgh Haymarket) (Fig. 5.7) and car-free housing in Edinburgh are clear signs of a realization of the importance of architecture to making cities good places in which to live. The award to Glasgow of '1999, Year of Architecture' is a fitting opportunity to demonstrate Scotland's housing renaissance.

[1] Willis, P., *New Architecture in Scotland*, p. 50.
[2] Based on information from Dr Peter Robinson, Construction and Building Control Group, The Scottish Office.
[3] Begg, T., *Housing Policy in Scotland*, p. 43.
[4] Ibid., p. 64.
[5] Donnison D. and Middleton A., *Regenerating the Inner City*, p. 221.
[6] Begg, p. 186.

FIGURE 5.7
Morrison Circus and Morrison Crescent: modern tenements in an appropriate setting.

ABERDEEN

St Nicholas Triangle, Union Street.
1994. Jenkins and Marr. R. Aberdeen.

The St Nicholas Triangle development in the Union Street Conservation Area lies in the historic and commercial heart of the city. Many of the buildings on the site were listed and their preservation was an essential requirement of the architect's brief to create a mixed-use development of retail, workshops, commercial, residential and ecclesiastical uses. Housing was accommodated above the shops and the buildings in Correction Wynd were refurbished to form seven residential units with individual car parking at the rear. The resultant scheme received a Civic Trust Award in 1995.
Prospect, Spring 1996, Issue 59, pp. 12–13.

BERWICKSHIRE (NOW SCOTTISH BORDERS)

Marine Square, Eyemouth.
1994. Swan Architects. R. Berwick-upon-Tweed.

This development of twenty-nine, mainly single-person flats, is located in the heart of Eyemouth Old Town Conservation Area overlooking the sea (Fig. 5.8). Formerly occupied by a network of old industrial buildings, the site had become derelict.

The design was influenced by a concern to reflect the townscape qualities of the area. It consists of five distinct buildings arranged along the Marine Parade frontage, with flats positioned to allow frequent expression of tall narrow gables, sometimes end-on to the sea. This creates an impression of height which is further emphasized by vertically proportioned windows, steep slated

FIGURE 5.8
Marine Square, Eyemouth: clustering of houses and view from the sea.

pantiled roofs and tall chimneys. External wall finishes are dry dash, the colours of which recall those of Gunsgreen House across the harbour.

Illustrative stained glass by Joanna Scott enhances the entrances to the buildings and designs by Eyemouth High School Art Department have been incorporated into ceramic medallions, made by Peter Thomas, for the dormer peaks.

Prospect, Autumn/94, p. 23.

CUMBERNAULD

Cumbernauld New Town.

Designated 1956. Master-plan, Sir Hugh Wilson and Cumbernauld Development Corporation; featured housing by Cumbernauld Development Corporation Architects. R. Cumbernauld.

Cumbernauld straddles a long, rounded ridge which lies on the watershed between the Clyde and the Forth. Hugh Wilson's master-plan (Fig. 5.9) rejected the neighbourhood principle adopted by earlier new towns and produced a single community of 50 000 people with two satellite villages to take the natural growth of the population up to 70 000. Up to 80 per cent of the population was overspill from Glasgow and the basic requirement to move to Cumbernauld was to have a job in one of the new factories.

Its key planning principle was to locate most of the housing within 10 minutes' walking distance from a linear town centre. There would be no

FIGURE 5.9
Cumbernauld New Town: plan of the central part of the town as it was in 1973. [AJ, 5/10/77, p. 640.]

local centres, merely a small number of local 'corner shops', one for every 300 houses. Schools were located where they were needed. Housing density was to average sixty persons per acre (148/ha) and eighteen to twenty dwellings per acre (44–50/ha) for two-storey housing, with higher densities for three- and four-storey housing. The use of Radburn layouts with segregated pedestrian and vehicular areas helped make these higher densities possible. The architecture emphasizes the Scottishness of the town and there is a common theme in the design of the housing based on the relationship of solid to void, and the use of materials and details for walls, roofs, windows and doors.

Today the houses are faring well, bearing in mind the initial cost constraints and the current maintenance costs of high density land use. The point blocks are very popular (never having accommodated children). In the high density two-storey housing, circulation areas, access, privacy, sunlight and variety are still appreciated. Jobs and factories are flourishing and the sense of community is strong [1].

Designed in the late 1950s, the small groups of family houses at **Seafar** were symbolic of the best in new town housing in Britain. The problems posed by the north-facing slopes and the objective of achieving higher densities gave impetus to the architects to take a fresh look at housing design. They examined the constraints: slope, daylighting and sunlight penetration, the need for privacy, views, vehicular/pedestrian segregation and character. They produced new solutions: single aspect houses, wide frontage terraces and 'upside down' houses. Their greatest success was the integration of houses, hard and soft landscaping and roads into one coherent design (Fig. 5.10).

Other housing projects that received acclaim for their design are those at Ravenswood at the west end of the town, the early parts of Abronhill, and at Westfield. The Development Corporation encouraged private development and Meadow View (Fig. 5.11) is a scheme designed in the early 1960s by its own architects.

[1] Based on recent observations of Derek Lyddon, former Deputy Chief Architect, Cumbernauld Development Corporation; *A&BN*, 29/3/61, pp. 413–424; *A&BN*, 26/1/66, pp. 145–153; *AJ*, 5/10/77, pp. 636–649.

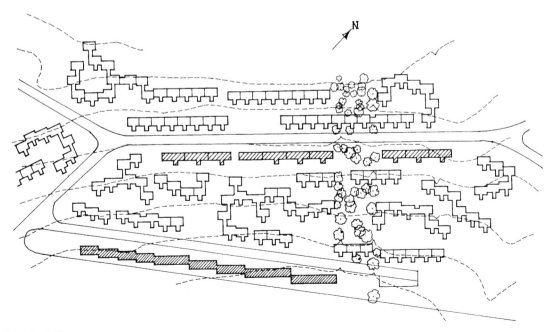

Figure 5.10
Seafar: 'The whole has matured over almost 40 years to be one of the finest environments in a new town anywhere' (David Cowling).

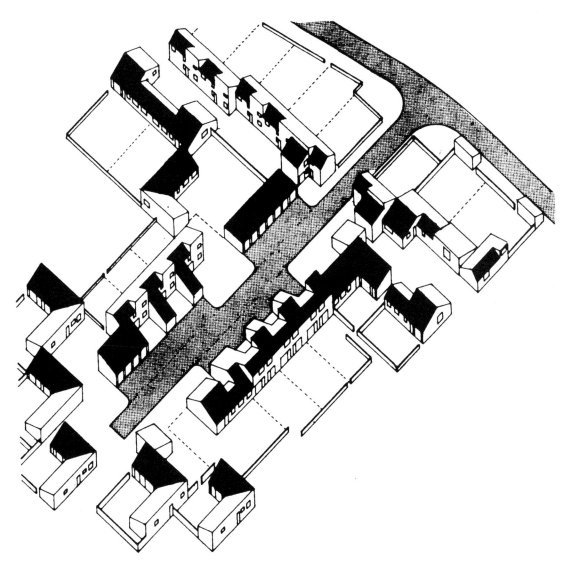

FIGURE 5.11
Meadowview: much admired new town private housing.

DUNDEE

Bell Rock Square, Broughty Ferry.
1973. James Parr and Partners.
R. Broughty Ferry.

These sixteen houses designed for the Tay Valley Housing Association Ltd reflect the tradition of Scottish vernacular architecture. The site faces over the estuary of the River Tay forming part of the old area of Broughty Ferry. Designed with rough-cast rendered walls and grey tiled roofs, the houses are in complete sympathy with neighbouring fishermen's cottages. They are grouped around a well planted pedestrian courtyard open on the water-front side, enabling most dwellings to have a sea view (Fig. 5.12 and 5.13).

Willis, P., *New Architecture in Scotland*, Lund Humphries, 1977, pp. 28–29.

FIGURE 5.12
Bell Rock Square: courtyard (photo by Alex Coupar).

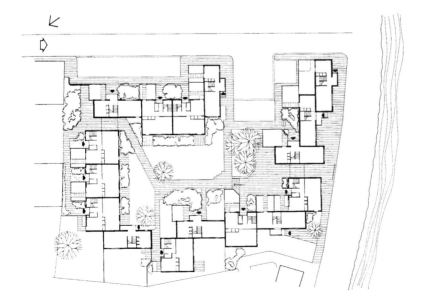

FIGURE 5.13
Bell Rock Square: site plan

FIGURE 5.14
*Sinderins Sheltered Housing,
Dundee. Photo: M. Anne Dick,
Building Pictures*

Sinderins Sheltered Housing, Sinderins, Perth Road, Dundee.
1989. Page and Park. R. Dundee.

This scheme, designed for the Scottish Special Housing Association, reinterprets the traditional Scottish tenement in a modern manner. It was the subject of an architectural competition restricted to young architects which was staged for the Festival of Architecture in 1984 by the Royal Incorporation of Architects in Scotland.

There are twenty-six one- and two-bedroom flats, with warden's accommodation plus a common room and ancillary spaces. The building has three parts – the 'tenement' block, the 'villa block' and the 'corner' block relating to the external spaces of a lane, a garden and a court-yard. It integrates well into surrounding features – the main Perth Road, gardens to an adjacent church, and garden walls. It is most imposing at the corner and the elevations possess many modern interpretations of traditional tenements (Fig. 5.14).

FIGURE 5.15
Westburn Avenue: glazed towers provide a focal point in the layout.

EDINBURGH

Estate regeneration, Wester Hailes (Westburn Avenue).
1995 with a later phase completed 1997. Smith Scott Mullan & Associates.
R. Wester Hailes.

Wester Hailes is one of Scotland's four Partner-ship estates established by the Scottish Office in 1988 (p. 283). Built between 1969 and 1975, it was the last of Edinburgh's ring of peripheral estates. The physical improvements to the estate include refurbishment of tenement housing and demolition of many of the unpopular high rise blocks, replacing them with new housing. Some of the best new development is at Westburn Avenue where refurbishment was considered non-viable.

The new housing reflects the community participation in the design which involved an enormous number of drawings, computer models and slides, as well as visits to other areas. The use of terraced housing and flats achieved a density of twenty-eight dwellings per acre (70 dw/ha), which was necessary for the scheme to be financially viable. The architecture has a strong sense of local identity with cultural prece-dents reflected in a distinctively modern way. This includes the use of render, Fyfestone and circular glass-block stair towers which resemble Scottish baronial architecture (Fig. 5.15). A sense of enclosure has been achieved, with the three-storey housing forming a focal point and centre at the lowest part of the site. A conventional pattern of streets and courts was adopted and the buildings were sited by the architects in a

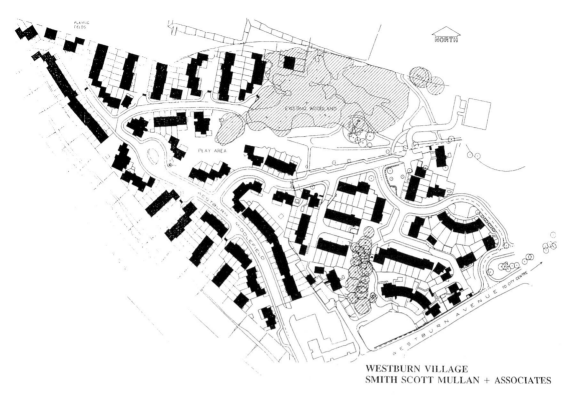

WESTBURN VILLAGE
SMITH SCOTT MULLAN + ASSOCIATES

FIGURE 5.16
Wester Hailes estate regeneration: site layout for new housing at Westburn Middlefield.

'pragmatic' manner [1], each responding to its own location (Fig. 5.16). Windows were positioned primarily to take best advantage of sunlight and to provide surveillance over adjacent spaces rather than to produce an organized composition. The design is likened by the residents to a traditional village and has therefore retained the name Westburn Village.

AT, 2/96, no. 65, pp. 16–19; [1] Ibid., p. 17.

Sheltered housing, Cameron Crescent.
1987. Nicholas Groves-Raines. R. Edinburgh Waverley + local transport.

This sheltered housing project was designed for the Viewpoint Housing Association in conjunction with Edinburgh City Council. Located on the site of a former church, it consists of twenty-eight one-person and fifteen two-person sheltered flats for elderly people on four floors. The building form was largely determined by the number of dwellings required to make the scheme financially viable but the site, and in particular a planning restriction to follow the church's old building line along Cameron Crescent, had a significant influence. The flats fronting the main road have bay windows to give good views up and down the street from the living rooms. On the top level these are replaced with a small balcony.

The construction is traditional brick cavity walls with extensive detailing of contrasting brickwork around the windows and eaves and in string courses at each floor level. This treatment of brickwork is unusual for Scotland but it is effective (Fig. 5.16).

FIGURE 5.17
Cameron Crescent, Edinburgh: fine brickwork detailing.

Craigwell Brewery, Calton Road.
1988. Nicholas Groves-Raines.
R. Edinburgh Waverley.

Craigwell Mews, close to the city centre, resulted from the conversion by Abbey Housing of some beautiful seventeenth century brewery buildings. The scheme comprises eight four-storey town houses with three bedrooms, three three-storey houses with two bedrooms and eight one- and two-bedroom flats. The roughly U-shaped development curves round one end of a linear courtyard paved with nineteenth century setts. The houses are in the brick-built brewery at the rear and most of the flats are in the red sandstone buildings, formerly the brewery offices, fronting Calton Road. Access to the courtyard is through the original pend. To the rear of the development a large and well-established garden slopes southwards to Regent Road.

FIGURE 5.18
Craigwell Brewery. Edinburgh: successful re-use of old buildings.

The architects have carefully restored the buildings and preserved the proportions of the window and door openings, and have added a small number of new details. The hoist housings on upper floors had perished but were reflected in the design of the new green-stained timber balconies which project from the two upper floors of the four-storey houses. These are matched by timber features around the courtyard (Fig. 5.18).

Mixed-use development, Calton Road.
1992. Rob Hunter Architects.
R. Edinburgh Waverley.

The design of this mixed housing and commercial scheme has three interwoven elements. The largest is a four-storey block which fronts Calton Road

and Lochend Close on the western boundary of the site. The ground floor contains offices whilst the three upper floors are flats with living and bedroom accommodation organized along the outer edges of the block. In the centre of the block is the service spine, containing staircases, light wells, kitchens and bathrooms. The second element is the L-shaped wing of two-storey office space linking the four-storey block to the Blair Brewery building which has been converted into housing. The third is the spacious court surrounded on two sides by the office wing and finished in granite setts.

The scheme is a benchmark of quality in Edinburgh, deriving its architectural language from the Old Town. Its twinned north gables and curved parapet fronting Calton Road would have unquestionably appealed to Charles Rennie Mackintosh (Figs 5.19 and 5.20).
AT, 4/93, pp. 31–32.

FIGURE 5.19
Calton Road mixed-use development in the shadow of Arthur's Seat.

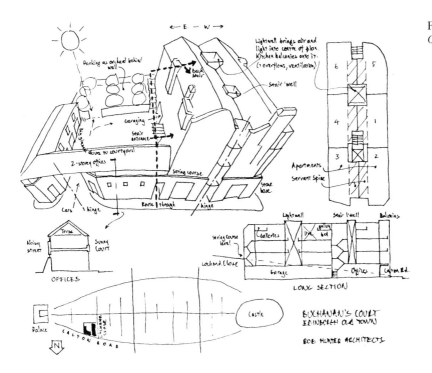

FIGURE 5.20
Calton Road: design principles.

Gogarloch Road, South Gyle.
1996. E&F McLachlan Architects. R. South Gyle.

Built by the Horizon Housing Association, this scheme was the subject of a design competition for young architects. The site is in a new suburb of Edinburgh and the architects felt that the design should be distinctive and reflect their interest in European modernism.

The scheme comprises twenty-seven dwellings; sixteen of these are adapted for disabled people and are fully integrated with the other dwellings. Half of all the dwellings were for sale on a shared-equity basis. The two- and three-storey housing is grouped around a green space with car parking pushed to the corners of the site. The projecting bays are a major element in the design which is repeated in a variety of

scales and locations around the central court. The materials – bricks, concrete tiles and the panels in the projecting bays – are not typically Scottish but rather reflect the architects' personal preferences (Fig. 5.21). In this they are fortunate to have clients who are supportive of modern architectural concepts.

RIBAJ, 12/96, pp. 40–45; *Prospect*, 10/97, pp. 44–46.

The Georgie Millennium Project, car-free development, Slateford Road.
2000. Hackland & Dore. R. Slateford.

Edinburgh's millennium housing project was the subject of an architectural competition in 1997 commissioned by the Canmore Housing Association, the Royal Incorporation of Architects in Scotland and Scottish Homes. The brief looked

FIGURE 5.20
Gogarloch Road, South Gyle, Edinburgh.

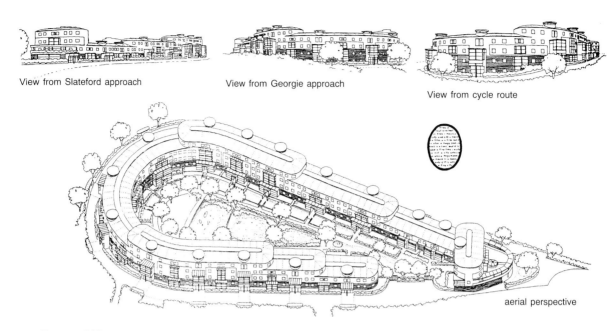

View from Slateford approach

View from Georgie approach

View from cycle route

aerial perspective

FIGURE 5.22
The Georgie Millennium housing, Edinburgh: car-free environment.

for architects to explore ways in which people will live in cities with limited natural resources. The winning scheme provides 121 flats and a kindergarten in a two- to four-storey form reflecting the traditional Edinburgh tenement block (Fig. 5.22). Its sheltering courtyard form was adapted to the site of the former Georgie railway sidings off Slateford Road.

The block encloses terraced gardens and is surrounded by natural landscape and allotments. It is skirted by a pedestrian street and a cycle route, which provides service, drop-off and emergency access throughout. No vehicles can enter the internal courtyard and minimal parking is located only for disabled people's flats and visitors. The residents will be asked to agree, as part of their tenancy, not to park cars within the scheme or in the streets around.

Flats are arranged in traditional stair clusters and closes. Each staircase is designed to include a furniture hoist and may be retrofitted with a disabled lift. Flats for disabled people are arranged around specifically designed gardens. All areas are barrier-free and routes ramped to provide access to public areas.

The design incorporates many low energy features. These include breathing walls, sun spaces or winter gardens, reed-bed ponds to treat surface and storm water, natural passive ventilation systems and stair lighting powered by photo-voltaic cells. Community heating will use waste industrial heat from a nearby whisky distillery to provide cheaper and more efficient heating and hot water. A low maintenance aluminium roof was selected as it can be recycled at the end of its life. Reed-bed ponds will be provided as part of the landscape to ernable the surface and storm water to be treated.
AJ, 10/10/96, p. 14.

GLASGOW

Spiers Wharf, Conversion of warehousing into housing, Craighall Road, Port Dundas. *1993. James Cunning Young & Partners and Nicholas Groves-Raines. U. Cowcaddens.*

At the mouth of the Forth and Clyde Canal, a row of twelve Victorian grain mills at Spiers

FIGURE 5.23
Spiers Wharf, Glasgow: conversion into mixed-use development.

Wharf have been sensitively converted into 150 flats for sale (Fig. 5.23). The design of the flats reflects the cast-iron column grid (3–4 m centres) and the window patterns of the original buildings. They are grouped around new stairs and every effort was made to give flats a view over the city. A leisure suite is located in the centre of the project and there are commercial uses at ground floor level.
Prospect, Autumn 94, Issue 53, p. 24.

Ingram Square, The Merchant Quarter.
1984–89. Elder & Cannon.
R. Glasgow Queen Street/Central.

The old Merchant City, close to the City Chambers and George Square, originally formed the residences

of Glasgow's tobacco lords who, in the eighteenth and nineteenth centuries, lived above their work. By the 1960s the area had become run down, blighted by highway proposals and was scheduled for comprehensive redevelopment.

A joint development company was established in the mid-1980s between the City Council, the Scottish Development Agency (SDA) and a developer, Kantel Developments Edinburgh (KDE). All three partners provided funding: the City Council from its housing improvement budget, KDE through a bank loan, and the SDA by providing an interest-free loan under the then existing 'LEG-UP' scheme (Local Enterprise Grants for Urban Projects – a flexible scheme aimed at encouraging private investment to create jobs or improve social conditions). The SDA also made a contribution towards the environmental improvement.

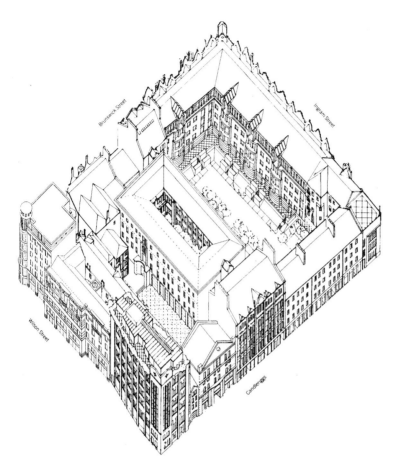

FIGURE 5.24
Ingram Square, Glasgow: axonometric drawing. [From AJ, *6/5/87, pp. 44–45.]*

This enabled fourteen separate buildings with a variety of ownerships to be redeveloped, principally as housing, with a total of 239 dwellings, mainly for sale but including twenty shops and parking for a hundred cars (Fig. 5.24). The redevelopment took three directions: the conversion of existing commercial buildings into flats, the demolition and rebuilding behind the retained listed facade of the Houndsditch building (built 1854) and new build on three gap sites. The largest of these, on the corner of Brunswick Street and Wilson Street, comprises an eight-storey corner block (no. 22 Wilson Street) linked to a five-storey building (no. 28) running along the east end of Wilson Street and butting up to the tall sandstone Nova building converted into housing in 1985. The spectacular glazed drum on the corner of Wilson Street and Brunswick Street is a new intervention into the street scene. The other new buildings on

the site are a five-storey building in Candleriggs and a student housing block for Strathclyde University overlooking the northern courtyard but entered from the southern courtyard. The Italian Centre with its fine sculptures and shops is the most memorable space in the complex (Fig. 5.25). *AJ*, 6/5/87, pp. 39–51; *AJ*, 3/5/89, pp. 35–59.

Community-based housing association development.
1970+. ASSIST Architects.

Carnarvon Street/St George's Road, Charing Cross (U. Charing Cross/St George's Cross). This 1993 scheme of seventy-three flats and three shops for the Charing Cross Housing Association filled two gap sites in a conservation area in East

FIGURE 5.25
Ingram Square: the Italian Centre.

LIVERPOOL JOHN MOORES UNIVERSITY
Aldham Robarts L.R.C.
TEL. 0151 231 3701/3634

FIGURE 5.26
Co-operative housing at Achmore Road/Katwell Avenue, Glasgow.

Woodlands. The scheme is divided into four distinct buildings on St George's Road and both sides of Carnarvon Street. Dwelling sizes range from one-bedroom flats to seven-person maisonettes with a number of the flats being purchased through equity sharing. The housing is four storeys in height with bay windows, tradi-

tional detailing and sculptured features to mirror the adjacent nineteenth century tenements, and it ties together the various views, corners and street frontages of the surrounding buildings.

Achmore Road/Katwell Avenue, Drumchapel (R. Drumchapel). Completed in 1994 for the Cernach Housing Co-operative, this is a low

FIGURE 5.27
*Achmore Road: tenement plans
(Cernach project).*

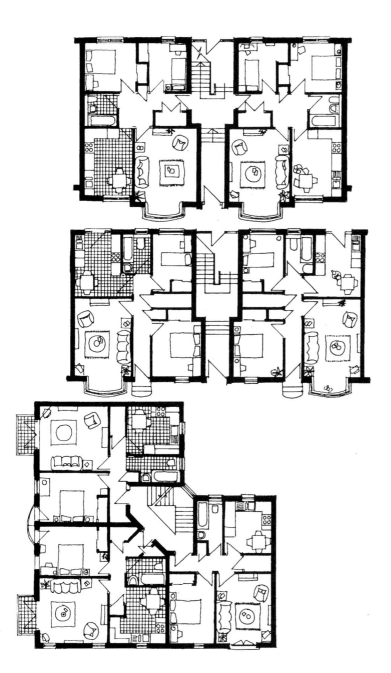

rise scheme in one of Glasgow's peripheral estatés. It comprises six two-storey houses, four three-storey houses and thirty-two two- and three-storey flats. The buildings are located around the perimeter of the site with a new vehicular access leading to parking courts. The project was designed to follow the line of the long, continuous blocks which were previously on the site. The street elevation to Achamore Road has been given a variety of scale and block size with a mixture of two- and three-storey dwellings (Figs 5.26 and 5.27). Corners and the central part of the terrace are given special emphasis. Colour is introduced by a pallet of brick colours, cast stone and render.

FIGURE 5.28
Co-operative housing: James Nisbett Street, Glasgow.

Elevations have 'close' entrances, bay windows and balconies highlighted as points of interest.

Tollcross Road/Sorby Street (R. Carntyne). This is a four-storey development completed in 1994 for the Parkhead Housing Association. It was the winner of a limited design competition and contains seventy-one flats and two shops. Its red brick and cast stone with high level pediments, oriel windows and glazed staircase screens were designed to harmonize with the surrounding buildings.

James Nisbett Street, Roystonhill (R. Queen Street + local transport). The refurbishment of these forty-seven post-war tenements in 1996 reflects the active involvement of the tenants in the design process. The use of 'green' materials and energy conscious design has produced housing that is pleasant to live in and economic to run (Fig. 5.28).

Pineview, 22–24 Jedworth Avenue and **18–34 Rozelle Avenue, Drumchapel** (R. Drumchapel). This 1997 scheme refurbished thirty-four flats on Jedworth Avenue and Jedworth Road for the Pineview Housing Co-operative. It included storey height reduction, insulated overcladding and new brick bay extensions to the main elevations. Some ground floor flats were combined to provide large family-sized dwellings. Externally, new enclosed front and rear gardens were created with railings and bin-stores designed to complement the main buildings.

Prospect, Summer/94, p. 25; *AJ*, 30/5/90, pp. 36–37.

Castlemilk Estate regeneration.
1988+. City of Glasgow Department of Architecture and Related Services, Director Chris Purslow. R. Kings Park/Croftfoot.

The peripheral Castlemilk Estate is located some 4 miles from the city centre. Its 9700 dwellings,

mostly four- and five-storey tenements, represented all that was paternalistic and monolithic about council house design in the city since the Second World War. After the publication of the government's 'New life for Scotland' report in 1988, the Castlemilk Partnership was established between Glasgow City Council, Strathclyde Regional Council, the Glasgow Development Agency, Scottish Housing, the Training Agency, the Employment Service, housing associations, representatives of the local community and Glasgow Opportunities which spoke for the private sector.

The key strategy was to diversify tenure, taking some two-thirds of the housing out of council ownership and passing it in roughly equal proportions to the housing associations and private tenure. The most unpopular housing was demolished and the remainder has been progressively improved. This has included taking a

FIGURE 5.29
Castlemilk: regeneration of one of Glasgow's peripheral estates.

storey off the height of buildings, converting flats into houses, re-rendering and cavity filling external walls, renewing roof tiles and gutters, upgrading security and insulation, part-enclosing balconies with glass blocks and curved metal roofs and reshaping the environment to create more defensible space and a higher standard of appearance generally (Fig. 5.29).

The aim of the Partnership was to transform the physical condition of the estate together with its economic and social life. To achieve this the Castlemilk Economic Development Agency (CEDA) was established. CEDA's task was to ensure that the economic regeneration moved in parallel with the physical development. Its work included training and job search provision. By supporting people wishing to set up in business through counselling and offering financial packages, it encouraged the private sector to become involved in the economic regeneration. It focused on the 16–18 year old school leavers aiming, through training and the establishment of local 'youth job clubs', to prevent long-term unemployment among the young of the area. The involvement of the tenants in the process of regeneration has clearly made an impact physically and has particularly helped change their attitudes, perceptions and personal awareness.

AT, 9/93, Issue 42, p. 43; *Prospect*, Spring/95, pp. 12–15.

The regeneration of the Gorbals.
1990+. Cooper Cromar Associates, CZWG, The Holmes Partnership, Elder & Cannon Architects, Hypostyle Architects, Page & Park Architects, Simister Monaghan Architects, Wylie & Court and Young & Gault. U. Bridge Street.

From Victorian tenements to 1960s tower blocks, housing conditions in the Gorbals area of Glasgow have been notorious. It is now in its second era of regeneration and is one of the largest and most significant projects in Britain, covering around 100 acres (250 ha). The overall plan for the area defines eight separate Regeneration Areas and envisages an eventual population

of approximately 16 000 (currently less than 9000). A full range of local shops, public services and community facilities will be provided and complemented by significant opportunities for local employment.

Management of the project

The eight project areas are managed by a number of community-based agencies such as the Crown Street Regeneration Project, the Gorbals Initiative, the New Gorbals Housing Association and the voluntary sector. The Greater Glasgow Health Board and the Strathclyde Police are also very active partners. Co-ordination is through the Gorbals Officer Group Working Party which includes representatives of Glasgow City Council, the Glasgow Development Agency and Scottish Homes.

The Crown Street Regeneration Area

The Crown Street project was set up in 1990 following the demolition in 1987 of Hutchinsontown 'E' which consisted of twelve linked, deck-access blocks known locally as the 'dampies'. The overall redevelopment proposals for this area came from a nation-wide urban design competition won by CZWG who then drew up the master-plan with the project team. The plan proposed mixed development, including almost 1000 new dwellings (75 per cent for sale, 25 per cent for rent), a new business centre, a new local centre, a budget hotel, some small office accommodation, student housing, light industrial units and a new local park (Fig. 5.30). The site was divided up into manageable packages which are released in a phased manner. Each individual package is subject to a Developer/Architect Competition, which is based on an Urban Development Brief and a fixed land price so that submissions can be judged on their design merits. Each development package has strict conditions regarding management and maintenance of the development, which ensures the long-term sustainability of the project.

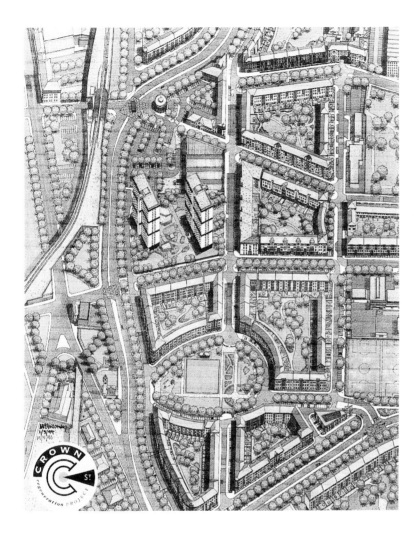

FIGURE 5.30
Crown Street regeneration: CZWG's master-plan.

The concept of the master-plan

The overall concept is to create the 'livable city' in which 'urban life can have vitality but also dignity and calm'. The elements of this are the traditional Glasgow street grid and the city block, where the front is clearly public and the back fully private; an important element is the tenement which the plan considers to be 'Scotland's, especially Glasgow's, traditional building form'. Its design will meet modern living requirements with the ground and first floors of a four-storey block comprising three-bedroom maisonettes with their own front and back door and a private rear garden. Above these the two upper floors are one-, two- and three-bedroom flats accessed by a separate communal staircase.

These principles were the basis of the design of the first development phases completed in 1995. **Ballaster Gardens** (Architects, Holmes Partnership) involved two private housebuilders and the New Gorbals Housing Association. It consists of three sides of a grid block and provides a total of 117 flats or maisonettes and three shops. The scheme forms the 'gateway' into the Crown Street Regeneration Project area, and the sweeping curves of the terrace and the corner turrets are most distinctive. **Errol Gardens** and **Pine Place** (Architects, Cooper Cromar Associ-ates) consist of a four-storey development of

FIGURE 5.31
Errol Gardens: new tenements in the Gorbals regeneration project.

ninety-two flats and maisonettes and five new shop units built around a private landscaped courtyard, with the elevations designed in line with the modern image of a tenement block (Fig. 5.31). The same approach was adopted by the architects (Hypostyle Architects) of the mixed rental/sale scheme at Cumberland Street, completed in 1997.

Gorbals East renewal area

Most interesting in this area is **Moffat Gardens** (completed 1998) on the corner of Moffat Street and Hayfield Street. This comprises a number of small housing projects grouped around a small urban square/garden. In a deliberate attempt to introduce diversity, the New Gorbals Housing Association appointed different architects for each site. Simister Monaghan's four-storey pivotal corner block and family dwellings contrast with Elder & Cannon Architects' 'cube and ellipse' (Fig. 5.32). The designs for these schemes were based on an imaginative client's brief for 'villa blocks' to form 'landmarks' within the development.

Social regeneration

This area of the work aims at improving the general well-being and health of the people. This has included upgrading the Gorbals Health Centre and establishing a food co-operative. The St Francis' Church and Priory has been converted into a community/learning/arts centre and housing for elderly people (Page & Park Architects, 1995). Many of the education and community development initiatives are based in the local schools. A youth drop-in cafe has been established at 556–558 Old Rutherglen Road (between Scottish Homes high rise flats). This offers training on video production, computing, dancing, golf, five-a-side football etc. It also provides information on training for work, welfare rights, housing, health issues and education.

FIGURE 5.32
'Cube and Ellipse', Gorbals East.

Economic regeneration

This important aspect of the project is managed for the whole of the Gorbals area by the 'Gorbals Initiative' which is a public/private partnership established as a local enterprise company. Construction on the site is linked to employment, training and the environment. Contractors are required to use local labour and a construction training programme ensures the possibilities of permanent employment. The Gorbals Initiative stimulates employment through counselling and supporting individuals as a means of personal development. It directly provides workspace at the new Adelphi Centre in Commercial Road (Architects, Wylie & Court), which was converted from the main classroom block of the former Adelphi Secondary School with the aid of European Regional Development Funding. Further business/office space was created in 1994 by Strathclyde Regional Council's conversion of the Grade 'B' listed McNeil Street Library into the Gorbals Economic Development Centre. At the same time the Twomax building, a former Category 'B' cotton mill at Old Rutherglen Road was converted into offices through a private sector initiative.

Prospect, Spring/95, pp. 18–21; *Prospect*, 10/97, p. 13; *AJ*, 5/12/96, p. 32; *Housing and Planning Review*, 10–11/95, p. 16; *AJ*, 4/5/94, p. 18.

Byers Road, infill housing.
1994. Simister Monaghan Architects. U. Hillhead.

The Byers Road project was the subject of an architectural competition in 1988. A narrow 15 m strip of leftover space now accommodates a most successful three- and four-storey development, clad on the street frontage in stone, thanks to a grant in 1989 from the Glasgow Development Agency. The handling of the corner with a 'pedimented gable pavilion' is most masterly (Fig. 5.33).
Prospect, Spring/95, pp. 22–23.

Carrick Quay, Clyde Street.
1991. Davis Duncan Partnership.
R. and U. Central.

This landmark project which overlooks the River Clyde is symbolic of the 1980s short-lived boom

and remains incomplete. The development, as planned, included ninety-three one-, two- and three-bedroom flats and penthouses in an L-shaped terrace enclosing a courtyard. Car parking is mainly located in the basement. The facade of the completed section is not typical of Glasgow, but its red brick walls and wide, black metal balconies are most distinctive when viewed from across the river.

Duke Street, housing and shops.
1993. Elder & Cannon Architects. R. Bellgrove.

Elder & Cannon's development of fifty-six dwellings and eight commercial units for the Reidvale Housing Association is a most interesting modern interpretation of the surrounding tenements. Designed in collaboration with the prospective tenants, this four- and five-storey development is grouped in a 'U' around a communal garden (Fig. 5.34). Its public facades are highly functional with a repetitive pattern of simple windows, softened only by large-scale openings of the gables. On the garden side, the wide living rooms have large floor to ceiling

windows which lead out to metal balconies. The buff brickwork of the external walls projects at every fifth course to relate to the module of the stonework of the adjacent tenements (Fig. 5.35). *AJ*, 9/2/94, pp. 43–53.

Annandale Square, Coplaw Street.
1994. Elder and Cannon Architects.
R. Pollockshields East.

Annandale Square is situated in the Govanhill area of the south side of Glasgow. The surrounding environment is characterized by an urban grid of typical four-storey stone tenements.

The design of the scheme was the subject of a competition promoted by the client, the Govanhill Housing Association. The brief called for a solution that would respond in a modern way to the existing character of the area, would satisfy local housing needs and would provide accommodation of good quality at an economic cost. The solution provided three four-storey blocks on each of the three sites, at Coplaw Street, Langside Road and Annandale Street/Butterbiggins Road.

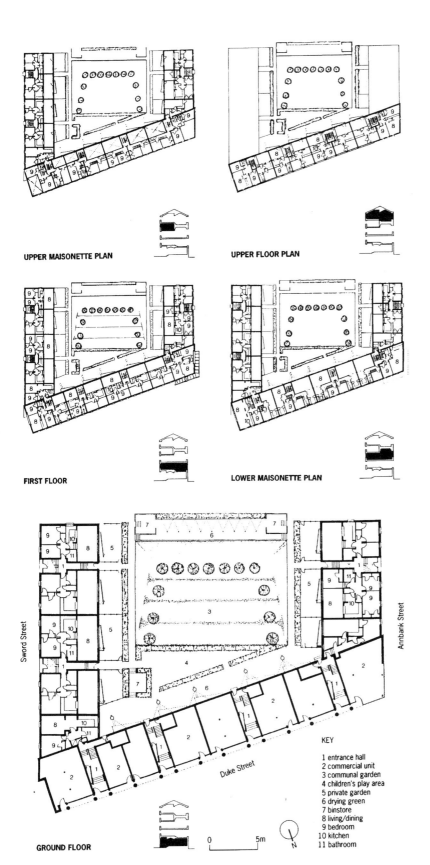

UPPER MAISONETTE PLAN

UPPER FLOOR PLAN

FIRST FLOOR

LOWER MAISONETTE PLAN

GROUND FLOOR

Sword Street

Annbank Street

Duke Street

KEY

1 entrance hall
2 commercial unit
3 communal garden
4 children's play area
5 private garden
6 drying green
7 binstore
8 living/dining
9 bedroom
10 kitchen
11 bathroom

0   5m

FIGURE 5.34
*Duke Street: modern
interpretation of the traditional
tenement.*

FIGURE 5.35
Duke Street: key floor plans (photo by architects).

FIGURE 5.36
Annandale Square, Govanhill, Glasgow (photo by architects).

The blocks were given a different appearance based on the local context. The Coplaw Street block (Fig. 5.36) is characterized by two pavilions at each end of the terrace with a curved centre element. The materials are red facing brick with concrete copings and sills. The brickwork is flush pointed and, at every fifth course, a strong horizontal emphasis is given by a brick projection. The Langside Road block is a terrace with an end pavilion block separated from the block on Coplaw Street by a high planted garden wall. The third block is a landmark building on the corner of Annandale Street/Butterbiggins Road. The Annandale Road frontage has large, slim windows which are repeated on Butterbiggins Road but on a smaller scale to reduce noise penetration. A curved, lead roof floats over a steel-columned colonnade which is substantially glazed in contrast to the solidity of the brickwork below.

FIFE

East Street, St Monans.
1969. Baxter, Clark and Paul. Local transport.

This scheme was important as it helped stimulate an awareness of traditional Scottish domestic architecture. The irregular roof-line of the buildings and its walls of harled brick and blockwork,

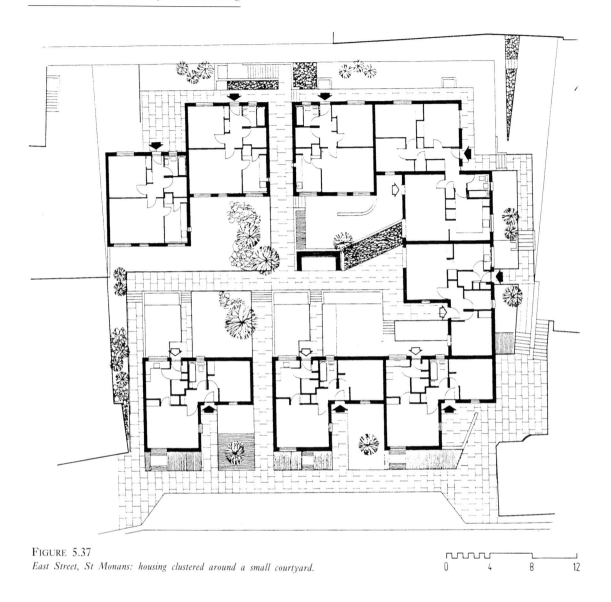

FIGURE 5.37
East Street, St Monans: housing clustered around a small courtyard.

0   4   8   12

for the most part painted white with a black base-course, are the hallmarks of the Scottish east-coast vernacular. The timber-framed windows appear as holes punched in the walls, emphasized by the surrounds picked out in black, brown or white. The layout is a simple square of housing around a courtyard in which the focal point is a three-storey block and chimney in the north-east corner (Fig. 5.37).

AJ, 20/3/74, pp. 588–590; Willis, P., *New Architecture in Scotland*, pp. 30–31.

Irvine New Town, Ayrshire.
1966–96. Irvine Development Corporation Architects, Principal Architect, Roan Rutherford. R. Irvine/Kilwinning.

Despite the Conservative Government's dislike of new towns, Irvine Development Corporation remained in existence well into the 1990s and continued to construct housing for rent at a time when authorities were prevented from building.

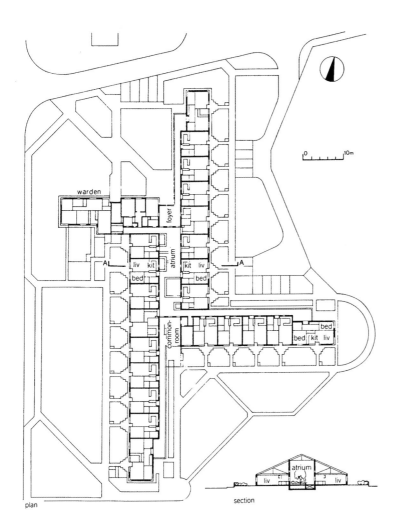

FIGURE 5.38
Hawthorn Place sheltered housing, Kilwinning.

Amongst the early schemes the daring use of colour at Bourtreehill (early 1970s) and the careful attention to traditional detailing at **Braehead** (1978) received considerable acclaim (Fig. 5.5). However, of far greater delight is the outstanding work of the Corporation's architects and consultants in later years.

Hawthorn Place, Nethermains, Kilwinning (Fig. 5.38), completed in 1988, is a single-storey, Category 2 sheltered housing development with warden supervision. The scheme provides seventeen two-person flats and two and three three-person flats capable of adaptation for wheelchair use. These are all accessed from three corridors which overlook well planted gardens. The corridors radiate from a central top-lit atrium

which forms the hub of the plan. Single-storey development with 'single banked' corridors and this quality of internal finish is a remarkable achievement within the cost yardsticks.

The same quality of internal space was repeated in the **Bryce Know Court** sheltered housing scheme completed in 1992. Here the atrium is sub-divided into different activity areas including a small library. The planting in the centre of the space creates the atmosphere of an indoor garden (Fig. 5.39).

The Development Corporation also carried out extensive rehabilitation and built new housing in small infill sites in the older parts of the existing settlements. This includes the **Harbourside** (Fig. 5.40), **Cochrane Street** (Fig. 5.1)

FIGURE 5.39
Bryce Knox Court sheltered housing: the internal garden can be enjoyed all year round.

redevelopment, Peter Street and Gottries Crescent and **Abbeygate** (Fig. 5.41) at Kilwinning, all completed in 1995/6. The schemes delightfully reflect influences of Charles Rennie Mackintosh. The white-painted harled blockwork walls and gateposts, cast-stone sills and plinth blocks, redwood joinery, natural slates, stained glass windows and decorative ironwork are wonderfully worked together to create compositions of great delight enjoyed by the local people.

PERTHSHIRE

Commercial Street, Bridgend, Perth.
1978. James Parr and Partners. R. Perth.

This design sought to emulate in a modern way the scale and atmosphere of the buildings which had existed previously on the site. It also endeavoured to ensure that all living rooms had a view of the river.

FIGURE 5.40
Harbourside, Irvine.

FIGURE 5.41
*Abbeygate, Kilwinning, Irvine New Town:
reflections of Charles Rennie Mackintosh.*

FIGURE 5.42
Commercial Street, Perth (photo by architects).

The accommodation consists of twelve five-person houses, twenty two- and four-person flats and eight four-person maisonettes, all clustered in one- to four-storey blocks to create a varied roof-line. The walls of the houses and the siteworks are of sand-blasted blockwork, relating to local stone, and the windows are of dark-stained timber. The roofs are covered mostly with second-hand grey Scottish slates which came from the demolished buildings (Fig. 5.42).

AJ, 13/12/78, pp. 1137–1149.

Scrimgeours Corner, Comrie Street and West High Street, Crieff.
1992. Nichol Russell Studios. R. Perth.

Scrimgeours Corner is a five-storey development built by the Servite Housing Association (Scotland) Ltd. The site was situated within the Crieff High Street Conservation area and the planning brief required the design to create a focal point on the corner of Comrie Street and West High Street.

FIGURE 5.43
Scrimgeours Corner, Crieff (photo by architects).

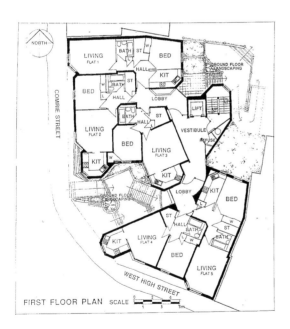

FIGURE 5.44
Scrimgeours Corner, Crieff, ground floor plan

The scheme comprises twenty-one two-person flats, one single-person flat, a communal laundry room and a shop. The dwelling plans are shaped in accordance with position on the site but living rooms and kitchens are placed to have good views (Fig. 5.44). Externally the building takes its shape, materials and colour from the neighbouring buildings. By slicing it into two apparently separate blocks, each aligned and grafted on to its neighbouring building, the corner was opened up to create a small, semi-public space which forms the entrance to the development. This also gives the impression of the development growing out of its surroundings which was a major aim of the design (Fig. 5.43). Towers complete each wing at the corner in a manner wholly in keeping with Crieff's traditional architecture.

Prospect, Winter/95, pp. 14–15.

FIGURE 6.1
Irish Street, Downpatrick: modern interpretation of Georgian street housing.

CHAPTER SIX

Northern Ireland

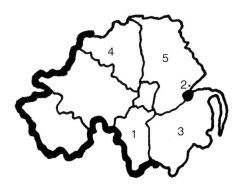

1 Co. Armagh
2 Belfast
3 Co. Down
4 Co. Londonderry
5 Co. Antrim

FIGURE 6.2
Northern Ireland: counties, towns and cities where the schemes are located.

Introduction

Despite a huge boom in house construction in Belfast at the end of the nineteenth century, housing was to prove a highly contentious issue throughout most of the 20th century. Between the wars very little was done by government nationally and locally to tackle the poor housing conditions in Belfast and Northern Ireland in general.

Civil rights campaign

Housing played a very prominent part in the civil rights campaign of the late 1960s, as public demonstrations pointed to poor housing conditions and a growing dissatisfaction with housing administration. Between 1969 and 1973 some 60 000 people were forced by the 'troubles' to leave their homes and territorialism became important as each community sought refuge in their historic districts. This added to the housing

pressures which, by the early 1970s, had become an overwhelming issue.

High density housing

Change came in the late 1960s when the Belfast Urban Plan of 1969 estimated that 75 000 new dwellings should be built in the city. The need existed due to the clearance of unfit housing, the consequence of motorway clearance programmes and new household formation. Even with population dispersal to designated growth areas like Craigavon New Town, designated in 1965, it was estimated that new developments built in the 'Urban Area' would need to be above four or five storeys. As a consequence, the pattern of development followed the mainland British model with similar disastrous consequences, but aggravated by the political unrest. Over forty high rise blocks were built in Northern Ireland. In Belfast this was reflected in a number of schemes, the largest and most notorious being the twenty-storey point block built amongst eight-storey deck-access Divis flats in the Falls Road area, providing more than 800 flats in one estate. The medium rise Lower Shankhill (known locally as the 'Weetabix boxes') and Unity were also built between 1966 and 1972. In Derry City, the Rossville flats were fortunately the only high rise development to be built.

The Northern Ireland Housing Executive (NIHE)

In 1971 the government undertook a radical reform of housing administration involving its transfer from local authority control to an entirely new, single-purpose body, the Northern Ireland Housing Executive (NIHE). This was given six key tasks.

1. Building new homes of a consistent standard across Northern Ireland.
2. Managing and maintaining existing housing estates.
3. Helping the private sector through grant aid.
4. Measuring housing conditions throughout Northern Ireland.
5. Undertaking housing research programmes.
6. Providing housing advice and information.

Today the NIHE is the biggest social housing landlord in Western Europe with over 140 000 dwellings and commanding a budget of more than 500 million per year with a staff of 2700 located throughout Northern Ireland. One of its cultural aims has been and still is the carrying out of its duties with fairness and equity in an otherwise divided community.

Progress 'Brick by brick' [1]

Its first house condition survey of 1974 painted a bleak picture of large areas of derelict and unfit housing with massive overcrowding. Northern Ireland was found to have the worst housing conditions in Britain if not Europe and comparisons were being made between Belfast and Naples. One in four houses in Belfast was classified as unfit with a ratio of one in five for Northern Ireland as a whole. The enormous task of

addressing the problem required the support of a sophisticated research and development facility. The crisis was of such a scale that a comprehensive approach was necessary. By establishing architectural groups drawn from former public housing bodies, an excellence in design was developed. This recognized regional differences yet utilized standard house types and details.

Until the mid-1970s most development was on greenfield sites. Planned in 1973, the controversial Poleglass development was built in southwest Belfast to alleviate pressure for housing in greater west Belfast and today it contains over 2050 homes. It initially met with hostile opposition from representatives of the majority community who feared an expansion of the minority community in west Belfast.

From 1979 onwards there was a radical shift of emphasis to inner-city regeneration which remains the major focus today.

Innovation and quality

The incoming Conservative Government of 1979 halted new housing development in Northern Ireland but by 1981 it had been persuaded to identify housing as Northern Ireland's first social priority. Poor housing conditions and long waiting lists demanded immediate and sustained treatment – an intensive programme directed at the core of the problem, which was rooted in Belfast. In 1982 the Belfast Housing Renewal Strategy paved the way for a huge programme of development in the city. It identified over forty small areas for redevelopment and a further fifteen as Housing Action Areas (HAAs) where the emphasis would be on refurbishment. A third dimension of the strategy related to areas of private housing where the Executive was eager to encourage the uptake of renovation grants and the injection of private finance to stimulate home improvements.

Low rise housing

During the peak years of the strategy's implementation in the 1980s and early 1990s, around 1500 homes were built annually in Belfast with

FIGURE 6.3
St George's Gardens, Sandy Row, Belfast, 1987, recapturing the best social features of traditional urban terraces.

a further 1500 in the rest of Northern Ireland. The policy of involving in-house and consultant architects to produce individual low rise design solutions, within the Executive's standard range of house types, was successful. Most schemes were small in scale and used bright, colourful brickwork and rendering and a wealth of imaginative detailing (Fig. 6.3). The general pattern was for the housing to be designed around pedestrian/vehicular mews courts using a variety of paviors, trees and shrubs. More permeable layouts with through streets and traffic calming measures have been introduced without any loss of quality. The new developments gained much from the participation of individual people and community groups and this has become a major part of the Executive's regeneration strategy.

The housing was built to the highest quality. The Executive retained Parker Morris standards which had been generally dropped by local authorities and housing associations in Britain. This policy was supported by the Department of Environment (Northern Ireland) which imposed the same standards on housing associations.

Improvement of public sector estates

This became a vital task for the Housing Executive. From 1982 it was implemented by designating 'Priority Estates' and 'Estate Based Strategies'. Both approaches tackled the physical and social stress with a range of improvements from modernization and environmental improvement to progressive clearance and renewal. In Belfast, eight Priority Estates, including the

Divis, Unity and Shankhill Estates, have now been significantly regenerated through this means.

Renewal of pre-1919 housing

In Belfast a total of fifty HAAs involving 21 000 dwellings were declared in the 1980s. Renovation grants were available to offer incentives to owner-occupiers to improve their homes. In addition, Private Investment Priority Areas (PIPAs) were created where the Executive could work with private owners to encourage urban renewal. In these areas it was hoped that young and economically active people would acquire, repair and improve their homes by the use of the renovation grant scheme and building society support. Enveloping (8000 dwellings in Belfast) and a small amount of homesteading were important parts of the programme.

Housing associations

The role of housing associations in housing regeneration was small in terms of quantity, but important nevertheless. Their involvement will now increase as the Executive passes the delivery of the new-build programme to them and concentrates on its role of enabler and co-ordinator. The Executive is determined that the high standards which it has worked so hard over many years to establish will remain.

Private sector housing

The development of private housing for sale is seen as important, particularly the need to draw the private sector into the development of brownfield recycled land in the inner city. In the 1980s private housing expanded in Belfast mainly in two new areas, Poleglass and Cairnshill, on the edge of the city. The housebuilding industry relies upon a number of local developers who construct 200–300 houses each per year and small builders who build around eight to ten dwellings per year. Few builders have land banks as in Britain. Generally, private sector housing in Belfast is designed by local architects and the quality is good (Fig. 6.4).

[1] Northern Ireland Housing Executive, *Brick by Brick*, NIHE, 1991.

Co. Antrim

Regeneration of Carnany Estate, Ballymoney.
1998. NIHE and CONSARC Design Group Ltd.

This is a typical example of the current problems which the NIHE is dealing with in many locations in Northern Ireland. Situated one and a half miles from the centre of the town, the

FIGURE 6.4
High quality private housing at Laurel Hill, Newforge Lane, Belfast (Lyons Architects).

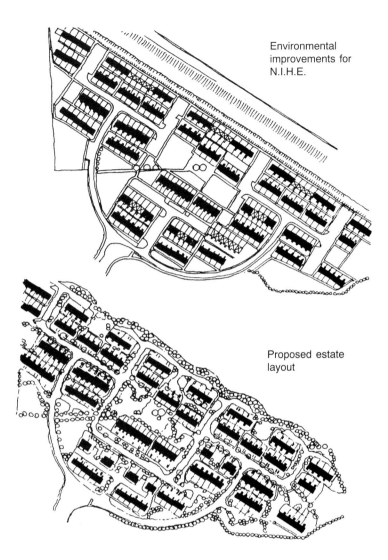

Environmental improvements for N.I.H.E.

FIGURE 6.5
Carnany Estate, Ballymoney: before and after regeneration.

DEVELOPMENT STRATEGY
- on plot parking to all dwellings
- create bus route loop road
- demolish mid-terrace housing to allow road penetration
- remove unsightly car parking areas and replace with spaces closer to the houses
- cut off some through pedestrian routes
- retain and enhance village green as a focal point
- provide better walling and fencing
- convert some houses into single person flats to meet demand
- provide variety in appearance and improve sense of individuality

Proposed estate layout

Carnany Estate contains 208 timber-framed, three-bedroom houses built in 1978. It had become unpopular for families and an analysis of the problems identified a range of issues. The houses were arranged in long rows with no individual identity, parking was remote from houses and unsupervised, pedestrian access was along windowless routes.

The imaginative design solution (Fig. 6.5) for estate regeneration involved selective demolition of remote and problematic 'back row' houses to create a more permeable road layout. This enabled more curtilage parking and small areas of supervised open space to be provided. Footpath-only routes were cut off by extending gardens. Single-aspect houses were converted to give a dual outlook and end gables were enclosed within private gardens along the sides of the dwellings. To meet the demand for housing for single people, a number of end terraced houses were converted into two-bedroom flats with independent entrances via new external staircases. Most important was giving more variety of appearance and individual identity through varied painting schemes, new door canopies and external stairs to flats. New planting also contributed, particularly a new serpentine landscape feature on the northern boundary of the site.

FIGURE 6.6
Castle Street, Armagh.

Co. Armagh

Castle Street redevelopment, Armagh.
1987. NIHE.

This redevelopment scheme of nineteen dwellings replaced a terrace of two- and three-storey stone-built houses which had become dilapidated. The design's aim was to respect the scale, style, tradition and materials of Armagh, recognizing the historic importance of the site in relationship to the adjacent Church of Ireland Cathedral. The occasional three-storey house was added into the two-storey terrace to create a varied roof-line which can be appreciated from a number of vantage points in the city (Fig. 6.6).

FIGURE 6.7
Balmoral Mews, Belfast: exceptional private housing development.

BELFAST

Balmoral Mews, Malone Road.
1986. Knox & Markwell.

This most exceptional private development comprises twenty-six town houses on a 0.5 ha (1.3 acre) site. The houses face Malone Road or into a courtyard served by a traditional cul-de-sac and footpaths (Fig. 6.7). The spatial quality of the scheme is enhanced by the treatment of the housing at the corners and by extending parapet walls above the roofs to help take up small changes of level between the houses. Its pleasant tree planting has matured well. The scheme is a good example of what is being achieved by private housebuilders in Northern Ireland.

Housing Design Awards 1987, A *Building* Publication, pp. 42–43.

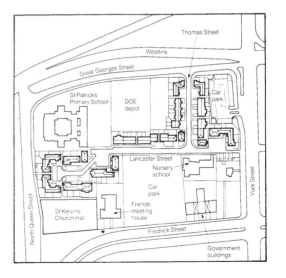

FIGURE 6.8
Lancaster Street, Belfast: an exceptionally well mannered and quiet scheme.

1–3 Lancaster Street and 1–19 Thomas Street.
1988. NIHE.

This development best illustrates the quality of new housing built by the NIHE in the 1980s. Built on a city centre site, it contains forty-three houses and twenty-eight flats grouped around two well planted block-paved courts (Fig. 6.8). These have a strong sense of enclosure and are safe places for children to play in. Car parking is located directly outside the dwellings where vehicles are overlooked.

The architecture is essentially urban, reflecting the character of Belfast's traditional terraced housing (Fig. 6.9). Multi-coloured brickwork detailing of the house elevations creates interest without fussiness and the overall affect is of calmness and tranquillity.

Housing Design Awards 1989, A *Building* Publication, pp. 30–31.

Carrick Hill (phase 2), Upper Library Street.
1994. NIHE.

Carrick Hill, which replaced the Unity flats, illustrates the NIHE's design approach to replacing the former deck-access housing. Community participation influenced the decision to provide predominantly two-storey housing around pedes-

FIGURE 6.9
Lancaster Street: site layout.

FIGURE 6.10
The new Divis Estate showing the remaining tower.

trian/vehicular courts, which was considered by the tenants to be the most effective means of cutting out through traffic (Fig. 6.10). Car parking in small, open bays close to the dwellings was also preferred. The houses were stepped and staggered to add variety to the design, which was further emphasized by the use of contrasting brickwork and render which gives individuality to each dwelling. Semi-mature trees and generous landscaping all add to the sense of place.

Housing Design Awards, *Building Homes*, 27/9/95, p. 29.

Divis Estate redevelopment, Milford Street/Cullingtree Road.
1998. NIHE.

The 795 Divis flats were built between 1966 and 1972 by the Northern Ireland Housing Trust. Its urgent need was to redevelop Belfast's slums by replacing the dense warren of streets known as the Pound Loney. The complex of twelve medium rise blocks and the twenty-storey Divis tower became the largest single development of flats in Northern Ireland. However, the drab concrete appearance never appealed to its residents and by the early 1980s parts were being demolished. In 1986, the result of an Investment Appraisal indicated a clear preference for replacing the medium rise blocks with around 260 new dwellings and the phased decanting of the residents from the old to the new housing. The tower would remain, to be refurbished and occupied by single people and couples.

Participation of the residents was essential – questionnaires, consultation with individuals and groups and door-to-door surveys were carried out. Several strategy layouts were then produced. The outcome was a clear desire for a mixture of one- to three-storey dwellings grouped along traditional

LIVERPOOL JOHN MOORES UNIVERSITY
Aldham Roberts L.R.C.
TEL 0151 231 3701/3634

FIGURE 6.11
The Cathedral is once more the dominant element in the new Divis Estate.

open-ended streets, with some residents asking for courts (Fig. 6.10). Both layout preferences were adopted and the street pattern now echoes the road pattern of the old Pound Loney, with a main street, Milford Street, running through the heart of the area with smaller link streets running off towards Cullingtree Road. T-junctions were used as a traffic calming measure. The residents also preferred traditional Belfast red brick housing combined with a measure of individuality. The housing is now complete and very popular. St Peter's Cathedral, previously overshadowed by the deck-access blocks, has again become the focal point (Fig. 6.11).

Perspective, 11–12/93, pp. 19–21.

Laganview Apartments, Bridge End.
1993. The Boyd Partnership.

A visit to Belfast's new concert hall offers the best viewing point for the first waterfront housing to be developed by the Laganside Urban Development Corporation. The brief for the developer-led competition called for tall buildings for the riverside, which resulted in a four-storey development with penthouse apartments and strong chimneys to give the scheme verticality when viewed across the river (Fig. 6.12). By orientating the facade south-west towards the curving River Lagan and installing full-length windows in every apartment,

FIGURE 6.12
Riverside private flats inspired by the Laganside Urban Development Corporation.

FIGURE 6.13
*Shore Street/ Union Street,
Donaghadee.*

the architects have given every occupant a view of the river. They have also provided every apartment with a private balcony off the living room. At the entrance to the site, close to an NIHE development at Rotterdam Court, are town houses built along the street frontage which link the public sector housing to the apartment block. *Perspective*, 9–10/93, pp. 56–58.

Co. DOWN

The following NIHE schemes in Co. Down were all winners of DOE National Housing Design Awards. They are indicative of the work of the Executive in remedying the housing problems that have existed in the smaller towns and rural areas. They demonstrate the NIHE's commitment to preserving Northern Ireland's distinctive architectural heritage through using housing designs which are in sympathy with the character of the old villages and historic country towns.

Shore Street/Union Street, Donaghadee.
1981. McAdam Design.

Donaghadee is a small coastal town at the mouth of the Belfast Lough and the new scheme involved the redevelopment of part of its water frontage (Fig. 6.13) along Shore Street and Union Street. This area had contained cottages dating back to the eighteenth century when the town

was the main sea trading link with Scotland. Unfortunately the cottages were far too dilapidated to be refurbished. Instead, the layout and the dwelling design follows their form and retains an old established pedestrian route (Schoolhouse Brae) across the site, which links the new housing with the town shopping area. The slope of the site meant that housing at the rear of the site could be at a higher level than the bungalows fronting Shore Street, which gives them extensive views over the roof-tops to the Copeland Islands and Donaghadee Harbour.

The twenty-nine dwellings for rent include a mixture of houses, flats and bungalows and are standard Housing Executive designs. The external treatment of the buildings and the landscaping embody local materials and features to keep the scheme in character with its surroundings; wall finishes are white-painted rough-cast with contrasting projecting plasterwork features, corner quoins, window and door surrounds and plinths.

A further twenty-seven houses by the same architects were built in 1984 at Bow Street/Manor Street.

Church Hill/Shore Street and Well Lane redevelopment area, Killyleagh.
1985. NIHE.

Killyleagh is a small Ulster village of considerable character and charm, located about 20 miles south of Belfast. Its architectural interest derives not so much from its individual buildings but from their compact grouping which the design endeavoured to reflect in terms of scale, character and use of local materials.

This small development of twenty-one houses and bungalows for rent was built on a clearance site close to the centre of the village. The site sloped steeply with gradients in excess of 1 in 8 in places which restricted car parking to Church Hill. An old pedestrian route was maintained through the new courtyard from Shore Street to Church Hill. This followed the line of the former Well Lane, the name of which was given to the courtyard. The proportions of windows and the materials all reflect the local vernacular. The external detailing is most charming, particularly the chimneys and gables, and the front entrances of the dwellings on Shore Street. Housing Design Awards 1987, A *Building* Publication, p. 80.

Cudgel Row, Ballylough Road, Annsborough.
1986. NIHE.

This small development of three houses and three bungalows is located on the main Ballylough

Road close to a local primary school in the village of Annsborough. It was built on land formerly occupied by the Cudgel Row Cottages from where there are good views of the Mountains of Mourne.

The design related the new dwellings to the school and retained the existing planting and dry stone walling which was rebuilt in the form of planters. The housing was sensitively mixed to vary the roof-line, and the architectural treatment was traditionally white-painted walls and natural slates with highly sculptured bargeboards.

New Bridge Street redevelopment, Downpatrick.
1986. NIHE.

This small redevelopment scheme, containing seventeen houses and five bungalows for rent, lies on the main road from Belfast into Downpatrick. There is a huge roundabout in front of the site but the housing design is sufficiently strong to ensure a prominence at this important entrance point to the town. The straightforward strip frontage site gave little scope for layout design

FIGURE 6.14
New Bridge Street, Downpatrick.

except building a single terrace with car parking at the rear, but within this constraint, the architects found a balance of one-, two- and three-storey dwellings that is visually attractive and reflects the character of Downpatrick.

The visual quality of the terrace was heightened by stepping the roof-lines to a climax at the highest point in the centre which was emphasized by the placing of strong colour on a single dwelling (Fig. 6.14). Here the footpath is also elevated to separate pedestrians from the busy road below. The landscape treatment at the front is extremely good, using heavy blocks of local stone and large areas of pebbles set in front of the windows and in the areas of attractive planting.

Housing Design Awards 1989, A *Building* Publication, pp. 62–63; *Perspective*, 5/94, pp. 15–17.

Main Street redevelopment, Killough.
1992. NIHE.

Killough is located some 6 miles south-east of Downpatrick on the coast of the Lecale Peninsula. In 1981 the harbour area was declared a conservation area but physically it was suffering serious decline. The NIHE took a leading role in improving the area with a number of small infill redevelopment areas at Palatine Row, Castle Street, and in 1992, thirteen houses and bungalows for rent at Main Street.

Built on the site of cleared cottages, the new dwellings kept the line of the former buildings fronting Main Street, except where access was required into a small court of houses built around a number of mature trees. The building materials – painted rendered walls, salvaged natural roofing slates, cast-aluminium rainwater goods and carefully detailed barge-boards on the entrance porches and over the glazed fanlights of the bungalows – were carefully chosen to be sympathetic to the rural seaside location. The result is a group of housing of simple charm and delight.

Housing Design Awards 1993, A *Building* Publication, 11/93, p. 28.

Redevelopment of 34–55 Irish Street, Downpatrick.
1992. NIHE.

The town of Downpatrick has a strong eighteenth and nineteenth century townscape structure. The architecture is a mixture of imposing civic buildings, town houses, and small-scale commercial and residential buildings, all of which offer great variety and a sense of enclosure. The centre of the town was declared a conservation area in 1985.

The redevelopment at Irish Street followed an options appraisal that considered but rejected the possibility of refurbishing the existing buildings. The planning requirements strictly called for the new development to maintain the building line and be designed to a scale and with materials that reflected the original buildings (Fig. 6.1). This was achieved through building a continuous terrace of two-storey houses and three-storey flats, with a single maisonette over an archway in the mid-point of the terrace through which access is gained to car parking at the rear. The bright colours of the rendering, which were intended to take attention away from the imposing security tower at the top of the street, are particularly effective. The natural Welsh roofing slates and granite kerbs and setts were salvaged from the previous buildings on the site and reused.

Perspective, 5/94, pp. 15–17.

Co. Londonderry

Redevelopment of the Rossville Estate, Derry City.
1991–92. NIHE.

The difficult housing circumstances in Derry City in the early 1960s did not result from its size (55 000 population) or its overall density. Instead, the problem was political, emanating from overcrowding in the Bogside area. In 1964 the City Corporation authorized the Northern

Ireland Housing Trust to build 178 dwellings in two ten-storey blocks and one seven-storey block at Rossville Street just outside the old city walls. Initially the scheme was popular as it was close to the city centre. However, the 'troubles' produced a high demand for transfers from the complex. Furthermore structural problems which appeared on the flat roofs, causing condensation and dampness, encouraged people to seek alternative housing.

By 1989 the housing had been demolished. Some of the people were rehoused in the new scheme of twenty-four dwellings and two shops at Creggan Street, completed in 1987. The site of the flats at Chamberlain Street is now occupied by a mix of forty-eight two-, three- and four-bedroom houses and smaller dwellings for elderly people. Instead of the grey concrete, the new development has traditional red brick houses with slate roofs, and is very popular. Once a byword for civil unrest, the houses on the Rossville site are now amongst the most sought-after in the city.

Perspective, 9/93, pp. 25–26.

Abbreviations

A&BN	*Architect and Building News*
AD	*Architectural Design*
AJ	*The Architects Journal*
AR	*The Architectural Review*
AT	*Architecture Today*
B	*Building*
BB	*Brick Bulletin*
BD	*Building Design*
BISF	British Iron and Steel Federation
CHAR	Campaign for Homeless and Rootless (recently renamed Natural Homeless Alliance)
CIOH	Chartered Institute of Housing
DC	Development Corporation
DETR	Department of the Environment and Transport
DOE	Department of the Environment
EH	English Heritage
ELHA	East London Housing Association
GEAR	Glasgow Eastern Area Renewal
GLC	Greater London Council
ha	hectare
HAT	Housing Action Trust
IBA	Internationale Bauausstellung Berlin
LCC	London County Council
LDCC	London Docklands Development Corporation
MoHLG	Ministry of Housing and Local Government
MoH	Ministry of Health
MT	Ministry of Transport
NFHA	National Federation of Housing Associations
NIHE	Northern Ireland Housing Executive
PSSHAK	Primary Support and Housing Assembly Kit
RIBA	Royal Institute of British Architects
SDA	Scottish Development Agency
SLASH	Scottish Local Authority Special Housing Group
SSHA	Scottish Special Housing Association
SRB	Single Regeneration Budget
UDC	Urban Development Corporation
UHRU	Urban Housing Renewal Unit

Travel Abbreviations

DLR	Docklands Light Railway
M	Metro (Newcastle upon Tyne)
R	Rail Station
U	Underground (London and Glasgow)

Bibliography

Aldous, A., *Urban Villages*, The Urban Villages Group, 1992.

Alexander, C., *The Timeless Way of Building*, New York, Oxford University Press, 1979.

Alexander, C., and Chermayeff, S., *Community and Privacy: Towards a New Architecture of Humanism*, Doubleday, New York, 1963.

Alexander, C. et al., *A Pattern Language: Towns, Buildings, Construction*, New York, Oxford University Press, 1977.

Balchin, P.N. *Housing Policy: An Introduction*, Routledge, 1989.

Barton, H., Davis, G., and Guise, R., *Sustainable Settlements – A Guide for Planners, Designers and Developers*, The University of the West of England/The Local Government Management Board, 1966.

Beattie, S. (GLC), *A Revolution in London Housing: LCC Housing Architects & their Work, 1893–1914*, The Architectural Press, 1970.

Begg, T., *50 Special Years: A Study of Scottish Housing*, Henry Melland, London, 1986.

Begg, T., *Housing Policy in Scotland*, John Donald Publishers Ltd., Edinburgh 1996.

Bentley, Alcock, Murrain, McGlynn, Smith, *Responsive Environments, a Manual for Designers*, The Architectural Press Ltd, 1993.

Bentley, I., Davis I., and Oliver, P., *Dunroamin: the Surburban Semi and its Enemies*, Barrie and Jenkins, 1981.

Boal, F.W., *Shaping a City, Belfast in the Late Twentieth Century*, The Institute of Irish Studies, The Queen's University of Belfast, 1995.

Borer, P., and Harris, C., *Out of the Woods: Ecological Designs for Timber-Frame Housing*, The Centre for Alternative Technology, 1997.

Borer, P., and Harris, C., *The Whole House Book: Ecological Building Design and Materials*, The Centre for Alternative Technology, 1998.

Broome, J., and Richardson, B., *The Self-build Book*, Green Earth Books, 1995.

Burnett, J., *A Social History of Housing*, Routledge, 1990.

Chapman, D., *Creating Neighbourhoods and Places in the Built Environment*, E & F Spon, 1996.

Charles, Prince of Wales, *A Vision of Britain: A Personal view of Architecture*, Doubleday, London, 1989.

Chartered Institute of Housing, *Housing Schemes Creation and Programming*, 1978.

Chartered Institute of Housing/Royal Institute of British Architects, *Homes for the Future*, 1981. Also supplements on the following topics:
Housing Design Brief, 1987.
Housing for Elderly People, 1988.
Housing for Disabled People, 1989.
Housing Rehabilitation, 1988.

Chartered Institute of Housing/Royal Institute of British Architects, *Tenant Participation*, The Architectural Press, 1988.

Chartered Institute of Housing (edited by B. Derbyshire, W. Hatchett and R. Turkington), *Taking Stock, Social Housing in the Twentieth Century*, 1996.

Church of England, *Faith in the City, a call for action by Church and Nation*, Church House Publishing, 1985.

Coleman, A., *Utopia on Trial: Vision and Reality in Planned Housing*, Hilary Shipman, London, 1985.

Colquhoun, I., and Fauset, P.G., *Housing Design in Practice*, Longman UK, 1986.

Colquhoun, I., and Fauset, P.G., *Housing Design – an International Perspective*, B.T. Batsford, London, 1991.

Colquhoun, I., *Urban Regeneration*, B.T. Batsford, London, 1995.

Conran, T., *The Essential Housebook*, Conran Octopus Limited, 1994.

Cooper Marcus, C. and Sarkisson, W., *Housing Design as if People Mattered – Site Design Guidelines for Medium-Density Family Housing*, University of California Press, Berkeley, 1986.

Cooper Marcus, C., *The House as a Mirror of Self: exploring the deeper meaning of home*, Conari Press, Berkeley, CA, USA, 1995.

Cowling, D., *An Essay for Today, the Scottish New Towns, 1947–1997*, Rutland Press, 1997.

Department of Energy, *Measures to Save Energy, Helping the Earth begins at Home*, 1992.

Department of the Environment, *Estate Action: Handbook of Estate Improvement*, HMSO, 1991.

Department of the Environment, *Quality in Town & Country*, HMSO, 1994.

Department of the Environment, *Construction Monitor*, Issue No. 9, HMSO, 1995.

Department of the Environment/Department of Transport, Design Bulletin 32, *Residential Roads and Footpaths*, (second edition) 1992.

Donnison, D., and Middleton, A., *Regenerating the Inner City: Glasgow's Experience*, Routledge & Kegan Paul, London, 1987.

Duncan, S., and Rowe, A., *Self Help Housing: The Housing: The World's Hidden Housing Arm*, Centre for Urban & Regional Research, University of Sussex, 1992.

Dunleavy, D., *The Politics of Mass Housing in Britain, 1945–1975: a study of corporate power, and professional influence in the welfare state*, Clarendon Press, 1981.

Edwards, B., *Towards Sustainable Architecture*, Butterworth Architecture, 1996.

Edwards, B., 'Green Product Specification', *The Architects' Journal*, 15/12/93, p. 30.

English Heritage, *Something Worth Keeping: Post War Architecture in England*, 1996. *Housing and Houses; New Towns and Rural Housing.*

Essex County Council Planning Department, *A Design Guide for Residential Areas*, Essex County Council, 1973 (2nd Edition 1997).

Girardet, H. *The GAIA Atlas of Cities – New directions for sustainable urban living*, Gaia Books Ltd, 1992.

Glendinning, M., and Muthesius, S., *Tower Block*, Yale University Press, 1993.

Goldsmith, S., *Designing for the Disabled: The New Paradigm*, Architectural Press, 1997.

Goodchild, B., *Housing and the Urban Environment*, Blackwell, 1998.

Greater London County Council, *Home Sweet Home: Housing design by the London County Council and Greater London Council Architects 1888–1975*, Academy Editions, 1976.

Greater London Council, *GLC Preferred Dwelling Plans*, The Architectural Press, 1977.

Greater London Council, *An Introduction to Housing Layout*, The Architectural Press, 1978.

Hackney, R., *The Good the Bad and the Ugly, Cities in crisis*, Frederick Muller, 1988.

Hall, P., *Cities of Tomorrow: An Intellectual History of Urban Planning and Design in the Twentieth Century*, Basil Blackwell, 1988 (reprinted 1993).

Home Office, *Safer Cities Progress Report, 1989–90*, HMSO, 1990.

Housing Awards Publications 1969–1998. These have been published in various forms and are available to see at the British Architectural Library, 66 Portland Place, London W1N 4AD. Between the years 1987–1995 they were published in *Building*.

Housing Development Directorate (DOE), Occasional papers.
2/74. *Mobility Housing*, HMSO, 1974, reprinted from AJ, 3.7.74, pp. 43–50.
2/75. *Wheelchair Housing*, HMSO, 1975.

Howard, E. *Garden Cities of Tomorrow*, Attic Books, (reprint) 1977.

Jacobs, J., *Death and Life of Great American Cities*, Jonathan Cape, 1962.

Jones, E., and Woodward, C., *A Guide to the Architecture of London*, Weldenfield and Nicholson, London, 1992.

Jung, C., *Memories, Dreams, Reflections*, Fontana Library, London, 1969.

Kern, V., and Sheridan, L., *Housing Quality: a practical guide for tenants and their representatives*, Joseph Rowntree Foundation, 1995.

Lawrence J.L., *Housing, Dwellings and Homes – Design theory, research and practice*, John Wiley & Sons, 1987.

Martin, L., and Marsh, L., *Urban Space and Structures*, Cambridge University Press, 1972.

Ministry of Health/Ministry of Works, *Housing Manual 1944*, HMSO.

Ministry of Health/Ministry of Works, *Housing Manual 1949*, HMSO.

Ministry of Housing and Local Government, *Houses 1952 Second Supplement to the Housing Manual 1949*, HMSO.

Ministry of Housing and Local Government, *Design in Town and Village*, HMSO, 1953.

Ministry of Housing and Local Government (Parker Morris Report), *Homes for Today and Tomorrow*, HMSO, 1961.

Ministry of Housing and Local Government, Design Bulletin 6, *Space in the Home*, HMSO, 1963 and 1968.

Ministry of Housing and Local Government, *Housing Subsidies Manual*, London, HMSO, 1967.

Moughton, C. *Urban Design – Street and Square*, Butterworth Architecture, 1992.

Muthesius, S. *The Terraced House*, Yale University Press, New Haven, 1982.

Neale, C. (former Essex County Planning Officer), *Essex Design Guide*, 1984.

Newman, O., *Design Guides for Creating Defensible Space*, The Architectural Press, 1976.

Northern Ireland Housing Executive, *Brick by Brick*, NIHE, 1991.

Noble, J., *Activities and Spaces – Dimensional Data for Housing Design*, Architectural Press, 1989.

Nutgens, P., *The Homefront*, BBC Publications, 1989.

Pearson, D., *The Natural House Book*, Conran Octopus, 1989.

Petherick, A., and Fraser, R., *Introduction to Living over the Shop*, The University of York, 1992.

Power, A., *Hovels to High Rise: State Housing in Europe since 1850*, Routledge, 1993.

Ravetz A., with Turkington, R., *The Place of Home*, E & F Spon, 1995.

Richards, J.M., *An Introduction to Modern Architecture*, Pelican Books, 1956.

RIBA, *Building Homes as if Tomorrow Matters*, RIBA, 1997.

RIBA Northern Regional Housing Group, *Housing North*, RIBA Northern Region, 1987.

Rogers, Richard, *Cities for a Small Planet*, Faber and Faber, 1997.

Rowntree, J., Foundation, *Housing Quality – A Practical Guide for Tenants and their Representatives*, 1996.

Rudlin, D., and Falk, N., URBED, *21st Century Homes – Building to Last*, a report for the Joseph Rowntree Foundation, URBED, 1995.

Scarman, Lord T. (Inquiry Report Chairman), *Brixton Disorders, April 10–12*, HMSO, 1981.

Scoffham, E.R., *The Shape of British Housing*, George Godwin, London, 1984.

Segal, W., *Home and Environment*, Leonard Hill Ltd, 1948.

Sherlock, H., *Cities are good for us*, Transport 2000, London, 1990.

Smith, Mary E.H., *A Guide to Housing*, The Housing Centre Trust, London, 1971 (third edition 1989).

Sudjic, D., *100 Mile City*, Flamingo, 1993.

Swenerton, M., *Homes Fit for Heroes*, Heinemann Educational Books, 1981.

Taylor, N., *The Village in the City*, Temple Smith, London, 1973.

Thorpe, S., *Designing for People with Sensory Impairments*, Access Committee for England, 1986.

Unwin, R., *Town Planning in Practice*, T. Fisher Unwin, London, 1909.

Vale, B. and Vale, R., *Green Architecture: Design for a Sustainable Future*, Thames and Hudson, London, 1991.

Valins, M., *Housing for Elderly People*, The Architectural Press, 1986.

Walker, D., *The Architecture and Planning of Milton Keynes*, Architectural Press, 1982.

Ward, C., *Housing – An Anarchist Approach*, Freedom Press, 1976.

Ward, C., *The Child in the City*, The Architectural Press, 1978.

Ward, C., *Welcome Thinner City*, Bedford Square Press, 1989.

Willis, P., *New Architecture in Scotland*, Lund Humphries, London, 1977.

Woolley, T., Kimmins, S., Harrison, P., and Harrison, R., *Green Building Handbook*, E. and E. Spon, 1997.

York, F.R.S., *The Modern Flat*, Architectural Press, 1937.

Index

The index provides the following lists:

1. Projects in alphabetical order followed by the name of the City, County or Borough in which they are located.
2. Cities, London Boroughs, Counties and Towns in alphabetical order with projects and locations.
3. Projects listed within categories of housing type where appropriate.
4. Architects or designers in alphabetical order followed by their projects.

Italic type indicates the page on which an illustration appears.

LIVERPOOL JOHN MOORES UNIVERSITY

LIVERPOOL JOHN MOORES UNIVERSITY